SERVICE IN
COMBAT, COURT,
AND HOME

A Memoir

BILL GIALLOURAKIS

Author of *Contracting with Uncle Sam*

PAGE PUBLISHING, INC.
New York, NY

First originally published by Page Publishing, Inc. 2019

ISBN 978-1-64424-527-9 (Paperback)
ISBN 978-1-64544-095-6 (Hardcover)
ISBN 978-1-64424-526-2 (Digital)

Printed in the United States of America

This text is dedicated to the memory of

1942–45 WWII Family Veterans. Jerry Caredis, who served in Europe during the Battle of the Bulge in December 1944, stopping the German winter panzer offensive in the Ardennes Forest of Belgium and Luxembourg; Phillip D. Giallourakis, who served in Europe also during the Battle of the Bulge under Gen. Eisenhower; Alexander Despo, who served in the South Pacific in the Philippines, New Guinea, and Solomon Islands under Gen. Douglas McArthur; Charlie Pappas, who served in the Air Force on B-17F Flying Fortresses as the rear turret machine gunner and flew numerous bombing missions into Germany from England.

1958 Cold War Service. Lt. Chris John Poulos, USMA West Point class of 1957 and brother-in-law, whose jet, on June 11, 1958, on a routine training flight with his flight instructor, Lt. Robert E. Irons, made their last flight for on their way back. They hit a storm where God reached out with His mighty hand and called them to His Legions. The plane crashed into a farm house five miles northeast of Ponca City, Oklahoma.

1968 Vietnam War. Major Floyd Spencer, my West Point roommate and 1958 classmate who answered the call for Vietnam, served with exceptional gallantry and valor (Silver Cross), sacrificing his life to save that of his fellow soldier.

1915–1998 my mother-in-law, Emorfia J. Poulos, born October 13, 1915, in Constantinople (Istanbul), an orphan Hellenic child refugee in Turkey during the Greco-Turkish War (1919–22), rescued from Smryna (Izmir) by the US Navy and transported to Athens along with other orphan children where she was adopted. She, later as a teenager, migrated to Kansas City from Leonidio, Greece, upon the death of her adopted mother. She stood strong despite the loss in 1958 of her only son, USAF Lt. Christ Poulos, USMA, West Point Class of 1957, followed by her husband, John, in 1966. She was the beloved grandmother of my three children, Stamie, Cosmas and Christina.

1944–2004 my beloved wife, Antonia, schoolteacher, artist, iconographer, beloved mother of three children, founder of Children's

Art for Children Cancer Foundation providing art therapy to children fighting cancer, who lived life to the fullest, finally herself succumbing to cancer.

1911–2013 my teacher, mother, Stamatia C. Giallourakis, born in Kalymnos, Greece, who taught her two sons, Mike and Bill, and hundreds of young Hellenes in Greece and Florida, the importance of their Hellenic heritage and culture, Greek language, need for higher education, physical fitness, and Eastern Orthodoxy, before succumbing at the centenarian age of 102.

1921–2015 My mother's sister, my second mother, and my aunt, Ypapanti Alexiou born in Kalymnos, emigrated to U.S.; lived in Tarpon Springs in our home, went to high school in Tarpon Springs; and marrying her husband, Anthony Alexiou from Nassau Bahamas. Together they not only were involved in raising a family but also were a team in all their business activities. Ypapanti lost her husband during a burglary of their home but courageously continued living her life in Nassau and traveled worldwide. She immersed herself in supporting charitable causes from children's schools to monasteries in her native Greece. Aunt Ypapanti was my brother Mike's and my second mother, and the mother of her two children, Kathryn and Emmanuel, who reside in Nassau.

Also by Bill C. Giallourakis

Contracting with Uncle Sam
The Essential Guide for
Federal Buyers and Seller

CONTENTS

PREFACE

This book is intended to be a memoir with a story and lessons learned about the key aspects of the molding of a young Hellenic-American who was swept up by the times between 1949 and 2017, serving other students, soldiers, clients, and his family.

This text, totally or for selected chapters therein, is intended for reading by multiple audiences as described in the preface table below:

Preface Table of Intended Memoir Readers

- American veterans of Vietnam, Iraq, Afghanistan, Syria, and other campaigns;
- Platoon, company, battalion, brigade, group, division commanders whether in the Army, Navy, Marine Corps, Air Force, or Coast Guard who are responsible for the training and leadership of their men and women under their commands in time of peace and war;
- DoD staff officers in all the uniformed services whether serving on their own service staffs, the secretariats of the heads of the major services or on the staff of the Office of the Secretary of Defense;
- Program managers, business executives, and lawyers;
- Civilian employees and civil servants planning on a promotion to a new job, career change whether to sales or marketing, accounting, research, health care, law, or other profession;

- Military servicemen and women returning to civilian life;
- Tourists visiting the Sponge Docks at the Sponge Exchange on Dodecanese Boulevard in Tarpon Springs, Florida;
- Any person who has been diagnosed with cancer and their family supporters to mentally prepare themselves for the struggle of a life ahead;
- Family caregivers undertaking the responsibility for the planning, management, and the hands-on care of a beloved wife, elderly parent, or seriously disabled family member, and;
- Some 1,319,188 Americans of Greek ancestry living in the United States in accordance with the US Census of 2010.

It is not limited to those in just uniform but to all those in our society that are taking care of an ill-loved one, planning for the geriatric care of a family member, or are actually taking care of an elder or disabled parent. As American society ages, the chances are that at least one reader out of five will, at one time or another, serve as a guardian or as a home health provider for a close family member. More and more Americans even will have attended or participated in an end-of-life discussion with their family, priest, and/or physician.

The battle of a life by a wife with cancer provides a trail of medical battle that others may gain insights in coping and supporting loved ones. The memoir reflects the pain and love of a husband who was devoted to his beloved wife and the subsequent coping to a void now some thirteen years that was not able to be filled, and the options that were taken to construct resilience and find acceptance and peace of mind.

In addition the memoir details the actions taken to care for an elderly mother and the options available for elder care are brought to the forefront in this text for others to review and gain insight for current or future use. Moreover, it presents the dilemma of a son who slowly is losing his closest sources of acceptance and love, from his brother, his beloved wife, and even his mother.

The text reflects the growth of a young man who constantly improved and molded himself to maintain a professional currency over a span of some sixty-five years, who became a professional in the Army, served in Vietnam and in other theaters in command and staff positions; performed duties of a nuclear weapons specialist; graduated from Purdue to teach Electrical Engineering at West Point; graduated evening Graduate Business School offered by Fairleigh Dickinson University, Teaneck, New Jersey and Law School at Seton Hall University School of Law, Newark, New Jersey; retired from the Army Service; practices law; and became the primary key caregiver to his beloved wife, who valiantly battled cancer, first and then later of his Centenarian mother.

The objective of this book is not to detail my story so readers may marvel at my accomplishments. Rather, it is hoped that readers of this book will be inspired to gain insights that may assist them in the duty of "caring" for others whether they be soldiers; family members; assisted living or hospital patients; or clients; and second, to reach deep within themselves to strive in maintaining their education, competence, and relevancy current over an extended life span. It is hoped that the "Sources" section at the end of this book will provide a resource for more in-depth review of various topics with access from the internet addresses provided.

The book mirrors contemporary events of thousands of refugees and orphans in camps in the Middle East and elsewhere as of the date of this text, through the experience of survivorship of a Greek orphaned child rescued by US Navy Destroyers from Constantinople after WWI and during the Greco-Turkish War and transported to an International Red Cross camp in Athens. The five-year-old orphan was destined to survive to become the author's mother-in-law.

Through the author's experiences in Germany, the reader will feel the pressures even today on soldiers, airmen, Marines, and sailors entrusted with the security and deployment of nuclear weapons. Likewise, through the author's experiences in Vietnam, the reader will gain an insight to the stresses faced by the servicemen and women who served or still are serving as advisers and trainers in Iraq, Syria, and Afghanistan. Through the author's service as the Army's action officer on the IHAWK Air Defense Program and later as project officer on the then Army's new tactical frequency hopping radio, the SINCGARS-V, one will gain an insight on the relations of the military industrial complex, the Pentagon, the Congress and even Western Europe and Middle East.

Thereafter, the author taught EE to cadets at West Point. Then he commenced teaching federal contracting from the first edition of the author's text, "Contracting with Uncle Sam," published by USNI Press to Navy, Army, and Marine corps officers and civilian engineers at AFCEA International Headquarters in Fairfax, Virginia; the Naval Warfare Surface Center at Carona, California; the Naval Air Warfare Center at Webster Field, Saint Inigoes, Maryland in the Patuxent area; the US Southern Command in Miami; and NATO Headquarters Staff in Brussels to mention but a few of the many defense procurement centers.

ACKNOWLEDGMENTS

Although the primary contents in this book are from my personal memories and notes, aside from the Internet and open government sources, materials in this book also have been gathered from libraries, including the Tarpon Springs Public Library and St. Petersburg College Library. The research staffs within these libraries are important to whatever success this book attains. The assistance of Salvatore Miranda at the reference desk of the Tarpon Springs Library was indispensable.

Two institutions were critical to my work. My file from the War Department, Adjutant General's Office, the Historical Service in Washington, DC, the "Officer Efficiency File," comprising Efficiency and School Reports, Awards, and Decorations was a true resource for a writer regarding the military matters contained herein.

Equally valuable was the Clinical Information Center at Memorial Sloan Kettering Cancer Center in New York City, which provided from its Memorial Hospital for Cancer and Allied Diseases archives pathology, surgical, medical reports and related data of the extensive cancer diagnosis and treatments received by Antonia over five years. Lastly, the records and my notes for Stamatia from Florida Hospital North Pinellas (formerly Helen Ellis Hospital) in Tarpon Springs, Florida, and from the office of Dr. Nicholas Pavouris, her general practitioner, were important for the geriatric care chapter of this memoir.

I also acknowledge the support and critique provided by my family, particularly Kathleen, Stamie, Cosmas, Christina, Aakash, and Aris. Of particular help was the review and corrections provided by my beloved aunt Ypapanti Alexiou, of Nassau, Bahamas, whom I visited in 2014 and, over a period of six days, read her my first manuscript draft, which she provided relevant critique.

Lastly, I want to thank the constructive comments, cheering, and encouragement by Bahamian cousins, Kathryn Klonaris, Manoli Alexiou; my West Point class of 1958 classmate, Alan Salisbury; my sister-in-law Janie Giallourakis, and my two nephews, Greg and Nick; my cousin, Duchess Arfaras and her daughter, Irene Steffas; my two cousins, Michael F. Giallourakis, Tony D. Giallourakis; and family friends.

A most grateful thanks,
Bill C. Giallourakis

ABBREVIATIONS

AFCEA	Armed Forces Communications Electronics Association
AHEPA	American Hellenic Educational Progressive Association
AI	Artificial Intelligence
AMTRAK	National Railroad Passenger Corporation
ARPANET	Advanced Research Projects Agency Network
ATBM	Anti-Tactical Ballistic Missile
ATDL	Army Tactical Data Link
BOQ	Bachelor Officer's Quarters
BSN	Bachelor of Science in Nursing Degree
CASCA	Cost Analysis Software for Contract Administration
CBR	Chemical Biological and Radiological
CCR	Central Contractor Registration
C^2	Command and Control
C^3	Command, Control, Communications
CECOM	Communications-Electronics Command
CIC	Combat Information Center
CNA	Certified Nursing Assistant
CINC	Commander in Chief
CT	Computed Tomography
CS	Capability Set-17
CTP	Coordinated Test Plan

DCSOPS	Deputy Chief of Staff for Operations
DDESS	Domestic Dependent Elementary and Secondary Schools
DISA	Defense Information Systems Agency
DMZ	Demilitarized Zone
DoD	Department of Defense
DoDEA	Department of Defense Education Activity
DSARC	Defense System Acquisition Review Council
EAR	Export Administration Regulation
EBG	Efficient Basing—Grafenwoehr Initiative
ECCN	Export Control Classification Number
EE	Electrical Engineer
EPLS	Excluded Party List
FADAC	Field Artillery Digital Automatic Computer
FDO	Fire Direction Officer
FEC	Florida East Coast Industries
FLIR	Forward-Looking Infrared Radiometers
FTX	Field Training Exercise
GAO	General Accountability Office
GMA	Georgia Military Academy
HAWK	Homing All-the-Way Killer
IBM	International Business Machines Corporation
IED	Improvised Explosive Device
IFF	Identification Friend or Foe
IHAWK	Improved Homing All the Way Killer
INF	Intermediate Range Nuclear Forces Treaty
INS	Immigration and Naturalization Service
IP	Intellectual Property
ISIL	Islamic State of Iraq and the Levant (ISIL)
IT	Information Technology
ITARS	International Traffic in Arms Regulations

JAG	Judge Adjutant General
JINTACCS	Joint Interoperability Tactical Command and Control System
KMT	Kuomintang
LKA	Amphibious Cargo Ship
LOH	Light Observation Helicopter
LPH	Amphibious Assault Ship
LPD	Amphibious Transport Dock
LSD	Dock Landing Ship
MRI	Magnetic Resonance Imaging
MBA	Master in Business Administration
MMR	Measles, Mumps, Rubella Vaccine
MNVR	Mid-Tier Networking Vehicular Radio
MOTBA	Military Ocean Terminal Bay Area
MP	Military Police
MSF	Medecins Sans Frontieres International
MSKCC	Memorial Sloan Kettering Cancer Center
MSN	Master of Science in Nursing Degree
MT&G	Military Topography and Graphics
MTMCWA	Military Traffic Management Command–Western Area
NASAMS	National Advanced Surface-to-Air Missile System
NATO	North Atlantic Treaty Organization
NGUTS	Never Give Up the Ship
ODCSOPS	Office of the Deputy Chief of Staff for Operations
ORCA	Online Certifications and Representations
QATT	Qualified Anti-Terrorism Technology
PEG	Percutaneous Endoscopic Gastrostomy
PET	Position Emission Tomography
PatFT	Patent Full-Text and Image Database
PDF	Portable Document Format

PSTA	Pinellas Suncoast Transit Authority
PTSD	Post-Traumatic Stress Disorder
PTRCP	Patent Trademark Research Centers Program
ROTC	Reserve Officers' Training Corp
SAM	System for Award Management
SBIR	Small Business Innovative Research program
SES	Senior Executive Service
SINCGARS-V	Single Channel Ground, Airborne Radio System—Very High Frequency
SRS	Stereotactic Radiosurgery—Cyber Knife
TADIL	Tactical Digital Information Link
TCJA	Tax Cuts and Jobs Act
TIWG	Test Integration Working Group
TOW	Tube Launched Optically Tracked Wireless
TPI	Technical Proficiency Inspection
UAV	Unmanned Aerial Vehicle
ULC	Underlying Learning Curve
USAEUR	US Army Europe
USAFA	US Air Force Academy
USAMRIID	US Army Medical Research Institute for Infectious Disease
USCIS	US Citizenship and Immigration Services
USMA	United States Military Academy
USNA	United States Naval Academy
USNI	United States Naval Institute Press
USPTO	United States Patent and Trademark Office
VA	Veterans Affairs
VHF-FM	Very High Frequency—Frequency Modulation

CHAPTER 1

The Spartan in Me

Growing Up in Tarpon Springs, My Hometown

As a fifth grader in 1941, I recall growing up in Tarpon Springs, Florida, a small town northwest from Tampa, where I was born. Tarpon Springs was known as the Venice of the South due to its natural sparkling waterways and bayous. In world events that same year, Germany had opened up its second front as it invaded the Soviet Union during World War II. Then president Franklin Roosevelt signed into law the Lend-Lease Bill allowing the US the unrestricted ability to supply the Allies in the fight against the Axis. Greece and Yugoslavia were invaded by overwhelming German forces. Finally, Japan with its attack against Pearl Harbor that "infamous" day, Sunday of December 7, 1941, the United States was brought into World War II. All these events and their impacts, I was only to understand many years later.

My hometown was the prime location for the golden years of the American natural sponge industry, which was the cause of the creation of a Greek community by immigrants that came from the Greek Islands of Kalymnos, Simi, and Crete. They built the sponge docks and its exchange to include the Saint Nicholas Greek Orthodox Cathedral. Tarpon Springs, also to this date, has the finest Greek restaurants, bakeries, and curio shopping markets in the country. The sponge docks and Greek restaurants thus daily draw numerous tourists to this colorful location on Florida's Gulf Coast, especially in the winter season.

We lived in a large Victorian-built home that featured steeply pitched roofs in irregular shapes, a full front screened porch, which wrapped around the house, patterned shingles, and a round front three-story turret.

I walked to English school in the morning and in the afternoon to Greek school each week day. The schools were across the street—one opposite from the other off Highway 19 North. Afternoon Greek school in those days took precedence even over sports such as football, baseball, music, dance, and even tennis classes. On my way back home, I played. We would play hide-and-seek with my school friends—Kate, Russell, Michael, and their sister Kea—and climb orange and grapefruit trees along the route leading and into our backyards. We were indeed naughty for during the season, we pulled grapefruits of their tree branches and watched them splatter on the ground beneath. We walked and ran in those days. Owning a bike would have been a luxury!

Halloween week was our favorite on our route back home from Greek school. We would knock on front doors and then run and hide in the nearby bushes. We marveled as we watched while in hiding the lights turn on the second floor, followed by the first-floor lights and finally the porch light of the homes. The frustrated owner would come out to the porch after the third time. We were mischievous, to say the least. Eventually, we all wound up in front of our Greek school principal for a ruler spanking, which in those days was an accepted disciplinary practice.

In the forties and early fifties, without any TVs and few cars, we were, in essence, free spirits with time to imagine, dream, and discover our neighborhood on foot. With our small dingy, which was moored on the Spring Bayou directly in front of our Victorian home, we oared. We fished with hand lines and crabbed with a pole net in and around the tidal Whitcomb Bayou, which provided an outlet into the Gulf of Mexico. The crabs and mullets in those days were plentiful.

Vivid in my mind was our backyard coop, which contained female chickens and even several roosters. I would enter the coop and pick up all the fresh eggs daily. My dad had also built pens for rabbits and a turkey. We also always had a sheep in season, especially for Easter.

I often reminisce about the annual gathering on Easter at our home on the Bayou at 170 Spring Boulevard whereat all of my dad's brothers (seven of them) with their families and friends would come. A whole large lamb was actually roasted by the grown men, my uncles, in our backyard near our chicken coop while I played with my brother and cousins hide-and-seek in the shrubs and trees of the large lawn, all around and even hide underneath throughout the crawl space under the large Victorian home.

Weekly, Elsie, our shared housekeeper, would come for her work day with us. Mike, my brother, and I behaved careful so as not to catch her stern attention. She actually spent one day of each week with one of the six Giallourakis families. She attended Baptist church every Sunday and rested. Elsie was stern but wonderful to us and was dedicated to helping my mom do her housekeeping and cooking.

On our family day, which fell on a Saturday, I would watch Elsie in awe as she would catch and spin overhead each chicken, snapping its neck, then scald each whole chicken in the open yard fire wood-built fire upon which sat the boiling cauldron. Thereafter, she would pluck all their feathers and gut their insides before returning to the main house to place the ready-to-cook chickens in the "icebox" in our kitchen. My dad would take me often to the nearby ice plant to pick up a large block of ice, which would fit into the insulated "icebox." Mass production of modern electric refrigerators, which were affordable and made their own ice, did not get started until after World War II.

Starting in the late 1930s, the radio on a small table in our screened porch was my brother Mike's and my favorite gathering place to hear the popular mystery detective radio series that ran until 1954 with the opening lines of *The Shadow*—"Who knows what evil lurks in the hearts of men? The Shadow knows!"

Those words would send a chill down my back as a young kid. The voice stretched our imagination. A figure never seen, only heard, the Shadow was an invincible crime fighter. He possessed gifts that enabled him to overcome any enemy. Besides his strength, he could defy gravity, speak any language, unravel any code, and become invisible with his ability to "cloud men's minds."

In contrast to today, youngsters are armed with iPads and are transported to school, followed by swim, karate, and music classes and then back home while each carries a smartphone in their hip pockets and even at church services.

Afternoon Greek language classes in Tarpon Springs at the St. Nicholas Cathedral have been even cut back to two hours just twice weekly rather than daily during the school year. Internet e-mail traffic viewing and texting between smartphones is a current theme. There were no worries of child kidnappings, strangers, transplanted citizens, or motor vehicle accidents with so few cars. I cannot help but contrast today's growing up climate where both parents have such worries and are working to assure not only the success of their child but even assure the child's happiness.

Still in the mid-1940s, there was time to explore and study but in a different manner than today's child has at his or her disposal. Tarpon Springs was sparsely populated and the neighbors knew each other. As a little boy, I had no TV to watch or any iPad to play games, much less an Apple iPhone to communicate with friends. I had time to read and explore Tarpon Springs. There is no intent to disparage or detract to the importance of the progress of technology, innovation, and entrepreneurship. These qualities and activities are essential to the creation of jobs, maintaining our standard of living and to our modern society—its living, economic well-being and security.

The Early Years of the American Natural Sponge Industry

John Michael Cocoris was a Greek businessman. He was born in Leonidio in Peloponnes, Greece. He came to New York in 1895 to work in the sponge trade. In 1905, he introduced Tarpon Springs to sponge diving with divers using the rubber suit and heavy copper helmet to which air was pumped via hose from the above sponge boat, allowing the underwater diver with relative safety, adequate time to harvest the sponges off the coral reefs. Eventually, improvements were made to the diving suits—metal helmets; breathing apparatus; and decompression procedures. Prior to that time in small boats operating in shallow waters, especially in the Florida Keys, the Bahamas, and Cuba, a fisherman would spear the sponges on the Gulf floor or used long poles with hooks at the end to pull them up after sighting the sponges through glass bottom buckets.

Cocoris recruited Greek sponge divers from the Dodecanese Islands, bringing them to Tarpon Springs. The sponge divers, boat captains and owners, and sponge packing house business owners were primarily immigrants from the Greek Dodecanesean Islands of Kalymnos, Symi, Crete, and Halki.

By the 1930s, the sponge industry of Tarpon Springs was very productive, generating millions of dollars a year. Diving boats from Tarpon Springs plowed the Gulf of Mexico from the Florida Panhandle to the Florida Keys. Tarpon Springs became a bustling small town with its Greek coffee shops and tavernas near the docks. The "golden" years of sponge diving had just begun.

A sponge is among the simplest animal organisms, having no organs such as heart and lungs and no locomotion. Sponges live attached to reef rocks on the sea bed. Natural sponges are found in different varieties such as sheep wool, yellow sponges, and grass sponges. Their bodies consist of skeletons made of a soft material called spongin and a leathery skin broken by pores. The sponge eats by pumping seawater in through its pores. It filters microscopic plants from the water and expels the excess water through one or more large holes called oscula. It also absorbs oxygen directly from seawater. Finding the sponge sea beds underneath the waters of the coast of Florida and its Keys was like a small gold find. It was competitive, serious, and dangerous work.

The sponge divers would remove the sponge off the reef or rock at the bottom where it was attached using a sharp knife, leaving a portion of the bottom of the sponge itself. This small portion then reproduced itself to grow again into a full-pledged sponge, thus ensuring the reproduction and maintenance of the overall natural sponge beds to include the reefs.

The Giallourakis Brothers Come to America

My dad was born on February 10, 1891, and at the age of sixteen, he and his brothers immigrated to the United States spread over a period from 1904 to 1912 and after WWI by ship all from Symi, one of the group of islands in the Aegean Sea between Turkey and Crete. Dad had seven brothers—Christos, Nicholas, Damianos, Vasili, Anthony, Nestor and Frank—and two sisters, Chryssanthi and Anika.

One of his brothers, Nicholas, had preceded him and worked both in New York City and then later came down to Florida to work in the leather tannery owned and started by his two brothers, Frank and Nestor, which was also funded for its start-up by the other brothers who worked in their sponge-packing company, known as Sponge Fishing Company, in Tarpon Springs. Uncle Nestor had been educated as a pharmacist.

Nicholas became despondent over his job at the tannery and how he was being treated by his two brothers at the new start-up leather tannery. Thus, he committed suicide by hanging himself in the backyard of the residence of his brother Vasilis, using a citrus tree. I distinctly recall walking by the home he had lived on my way to school daily and thinking about the loss of my uncle Nicholas.

Dad worked his way down from New York City into Georgia. In Georgia, Dad worked in a southern plantation, which housed a pine forest lumber mill where turpentine was a by-product. He was horrified at the lack of safety with the loss of human limbs due to timber saw accidents; hence, he left as soon as he could. From there, he finally arrived in Tarpon Springs where he and his brothers lived together, until they got married, in Damianos home on Hibiscus Street. Hariklea, their sister-in-law, who prematurely died in 1938 at an early age, was a true sister to all the brothers. Multifamily living together in a single home until one got financially started with a job was a natural phenomenon for various ethnic immigrants such as from Greece, India, who initially entered the United States especially then and even now to this very day.

Dad had not finished grade school; however, he had a sharp mathematical mind and could do calculations in his head. As a student, I would sit next to him while he was in his favorite rocking chair in our salon at our Victorian home and do my arithmetic homework with him. I was always amazed on how he could give me the correct answer without lifting a pencil. I often reflect that my love of math came from his genes.

He had a business acumen and rapidly moved from working as a hired help on sponge diving boats as a diver to being a boat owner and then a sponge merchant with his brothers in Tarpon Springs. Initially, with the financial support from sponge dealer and financier Ernest Meres, three diving boats and a mother boat were acquired. Some of the brothers had knowledge of sponge diving and others learned quickly.

Sometime thereafter, around 1925, the brothers suffered a major loss working off the Florida Southwest Coast and Keys. The mother boat, a schooner, which was berthed in Key West was overwhelmed by the "Key West Conchs," was set on fire and destroyed. "Conch" was applied initially to the descendants of Bahamian immigrants in Florida. The white Bahamians in the Keys continue to be known as conchs. The term "Conch" is generally applied now to all residents of Key West, and even applied to a number of different medium-to large-sized sea snails or their shells.

This action was in retaliation by the Conchs against the Greeks for fishing in their sponge waters. Although the diving boats and their crews returned back to Tarpon Springs without any loss of life, the brothers had received a serious financial loss. Due to their industriousness, they rebuilt themselves, and thereafter, they even acquired another diving boat, the *Liberty*.

Some readers may recall the 1953 film *Beneath the 12-Mile Reef*, an adventure film starring Robert Wagner and Terry Moore made in cinemascope depicting two Greek families involved in sponge diving and the vicious competition for diving and finding profitable sponge beds, which took place. It was filmed in Key West and at the sponge docks and exchange in Tarpon Springs. It is a classic, especially with its actors, being in cinemascope, and sound track, worth revisiting by both old and first-time viewers through www.amazon.com/dvd.

Dad's word was his honor, and the banker, Mr. Alpheus Lee Ellis, president at the local First National Bank of Tarpon Springs, and Mr. Nixson, of Florida National Bank of St. Petersburg, loaned him and his brothers business loans to start and grow their own sponge-packing house, Sponge Fishing Company Inc., located on North Pinellas Avenue in Tarpon Springs. In the years to follow, Louis Smitzes who started up his own bank, First National Bank of Tarpon Springs, was a key supporter of my father in his business operations, and also my mother, especially after my father died and the need arose to orderly close down the family sponge business with the help of Gus Cocoris, a sponge merchant who also supported my dad.

History of the Tarpon Springs Public Sponge Exchange

At the Tarpon Springs Sponge Exchange, public auctions of the sponge lots of sheep wool, grass and yellow sponges were a weekly event. The exchange was built by the sponge boat owners and their captains. The exchange was a gated facility. It provided secure facilities to prepare the sponges for the auctions and to secure them in separate locked storage rooms built to hold sponges. The exchange issued some twenty-five permits to selected firms and individuals, which allowed them to participate in the public auctions.

However, during WWII, in as much as the limited availability of permits constituted restrictions of trade, precluding many others from the public bidding, a federal suit was filed in Tampa at Federal Fifth Circuit Court in 1944 known as the *United States v. The Tarpon Springs Sponge Exchange*. The suit claimed violations of the Sherman Anti-Trust Act. A disgruntled merchant, the Tsangaris family from Chicago, played a key role in the suit bringing the restrictive practices of the Sponge Exchange to the attention of the US attorney general. The court found the rules of the exchange restricted trade and ordered that the twenty-five permits would be converted into fifty stockholder shares and the exchange would be required to issue permits to any other person or entity that wanted to participate in the frequent public sponge auctions for a reasonable fee.

The exchange became a corporation with a board of directors and with fifty outstanding shares, which were individually valued at eight thousand dollars. The shareholders were primarily the former permit holders, the various sponge-packing companies in the area. Sponge Fishing Company, my father's and uncles' firm, owned two shares. Buyers came to Tarpon Springs thereafter from as far away as New York City, Chicago, and St. Louis to bid at the open auctions using specially issued permits.

The sponges were shipped from Tarpon Springs to wholesale agents in the Midwest and Northeast and directly to consumer stores throughout the United States such as Woolworth, JCPenney, and Sears. In those days, Amazon or Walmart had not yet come to fruition. More importantly, DuPont had not as yet mass marketed the synthetic cellulose sponge.

After each auction before the sponge boat owner received his money, 2 percent of the accepted sale price was deducted by the buyer. Of the 2 percent, 1.5 percent would be forwarded to the Sponge Exchange. The remaining .5 percent would be forwarded to Saint Nicholas Greek Orthodox Cathedral, at that time a separate wooden structure, as membership fees for the crews and captains of the sponge boats to be used to fund the operation and maintenance of the church.

Separately, donations were made by the sponge boat captains and their crews plus the sponge merchants to a special building fund for the construction of a new orthodox cathedral using Neo-Byzantine architecture modelled after the Saint Sophia Cathedral in Istanbul. The Saint Nicholas Cathedral, completed in 1943, with its tall brick tower, interior Pandocratoras Dome, numerous stained glass windows, marble Narthex and Ikonostasis, with elaborate Orthodox icons, stands as a classic edifice of Eastern Orthodoxy in America.

To this very day, the cathedral remains not only as a must-see historical site for Florida-bound tourists, but an active, liturgical center standing as a testimonial of the generosity and faith of those early sponge divers, sponge captains, boat owners, and sponge buyers or merchants.

Migration of the Nephews and Remaining Two Brothers from Symi, Greece

Dad and his brothers were responsible for sending earned money to Symi, Greece, to support his mom, sisters with their children, and sending for any remaining brothers (Frank and Nestor) in 1932–'33 to join them in Tarpon Springs. In addition, the brothers eventually sent for their four young nephews, starting in 1934 with Michael, followed by Teddy, Deno, and Karalos Cantonis, who joined Sponge Fishing Company in Tarpon Springs and were taught by the uncles the sponge business. Eventually, these nephews initially moved to New York and then Chicago, starting their own independent sponge and chamois business under the name Acme Sponge & Chamois Company Inc., a New York corporation that was founded in 1938. Acme, under the leadership of Michael Cantonis, evolved to currently become the largest distributor of both natural chamois leather and natural sponges in the United States and largest chamois tanner in the world according to Acme's website. The firm consolidated most of its operations and headquarters in Tarpon Springs at 855 East Pine Street by 1979 from Chicago.

On September 13 and 18, 2009, Michael and I, being his cousin, met at his home for the first time in some sixty years in Tarpon Springs, where we exchanged his family autobiography and my first text book, *Contracting with Uncle Sam* (2008, USNI Press) and critiqued them. For more information on Acme, one may want to read the autobiography *Michael G. Cantonis: My Ancestors & My Life* (2008, Star Graphics, Seminole, FL). Some two months later on November 17, Michael died in his home at the age of ninety-four.

He will not only be remembered as a successful businessman, but Michael will also be remembered as a philanthropist for his multiple donations from the Saint Nicholas Greek Orthodox Cathedral, the new Tarpon Springs Library, the emergency room of Morton Plant Hospital, the University of Florida in Gainsville for the Department of Greek Studies to the support of various needy families.

The remaining two brothers, Frank, who was a tanner, and Nestor, the latter who had been educated as a pharmacist, in 1938 started a tanning factory on Twenty-Four South Walton Street in Tarpon Springs by purchasing an old remote railroad warehouse with the financial aid of the other brothers. There were no neighbors but a nearby swamp that had snakes and mosquitoes. The start-up tanner factory, Florida Tanning Company, was in keeping with the tradition that their father operated a leather shoe shop in Symi, Greece.

The plant participated in the World War II effort by producing leather by tanning the hides of cattle for the manufacturers of boots for soldiers. The Lykes Brothers Inc., a family-owned business with substantial land and livestock holdings from Tampa, began supplying cattle hides to Frank and Nestor under government contract for boot leather.

After the war, the plant shifted to the tanning of alligator hides, producing luxurious leather for the manufacturer of handbags and shoes. It was Uncle Frank's skill and diligence as a tanner, plus the help of a German tanner, that Frank determined the formula in turning the hide of the alligator into luxurious leather.

I recall as a small boy hanging out at the tannery plant under the watchful eye of my uncle Frank, who, at that time, was unmarried, having no children of his own. I had to be watched for due to my curiosity. I would attempt to climb on the top of the large vats to see what was contained therein. There was fear that I would lose my footing and, even, fall in one of the chemical-filled vats. The plant had numerous vats full of hides. Each vat contained a variety of chemicals and hides being treated at various stages of the tanning process. There was quite a strong smell due to the murky chemical contents of each vat. My uncle Frank would be wearing rubber boots and a heavy plastic apron. On occasion, there were live alligators that had just been delivered and some even were crawling on the plant floor. On these later occasions, I would be ushered quickly to the plant office to be under the watchful eye of my uncle Nestor while I played on a typewriter.

Uncle Nestor took tanned leather samples to New York at the trade shows for manufacturers of handbags and shoes. They were amazed at the look, feel, and quality of the alligator leather. Florida Tanning Company became the second largest company in the United States specializing in this high-quality leather. Their customers were such famous names of that era as Florsheim, Amity, Andrew Geller, and Buxton for shoes, purses, and other accessories such as wallets for both men and women.

In 1963, my two uncles, Nestor and Frank, separated. Uncle Nestor kept the realty and physical plant. The original plant was eventually closed. Uncle Frank, with his share of the original business, opened a small tannery known as F. M. Giallourakis Leather Works, at 25 West Dodecanese Boulevard near the Sponge Docks. However, with the passage of laws in 1967, followed by the US Endangered Species Act of 1973 (ESA), the alligator as part of the crocodile family, was protected, thus precluding any further availability of alligator hides for tanning.

The alligator was removed on June 4, 1987, off the federal ESA and are regulated by each state. Alligators in Florida are now regulated by the state of Florida under Chapter 379.409 Florida Statutes, Florida Senate and the Florida Fish and Wildlife Conservation Commission. The original tannery that used various toxic chemicals in the tanning process, which were dumped in the immediate vicinity of the plant, to this day remains shuttered and designated as an environmental hazard area that requires cleanup before the property can be used or sold for any purposes.

The second factory in Tarpon Springs that used toxic chemicals was the Stauffer Chemical factory, which produced elemental phosphorus from phosphate ore and operated from 1947 until 1981. As a small boy, my brother, Mike, and I would often watch the smoke stacks from even miles away of the plant puffing tons of smoke into the atmosphere while we were swimming at the Fred

Howard Park Beach. The factory was originally operated by Victor Chemical Company and was acquired by Stauffer Chemical in 1960. The United States Environmental Protection Agency reported that site operations resulted in the contamination of soils, ground water, and waste ponds on the property. The main contaminants of concern in the soil include arsenic, antimony, beryllium, elemental phosphorus, polynuclear aromatic hydrocarbons. The plant was eventually closed and some one hundred local plant jobs were lost.

EPA placed the site on the Superfund's National Priorities List (NPL) in 1994 because of contaminated groundwater, sediment, and soil resulting from facility operations. EPA, the Florida Department of Environmental Protection (FDEP), and Stauffer Management Company, the site's potentially responsible party, have investigated, taken steps to clean up the site to protect people and the environment from contamination. Site contamination does not currently threaten people living and working near the site.

My Dad's Return to Greece to Find a Bride

It was not until Dad was some forty-five years old that he returned to his home in Symi, Greece, in 1933, specifically to get married. When Dad had now finally returned to Greece after some twenty-nine years, his father and mother had died, leaving his two married sisters whom he visited. His father's brother, Alexandros, befriended Dad. Dad's relatives had arranged for him to view from a café balcony overlooking the boardwalk a possible bride whom they considered eligible to be his future wife. The prospective bride, Irene, was a preschool and primary teacher. Dad was to see her on her way home after school as she walked through the plaza that afternoon. Both families, to include Irene, were aware that the prospective groom would be watching from his perch on the balcony.

As fate would have it, when Irene was approaching the plaza in the vicinity of the café's balcony, another schoolteacher appeared from behind running to catch up to Irene. She too was on the way home after teaching in the same school but unaware of the planned viewing by the American *groom*. Dad's eye caught the second teacher in particular, Stamatia Gerakis, in lieu of Irene. That evening Stamatia and her father, as prearranged, walked by the same café balcony so that Irene could see the groom too. The very next day, by the time my mom returned from school, my dad was sitting in the living room with my grandfather, Michael, and grandmother, Nomiki. By the end of that evening, my dad had found his wife.

My mom was born on January 17, 1911, on Saint Anthony's, celebrated name day. Her father originally was from the Island of Symi, Greece. His name was Michael Gerakis. He came to Kalymnos in 1905, which was a larger island recognized as a haven for trade, and opened a retail paint store. Many traders came to the island to ply their wares. In 1909, in Kalymnos, he married Nomikis Cretekou, my grandmother, in the Church of Christ (Sotiras) with whom he had four daughters—Stamatia, Katina, Ypapanti, and Kaliope—of which Stamatia was the oldest.

When my mom married, she had already completed college in Athens (at En Kallithea) and was a practicing schoolteacher. From Athens, she was initially assigned to teach on the island of Symi, where the entire family moved. My grandfather at that time was sick with his stomach and unable to continue to operate the paint retail store in Kalymnos. When my dad asked to marry my mom, he recognized the responsibility he took on, since my mom, Katina, and Kaliope were the primary bread earners for their parents and youngest sister, Ypapanti.

One can imagine the excitement in that household, where my mom also had three other younger sisters, Katina, Kaliopi, and Ypapanti. My grandfather had decided that my mom was to use the family dowry set aside for the marriage of the four children to defray the cost of her college education in lieu of a dowry. Hence, Stamatia first attended and graduated from En Kallithea Teacher's College in Athens and was assigned a teaching position on the island of Symi. It was common in those days that to get married, the prospective bride required a dowry in the form of money or a home or apartment to provide the groom to live.

The Gerakis family agreement was that once my mom graduated, she would work as a schoolteacher to earn funds to defray the cost of the next sister's professional education. The family philosophy was that no dowries were to be paid, but rather each sibling was to use family funds and the earnings of each sister to graduate each of them in order. A prospective groom would have to be wealthy enough not to demand a dowry.

My dad was married to Stamatia in Symi on October 2, 1933. En route from Greece, on their return to Tarpon Springs, the married couple stopped off in Paris for their honeymoon. Adolf Hitler had seized power in Germany that year, and President Franklin Roosevelt had his first radio "fireside chat" with America. Such "chats" were periodically conducted as the "New Deal" was being implemented and later during the war years. When the newlyweds arrived in Tarpon Springs, my mom, as she relayed to me years later, was horrified. The wild sponge fisherman and diver environment at the sponge docks on Dodecanese Boulevard and the rural, unsophisticated nature of Tarpon Springs were a surprise. No classic theaters, dirt, unpaved roads, few cars, swamps, mosquitoes, and lots of brothers-in-law who were unmarried and lived with the newly married couple in their large Whitcomb Boulevard home for extended periods of time!

Years later, Irene married my dad's brother, Damianos, who also had returned to Symi to become married after the early death of his first wife, Hariklia. In America, Irene taught school for Saint Nicholas Greek Orthodox Cathedral where my mom was also teaching. Then both, being married to Giallourakis brothers, found themselves teaching in the same school as they had back in Greece.

Three Gerakis Sisters Unite in Tarpon Springs

Being lonely, my mom, asked one of her sisters to come to America and live with her and my dad. Ypapanti, the youngest of the four sisters, at the age of eleven years old, came to live with her sister Stamatia. She grew up as a teenager in Tarpon Springs and attended high school. My aunt Ypapanti was in essence my brother's and my very own sister—our "second" mother. She played with and took care of us.

Aunt Ypapanti secretly wrote letters to her mom and dad back in Symi, reflecting that she too was very lonely. Both my dad and mom left for work daily—Dad to the sponge packing company and Mom to Greek school. Because Ypapanti was lonely, Katina who had finished the University of Athens and was a certified Greek school-teacher unexpectedly came from Symi to join her two sisters in America.

This left Kaliope, who had trained as a professional tailoress, seamtress, and fashion designer in Athens. Before World War II commenced, the family moved back to Kalymnos where Kaliope took care of her parents through the war years. Kaliope became a nun at the Panagia Cloister in Kalymnos. With the death of my grandfather Michael, her mom, Nomikis, accompanied Kaliope into the cloister where they both later died some fifteen years after WWII by 1962. My grandmother, Nomikis, was a centenarian at 105.

Aunt Katina served as a Greek teacher and taught in Tarpon Springs for the St. Nicholas Greek Orthodox Cathedral. She died as a young woman in an automobile accident in Tampa on January 18, 1939, when I was just a little over two years old. My mom was in the same car accident with Katina and was seriously injured; however, after almost six months of hospitalization, she recovered. I never got to know Katina, but the entire Greek Tarpon Springs community at that date turned out to mourn at their twenty-six-year-old Greek teacher's funeral. To this day, parishioners often come up to me on Sunday services at Saint Nicholas Cathedral to relate that they still remember Katina as their Greek language teacher to this very day.

Katina's class photograph with her students, priest, and bishop hangs in the Father Tryfon Hall foyer adjacent to the St. Nicholas Cathedral. Nearby in the same church hallway, now hangs my mother's plaque and her school class picture too. The two sister Greek schoolteachers are now once again in memoriam seen together by two generations of parish former students. Although now middle-aged or elderly, they have stories to relate to their children and grandchildren about these two Symian teachers—both who were ahead of their times. Between these two teachers' class photographs, numerous children of former students will for years be able to see their moms and dads.

Expanding the Family Ancestry Tree to the Bahamas

Aunt Ypapanti went on to marry a young start-up Greek merchant in Nassau whom my dad had met earlier in Cuba who had moved with his brother, Harry, to Nassau. In those years, the sponge beds found in the Great Bahamas Bank off Andros Island's west coast were rich and plentiful. The Bahamas were a British crown colony from 1717 until they were granted internal self-government in 1964. The self-government eventually negotiated a new constitution with Britain under which the colony became the Commonwealth of the Bahama Islands in 1969. On July 10, 1973, the Bahamas became an independent nation.

Ypapanti had to make her mind up whether or not to marry Anthony while my mom, my brother, Mike, and I waited with my dad in the then only Tampa Walgreens Drugstore. Ypapanti and Anthony took a stroll to decide whether or not they matched. At the end, within an hour from their departure, we saw them walking back to the Walgreens holding hands. The union was sealed with an engagement party that same afternoon in Brooksville, Florida. Even a trusted dating site such as e.Harmony.com/ or www.lunchdatingtips.com/ could not have been more successful.

The wedding took place in the Greek Orthodox Church of the Annunciation in Nassau a year later. Aunt Ypapanti, at the age of eighteen, had been sent within a year to Nassau all by herself to get married to Uncle Anthony whom she had met for several hours in Tampa and at the subsequent engagement party in Brooksville.

However, as an omen of events to come, starting her first night on her honeymoon and intermittently over some thirty years thereafter, Ypapanti dreamed that she would lose Anthony by being shot. Ypapanti furthermore relayed to me, when she had this nightmare, she would be awakened up by Anthony when he heard her screaming at which time he noticed her tears.

My dad had given Ypapanti funds to return back from Nassau in the event she changed her mind once she had gotten to Nassau. My aunt Ypapanti though considered Uncle Anthony to be an honest, kind, poor, but industrious person. Based upon those qualities that she saw in him, she remained in Nassau, returned the some $3,000 back to my dad at the insistence of Anthony. It turned out that Ypapanti had been blessed with a wonderful teammate.

Uncle Anthony and his brother, Harry, eventually went into the retail and wholesale grocery and dry goods business. They prospered. They imported into Nassau products for resale from the United States, the British Commonwealth of Nations with much of it coming from Australia, England, and Germany. Many of their retail and wholesale customers came by boat to Nassau from the numerous outer islands of the current Commonwealth of the Bahamas, such as Abaco, Andros, Grand Bahama, Cat Island, and San Salvador to mention but a few. They purchased in large quantities such groceries as coffee, lard, rice, sugar, flour, bacon, tobacco, and other staples of the times for themselves or to resale to their customers.

As a small boy, I often jumped on an open wagon pulled by a horse whose wooden flatbed was loaded with bales of flour and rice. The wagon was loaded from my uncle Anthony's dry goods warehouse then headed to complete the delivery of the merchandise to the customer's boat side at Nassau's midtown docks. The loaded open horse cart rides through downtown Nassau were thrilling to me despite the risk due to the absence of any belts or side rails. Once in a while, I was caught by Uncle Anthony. The horse ride was worth the subsequent discipline.

Aunt Ypapanti raised her family and concurrently grew herself from running a small grocery store annex near that of Uncle Anthony's main grocery store to purchasing, expanding, and operating a successful Nassau hotel. She became what one would label today a true small business entrepreneur in promoting her boutique hotel, "Gleneagles," by her dealings with the then nearby Montague Hotel and other major Nassau hotels to handle their overbooked guests. She even found financial support from foreign international banks with branches in Nassau and individual wealthy Canadians.

I considered my aunt's home in Nassau my second home and spent quite a few of my summer vacations as a small boy with my brother Mike in Nassau. We had quite a bit of fun with my two cousins, Kathryn and Manoli, with whom I played and later tutored in mathematics. Kathryn went on to become a schoolteacher, and Manoli became a lawyer and successful businessman in Nassau.

Many evenings while in Nassau, I would sit with my uncle and his relatives and friends, "Uncles" John Psilinakis, Pandelis Psilinakis, and Mekai Klonaris, on Nassau's east side beach park or on the family second-story porch listening to these grown-ups telling stories and jokes.

On the weekends, my uncle and I, along with Pantelis Psilinakis, often went underwater, spear-fishing for lobsters (crawfish), grouper, and hogfish at a special cove with reefs called the Rocks.

I, in particular as a small boy, was mystified by my uncle's heavy eyebrows, which, on many occasions, precluded me from being naughty. Uncle Anthony befriended my brother Mike after my dad in 1956 had died. Mike, for a while, worked in Nassau before attending college in Mexico City.

On the thirty-year anniversary of my uncle and aunt's marriage, a burglary occurred in their then east-end home in which my aunt Ypapanti survived a bullet wound to the chest while attempting to shield Uncle Anthony. Uncle Anthony was still, however, mortally wounded. My aunt's dreaded premonition of losing her Anthony played out that dark night. It was by God's grace that no other family member was lost on that traumatic evening.

Inside the Sponge Packing House

On many a Saturday morning, as a small boy, I sat on a wooden stool next to my dad and handed him sponges so that he would not have to stoop. At the sponge-packing house incorporated under the name Sponge Fishing Company, my dad would sort the sponges by quality and also decide and cut those he selected into smaller ones. He would then toss them into several separate bins made of wire mesh, depending on their size and quality. My brother, Mike, and I enjoyed going to Dad's sponge-packing house owned by my father and his three brothers: Tony, Damianos, and Vasilios—the four shareholders. We played hide-and-seek in the various sponge bins hiding under the fluffy but smelly sponges. There was no better place to hide.

I was amazed at the large hand hydraulic presses that compressed the dry sponges placed in variable built wooden containers covered internally with large canvas into fifty- to seventy-five-pound bales. They were similar as if they were cotton bales for shipment. The bales were shipped to the northeast client base. It was better than playing with large wooden building blocks. In those days, my cousins Tony, Duchess, Phillip, and Mike were in high school or already graduates of Tarpon Springs High School and were employed at various times at the sponge-packing house.

In 1947, Duchess, in her senior year in high school, served as an intern in the front offices doing typing and book keeping. She and her brother Tony were to later start their own curio stores and sponge business on the Tarpon Springs Docks, catering to tourists.

I distinctly recall watching, as a ten-year-old boy, Phillip loading up his new van with sponges in the parking lot of Sponge Fishing Company. Phillip, my cousin, had returned in 1945 from serving in the US Army in Europe where he had participated in the defense of the German offensive known as the Battle of the Bulge in Belgium. He was hospitalized for frostbite, along with numerous other soldiers during that campaign, and later transferred to the VA Hospital at Daytona Beach. After a year of treatments, Phillip recovered and was released from the Army.

Years later, I better understood the significance of that day when Phillip was loading his van. He had decided to embark on his own adventure as a sponge salesman traveling to the Northeast and Midwestern states. He wanted to be independent from his uncles at Sponge Fishing Company and start his own business. Phillip wound up in Cleveland, Ohio, where he met Catherine, with whom he had five children. Phillip eventually joined his father-in-law's small independent business, installing railroad tracks and performing track repairs for rail access into industrial sites in Ohio and other states.

Phillip also befriended my brother Mike as his mentor. Mike eventually went to Case Western University in Cleveland, Ohio, where he was working in the Sociology Department in an administrative position. It was at Case Western University that Mike met Janice Faye Nussbaum who, at that time, was a graduate student earning her master degree in mental health nursing; and they were married. Phillip served as the best man upon Mike's marriage to Janice. Their children, Nick and Gregory, were born in August of 1976, 1980, respectively in Neenah, Wisconsin.

The couple lived initially in Bloomington, Indiana, where Mike was a graduate assistant at Indiana University for four years; thereafter, he served as an assistant professor at the University of Wisconsin at Oshkosh, Wisconsin, for six years and then associate professor in the College of Business at Mississippi State University from 1982 to 1995 at Starkville, Mississippi.

Janice had earned her bachelor of science in nursing degree (BSN) at Alverno College in Milwaukee, followed by her master of science in nursing degree (MSN) focused on mental health nursing at Case Western University. Thereafter, she held various mental health clinical and teaching positions in Madison, Wisconsin, and Indianapolis, Indiana. Janice served as an assistant professor at Mississippi University for Women from 1983 to 2013 and then part-time since 2013.

Mike upon his death on June 30, 1995, was thereafter laid to rest at Cycadia Cemetery in Tarpon Springs, Florida next to his father, Cosmas, who passed on January 25, 1956 and mother Stamatia, who had passed on August 13, 2013.

Life on the Whitcomb Bayou

On Saturday evenings, my dad would drive us in his car, a LaSalle, a General Motors low-priced look-alike cousin to the then

1939 Cadillac, to the ice cream store in downtown Tarpon Springs with my mom and Mike.

There was always men's gatherings seven days a week at the city park each evening next to the Baynard Rexall Drugstore at the western end of Tarpon Avenue in downtown Tarpon Springs. In the summertime, when schools were closed, my brother and I would accompany Dad where we would sit and be treated at the Baynard's ice cream counter on the rotating stools where we would also play. Dad would smoke his Havana or Tampa Nugget cigar outside in the adjacent park and chat with friends and business acquaintances.

We lived on the Whitcomb Bayou in Tarpon Springs at 170 North Spring Boulevard, in a large Victorian two-story home built in 1885. The home was bordered in the front by a winding narrow dual-lane road around the periphery of the bayou and, in the rear, by a dirt trail that was used as shortcut to primary English and afternoon Greek schools. Our home was some four thousand square feet with four large bedrooms, three wood-burning fireplaces, two kitchens, and a waterfront front viewing, wrap-around screened porch.

The main sitting room had a stuffed male moose head with onerous antlers mounted over the fireplace mantel. The moose is the largest of all deer and is easily identified from other deer not only by its size but by its huge palmate antlers and by its bulbous, overhanging nose. The taxidermist had done a great job. Especially when the fireplace was roaring with firewood, the mounted deer presented a formidable enticement to my younger cousins, Kathryn and Manoli, visiting with their mom, Ypapanti, from Nassau, to eat for fear of the moose's eyes, antlers, and mouth.

The wrap-around screened porch provided an excellent playground for my brother Mike and me. It was large enough for us to pedal all our carts, play ball, and wrestle with each other—lots of space for two boys, my brother and me, plus friends to play. The porch had direct access to the kitchen and our outdoor supper dining table was located on the northern side of the porch adjacent to that kitchen door. The porch not only provided a beautiful panoramic view of the bayou but access to the icebox.

The tidal Whitcomb Bayou was an escape for me as a teen-ager, especially when schools were closed and on weekends. My dad had provided my brother, Mike, and me a small wooden dingy row boat, which we used to oar around the bayou to use our pole net for crabs when they were in season and for line fishing for sheephead and mullet too. We were careful not to be drawn by the current into the nearby Anclote River, which remains a major tidal tributary into the open Gulf of Mexico. My brother was some two years older than me and was gifted playing football and running track in contrast to my ability to rope-climb and tumble on the mats and perform free exercise calisthenics on the wooden floor at the gym.

On Sundays, my brother and I would attend St. Nicholas Greek Orthodox Church and serve as altar boys under Father Theophilos Karaphillis, who, at times, was amazingly very tolerant of our naughty behavior. Father Karaphillis was beloved by all the parish serving for some thirty-two years from 1922 to 1954. He would travel to the docks to bless the sponge boats and their crews on Epiphany Day and before they would depart for extended sponge diving periods. Epiphany celebrations are held by many Christians in remembrance of the baptism of Jesus Christ in the water of the Jordan River some two thousand years ago. Epiphany continues to be celebrated annu-ally by thousands of Tampa Bay area residents in Tarpon Springs at Whitcomb Bayou on the first week of January, over several days of celebrations, generally between January 5–7 each year.

My mom was a staunch supporter of attending church each Sunday. After all, she was one of the parish's Greek schoolteachers. I enjoyed the comradeship of the other altar boys. Once leaving Tarpon Springs to attend Georgia Military Academy (GMA), my brother and I, through high school, continued serving as altar boys in the Annunciation Greek Orthodox Church on 524 Pryor Street in Atlanta.

To this day, now that I have returned to Tarpon Springs, on Sundays in St. Nicholas, I always reflect on those days as an altar boy. I was ordained as an altar boy by the Revered Archbishop Spyrou Athenagoras, of the Greek Orthodox Church in America, who blessed and announced us as "Axios" (worthy) during the ordination ceremony, which included cutting a few locks of my hair in the ceremony before the entire congregation.

Being an altar boy created my first experience of being on an important working team, the size of a seven-man infantry squad—all in the uniform of white robes. Our mission was to support the priest. We ensured we were on time and ready to perform our duties in front of the congregation, in the rear altar area, and stood at the ready around the altar. By the time I had graduated from high school, I had become the squad leader of the altar boys at church. You need a team to be successful. A lesson that I carried forward in my approach to my assignments in both the Army and civilian endeavors from those days as an altar boy.

The Twilight Years of the Sponge Diving Industry in the Gulf of Mexico

After World War II in 1947, the sponge beds in the Gulf of Mexico had become contaminated, causing the sponges attached to the reefs to rot due to the so-called red tide algae bloom, which hit the West Coast beaches of Florida as evidenced by the dead fish that came ashore. Unlike the BP explosion and release of oil into the Gulf of Mexico from the Deepwater Horizon drilling rig oil in the gulf on April 20, 2010, this red tide phenomena, although not confirmed, was blamed by some on Navy munitions dumped in the Gulf of Mexico during live training exercises or created by various underwater sea algae species. Others blamed the damage due to fungoid microscopic organisms, which poisoned the fertile sponge beds of the Gulf of Mexico and West Indies to include Cuba, Jamaica, the Bahamas, and Grenada among others.

The cause and effect, whatever its origin, in the ensuing years impacted the Gulf Coast's sponge beds and fish wildlife, destroying them. When the red tide algae bloom occurred, wiping out the sponge fields in that region of the Gulf of Mexico, between 1951 to 1980, most of the sponge divers and their supporting crews from some one hundred or more sponge boats had departed from Tarpon

Springs to seek jobs in the factories, construction firms, and painting firms in Akron, Cleveland, and other midwestern cities such as Toledo and Chicago.

A small residual fleet and sponge fisherman remained. Some former sponge boats and divers switched to fishing and shrimping for a livelihood. Tarpon Springs then converted most of its sponge-related activities, especially the warehouses where they were sold, into tourist attractions. Along the sponge docks are now mostly shops, restaurants, and museums dedicated to the memory of Tarpon Springs's earlier industry. The Sponge Exchange was sold to the Pappas Brothers (descendants of Louis Pappas, the founder of the famous Louis Pappas Restaurant in Tarpon Springs) and was converted into a small mall with numerous boutiques, curios, restaurants, and cafes for tourists. The tourists keep coming to the sponge docks of Tarpon Springs to get a glimpse of America's glory days of open-sea sponge diving and to enjoy Greek cooked meals and pastries.

Concurrently in the 1950s, the mass-produced cellulose sponge, made of wood-fiber material, first produced under patents by DuPont came to the forefront. With its lower price, despite not of the same quality as a natural sponge, the synthetic sponge undercut the natural sponge market for household and industrial uses. As fortune would have it, with the end of World War II, the natural sponge market around the periphery of the Mediterranean, primarily from Greece, Turkey, Tunisia, Egypt, Cyprus, and Crete, reopened to supplant that of the Tarpon Springs Exchange.

Hence, after World War II, my dad traveled throughout the Mediterranean peripheral states and Middle East buying by the lot Mediterranean wool sponges that had been cleaned, dried, and stored up over the war years. He imported them to Tarpon Springs for resale to wholesale sponge dealers in Chicago and New York. As a small boy, I recall using a hose to wet the imported bales, which would then spring to life as the flattened, dried Mediterranean sponges swelled and "popped" to life.

New Beginnings for the Entire Family

It was in 1952 that the brothers in Sponge Fishing Company decided to split apart. My father was the first to go and later his brother, Damianos, each on their own separate ways. However, they were not fairly compensated by the two remaining corporate officers and brothers, Uncle Anthony and Uncle Vasilios. Dad was given the majority value of his stock (one hundred fifty thousand dollars) in the company in undervalued sponges, a minimum residual amount (some twenty-five thousand dollars) in cash, and the remainder in promissory notes (twenty-five thousand dollars).

Damianos retired due to his eye disabilities. Sponge Fishing Company agreed to pay him a monthly pension of one thousand dollars, plus some five thousand dollars in sponges and cash and some ten thousand dollars in promissory notes. As it turned out, Damianos's promised monthly pension was progressively reduced and never fully paid by the firm.

Dad started then his own sponge-packing company at age sixty with my mom as his secretary and bookkeeper. That was when he discovered that the sponges in lieu of cash for his stock were under-valued due to their quality. Their fair market value was substantially less. My mom came to the full-time support of my dad at the sacrifice of her public and private Greek school teaching. She also sacrificed two summer beach houses she had built on Clearwater Beach to raise the capital to fully provide the funds for my dad's new enterprise. She really loved the beach houses for our personal family use and as lucrative income-producing rental properties. There was to be one beach house for each Mike and Bill. Yet she saw how nervous and frustrated her husband was that she did not hesitate to sell the twin yellow brick houses to raise the capital. My dad wanted to stay in business despite his age of sixty years. She did not want him to have a heart attack.

My mom was family focused even with her teaching and devotion to my dad's business endeavors. She was considered stern but highly respected by the children and the grown-ups—she taught Greek as a second language. She stressed to Mike and me the importance of school and physical exercise. She was probably the first Greek schoolteacher in Tarpon Springs to teach students in our home while riding her stationary bike.

My father, who was accompanied by my mother, pursued the European sponge markets year round; hence, my brother and I were enrolled in 1949 as boarding students, seventh and ninth graders respectively in the then all-male private Georgia Military Academy(GMA) (now known as Woodward Academy and coed) located in College Park, Georgia, just outside of Atlanta.

My mom and dad had researched a number of private secondary and college military boarding preparatory schools in the Tampa and St. Petersburg area, such as Admiral Farragut Academy and Riverside Academy. With the help of a former alumni of GMA, my dad and my mom agreed that GMA, although in Atlanta, was worth the sacrifice of parting with their two sons for their educational advancement.

Moreover, my mom considered Florida's high schools to be substandard and was instrumental, more than my dad who wanted to have his two sons close to him, in our being sent to GMA as boarding students to receive our seventh through twelfth grade educations. Mom felt that we had to be educated outside of Tarpon Springs to have a chance elsewhere to be more successful in a modern world in whatever endeavors we undertook.

CHAPTER 2

Waiter to House Mother's Assistant

At Georgia Military Academy (GMA), I wore a school uniform to classes and was instructed by ROTC instructors (both regular Army officers and enlisted personnel), retired military officers, and civilian teachers. Moreover, it was at GMA that I learned not to cry when I was lonely despite the fact that my brother, Mike, was with me. I attended GMA from the seventh grade until I graduated from high school. It was at GMA where my brother Mike and I were awarded scholarships and worked in the dining hall as waiters. Later, I was assigned as an assistant to a housemother for some thirty young elementary school boarding students. GMA was where I mastered high school sciences, mathematics, history, and literature and where I joined the gymnastics and boxing teams.

I attribute my early interest in mathematics (plane and solid geometry, trigonometry, and calculus) to my math teacher, Lottie Wilson. Her love of the subject was infectious. Little did I realize that Mrs. Wilson was developing and building my foundation for critical thinking and problem solving to be able to resolve issues and conflicts without depending on technology to discover answers. There was no Internet to provide a database for solutions or Google to search for a comparable problem. There was no Chegg, online study aid covering calculus, physics, chemistry, or unlimited access to guided solutions plus textbooks, or solutions from textbook publishers or Chegg-qualified experts (composed of professors, graduate students).

The Golden Gloves Challenge

As a one-time adventure, I joined the boxing team to fight in the amateur championships in downtown Atlanta. My weight class was featherweight or under ninety-nine pounds. I recall working out daily and looking forward to fighting in the Golden Gloves amateur boxing championships. I am not sure how my boxing coach got me qualified, but I recall that special evening being at the championships in the Atlanta Convention Center in 1952, which for the first time were to be shown on television. TV had just come to Atlanta.

Despite all the excitement, I was matched up with the prior year Golden Gloves Champion at 110 pounds. During the first round, I was punched directly in the throat, taking my breath away, causing me to be knocked down onto the ring's floor mat. I survived the referee's count to fight another four rounds without getting knocked down again only by pure mental determination, "grit."

Although I had lost the fight in a decision by the referee, rather than a technical knockout (TKO), I had learned an important lesson that evening. Never give up, even if you are exhausted and getting beat up. By the end of that evening, I realized also that boxing was not to be my career. The very next week, my classmates, contemporaries, upperclassmen, and church members, many who had watched the fight on television, treated me as a hero despite the loss! The Atlanta audience had gotten a glimpse of the Spartan in me.

Thereafter, while my brother played football, not to be outdone, I took to gymnastics focusing on the flying rings, balancing beam, parallel or high bars and free exercise on the gym floor. Before graduating from high school, I would have become a Georgia state high school gymnastics champion.

Our Boarding High School Scholarships

After our second year at GMA, my dad and my mom could no longer afford to keep us in a private boarding school in Atlanta. However, the GMA school's administration so much liked the team of my brother and me that they awarded us a need-based boarding and tuition scholarship annually for three years to complete high school. The scholarship required us to study and also work in the dining room as cook's helpers and dining room waiters nine months out of the year.

In the summer, we both worked on campus doing work on the maintenance of the grounds and even accompanying the football team in its annual four-week August summer training camp. Mike and I went with the football team to Kissimmee, Florida, to the estate of a GMA alumni who not only had a ranch that housed the football team, but had a manicured full-size football field with goal posts all built specifically for summer practice.

Kissimmee is located adjacent to the world-famous theme parks of Walt Disney World, Sea World, and Universal Orlando. I worked in the kitchen with Mike, who also was on the team as its right end. We both served the football players. We were also the assistant cooks for the one assigned GMA cook. In fact, when the GMA cook was a bit inebriated on occasion, we covered for him and cooked for the team meals.

At the end of the practice month, we played a game against a local Orlando High School team in the Tangerine Bowl Stadium, now known as the Florida Citrus Bowl, in Orlando. My mom had come up from Tarpon Springs to see her two sons and not only did she see us, but also when they carried me off the field. I had delivered a best effort to what one would classify as an ineffective body block. However, I was run over by the leading interference of the offensive opponent's full back, which steamrolled over me. The coach regretted that he had given in to my pleadings to let me one time suit up and be a substitute on just one play on defense for the game.

Eventually, I was "promoted" out of the dining room to become a resident counselor during my junior and senior high school years to the main boarding house, which housed only first through seventh grade students. I was assigned as the assistant to the "house mother." Mike got promoted to the school's motor pool where he became a bus driver in his senior year. I was like a "mother" to young children, the fourth through seventh graders, placed in GMA's boarding school from wealthy families that were in the midst of divorce or already separated. I even coached the junior football team.

The students needed consoling and empathy due to home sickness. I tutored them in math and even ensured their bathing took place. By the time I had made my evening rounds of each student room, my studies would start at about eleven o'clock each evening and go into the wee early morning hours of the next day.

Concurrently, I also received the cadet military rank of cadet battalion commander in the Reserve Officers' Training Corps (ROTC) in my senior year. It was an honor to be selected to that post by the ROTC active military Army faculty. During the weekly parades in the fall and spring, I enjoyed leading the cadet battalion. Being a house counselor and the cadet battalion commander were the beginning of my introduction to care giving and leadership. I had made several college applications in my senior year with intent to become a doctor. By the spring of 1954, I was elated to have received my college acceptance for attendance at John Hopkins University and its School of Medicine in Baltimore under grants of full scholarships for undergraduate and graduate studies in biology and medicine.

My Brother Mike's Circuitous Journey to Professorship

Mike graduated from GMA in 1953, a year earlier than me. He left GMA with the rank of cadet captain in the ROTC. He then went on to attend heating and air-conditioning engineering at Southern Technical Institute in Chamblee, Georgia. Southern Technical Institute was an extension of Georgia Institute of Technology. It is currently known as the Southern Polytechnic College of Engineering and Engineering Technology located at Kennesaw, Georgia, devoted to the instruction of technical arts and applied sciences.

Thereafter, Mike spent a stint in the Army where he underwent basic training at Fort Ord, California. Later, Mike also worked in Nassau alongside Uncle Anthony and Aunt Ypapanti in the hotel management business. Despite the fact that my mom always worried about Mike's academics, he received his bachelor's degree from the University of Mexico in Mexico City, his master's degree from the University of Illinois, and his doctorate degree from Indiana University.

These accomplishments were due in part to his relationship with my uncle Anthony in Nassau; cousin Phillip who lived in Cleveland; and especially, his subsequent marriage to Janice Faye Nussbaum, a nurse and later assistant nursing professor at Mississippi University for Women. Janice received her master of science in nursing, and Mike worked at Case Western University. Phillip was our first cousin whose dad, Damianos, had been his business partner at Sponge Fishing Co. with my dad.

Mike and Janice were blessed with two wonderful sons, Gregory and Nicholas. Gregory serves as the manager head at the nation-wide firm Maxim Health Care Services with offices serving Northern Virginia, which focuses on providing homecare, companion care, medical staffing, and wellness services nationwide to include providing pediatric nursing services. Nicholas practices law as counsel with the national commercial and tort litigation law firm of Forman Perry Watkins & Krutz LLP in Jackson, Mississippi.

Mike taught at Mississippi State University in Starkville management and international business as an associate professor. Mike died on June 30, 1995, at sixty years old due to heart issues. Mike was laid to rest at Cycadia Cemetery in Tarpon Springs next to his dad, Cosmas, on July 5, 1995. Despite the fact that we were close as small children and especially at GMA, after I entered the Army, as brothers, we lost that closeness.

This loss was inexcusable only to be regained when he was ill and on the last leg of his life's journey. Before Mike had died, he had reached out and consulted with me to be designated in his last will and testament as his personal representative. In that capacity, I did my best to assist Mississippi counsel and was instrumental in settling his estate as described in his will in a fair and intended manner for his children, Greg and Nick, and wife, Janice. Complex issues were settled related to insurance matters with the Teachers Insurance and Annuity Association (TIAA) and other claims by Mike's second wife,

Joannie Erickson, whom Mike had married several years before his death.

Because of this haunting, unpardonable neglect and lack of frequent, meaningful communication between Mike and myself, I have attempted to instill in my three children the importance of always talking to each other. In addition, they should coordinate among themselves often and at least once a year conduct a family reunion at a summer beach house of their choosing. It was also the explicit wish of their beloved mom Antonia to do so. With the advent of the internet, tablets, and smartphones, there is no excuse for siblings not staying in touch by at least texting often.

A Mentor's Impact on a Student

By the spring of my junior high school year, I had come to the attention of the President of GMA, Colonel William R. Brewster, who had been a West Point graduate. My boarding room faced the president's home and he could see my lights on as I was studying in the late evening hours every day of the week. He wanted me to attend college at the United States Military Academy. He sent me with his stern direction at his expense even to an optometrist in downtown Peachtree Street in Atlanta to undertake five months of special eye exercises in the afternoons to strengthen my eyes. He wanted assurance that I would be able to pass the West Point eye exam, which at that time required twenty-twenty eye vision on both eyes without glasses.

Initially appointed as a Distinguished Reserve Officers' Training Corp (ROTC) graduate to attend West Point, I later concurrently also received a senatorial principal appointment to West Point from the Honorable George Smathers, Democrat of Florida. US senators, as of this writing, by statute are allowed five "principal nominee" appointments to each of the three principal service academies (US Naval Academy at Annapolis, US Military Academy at West Point and Air Force Academy at Colorado Springs).

I had turned down the Distinguished ROTC graduate appointment, since I thought I would not be able to pass the West Point eye exam. That action allowed another fully qualified candidate to take my seat. However, I accepted the senatorial "principal nominee" primary appointment in as much as there were several backup "competing alternate" qualified candidates in the wings, anyone of which that could take my seat in the event I was unable to pass the physical exam.

I found myself taking the special West Point Physical and Academic Admission Entrance exams at Fort McPherson in East Point, Georgia, and continued the heart medical portion at Martin Army Community Hospital at Fort Benning, Georgia. West Point developed and used its own special admission exam. Neither the college entrance Scholastic Aptitude Test (SAT) or American College Testing (ACT) exam were used by the academy for admission in those years. Currently, both the SAT and ACT are taken and provided to the academy for admission selection.

The eye doctors at Fort McPherson were amazed when they noted the difference in my eyesight on the second exam. My eyes even passed the color plates and yarn test for color to my amazement. The doctors, after a week of observations and tests at Fort Benning, confirmed that my heart was in great shape and the escalated blood pressure measurements at Fort McPherson were because of my anxiety in taking the eye exam, which subsided once I had passed that medical exam.

Unbeknown to me years later, I found that my mother had lobbied through Mr. Emmanuel Johnson, the well-known family insurance broker in Tarpon Springs, for the 1954 principal senatorial appointment to West Point of then Democratic senator George A. Smathers. I was surprised to have received a coveted "principal nominee" senatorial appointment. In retrospect, it was surely politically motivated to please the Hellenic-American community in Tarpon Springs.

It was not until high school graduation that last Sunday afternoon in May of 1954 while walking to the commencement ceremony at the GMA gymnasium and to meet my parents, that a special courier intercepted me. The courier handed me the Army's acceptance envelope to West Point. This event thus derailed my college acceptance attendance to the John Hopkins University.

Rather, I decided that afternoon and at that instant of time, 2:00 p.m., May 30, 1954, that that *Spartan* Hellenism in me from Alexander of Macedonia, conqueror of the Persian Empire to Theodoros Kolokrotonis, preeminent leader of the Greek War of Independence against the Ottoman Empire, would prevail. My afternoon Greek school history supported the decision.

My study of American history at Georgia Military Academy sealed the decision. The Civil War and World Wars I and II legends of Generals Lee, Grant, Pershing, McArthur, Patton, and Eisenhower, who had all been cadets at West Point, were too great to ignore. It was my belief and dream that West Point would be my very stepping stone to a place in American history too!

By the time I returned from Atlanta to Tarpon Springs after graduation, every immigrant Greek-American, to include sponge divers, knew I was going to West Point. My dad and mom made sure! It was the talk at the local cafés and tavernas on Athens Street and Dodecanese Boulevard just off and on the sponge docks. I was proud to represent the Greek community.

GMA had served my brother and me well in preparing us for our future educational growth. In 1964, GMA became coeducational, and in 1966, it changed its name to Woodward Academy in honor of GMA's founder, Colonel John Charles Woodward. Woodward Academy is no longer a military or boarding school. However, it remains a foremost, vibrant private educational school for day students in the Atlanta area.

CHAPTER 3

Plebe to Lieutenant

Train Service to New York City

By noon on July 5, 1954, I arrived for the first time in New York City by train. In that year, trains operated by the National Railroad Passenger Corporation (AMTRAK) stopped at the Tarpon Springs Train Depot from where my rail journey took me northeast through Jacksonville to New York City. I was to use AMTRAK for the next four years, along with numerous other West Point cadets living on the West Coast of Florida, going and returning from New York City. AMTRAK in those years also allowed residents from Tarpon Springs to travel south to Tampa, east to Orlando, and onto the east coast to Miami. Today, the rail tracks into Tarpon Springs have been removed and paved over for use as the Pinellas County bicycle trail between Tarpon Springs and St. Petersburg in the south.

The Tarpon Springs Area Historical Society, organized in 1967 as an Internal Revenue Code 501 (c)(3) non-profit, with the help of the city and federal grants, rescued the historic train depot at 160 East Tarpon Avenue after many years of neglect, transforming the neglected, dilapidated building into the Historic Train Depot Museum. The museum now houses the archives of the Tarpon Springs Area Historical Society. The historical society has filled the old station with exhibits telling the story of Tarpon Springs' past.

Tourists, schoolchildren, and locals visit the depot to learn more about the city's heritage.

Despite overtures related to the construction of a high-speed rail system in Florida by various federal officials and past and recent Florida governors, the project connecting Tampa, Orlando, and Miami for various political and budget pressures remains elusive to this day. Hence as a starter, the private investors of Florida East Coast Industries (FEC) have stepped up to finance a high-speed train connecting Orlando International Airport and Miami with stops at Fort Lauderdale and West Palm Beach—the All Aboard Florida Train. The first leg of this effort is labeled Brightline, an express train service using the FEC Railway corridor between Miami and Cocoa, Florida, and a new forty-mile track along State Road 528 between Cocoa and Orlando with projected service first extending between Miami and West Palm Beach by 2018.

Once arriving at Penn Station in New York City that afternoon, I took my first taxi in New York City to Times Square. I had reservations for one evening at the then well-known Times Square Hotel on Fifty-Ninth West, Forty-Sixth Street where my father had always stayed on his business trips to market sponges. I was seventeen years old and overwhelmed by the sight of the multitude of skyscrapers and Times Square's crowd.

The very next morning, an unfamiliar uncle of mine, Uncle Vasili, my grandfather's brother, appeared at the hotel, identified himself, and escorted me to the Port Authority. He placed me on the bus at the Port Authority for the trip along the Hudson River to Fort Montgomery and Bear Mountain, then Highland Falls and the West Point Main Gate.

On July 6, 1954, as the bus traveled north, winding along the Hudson River on Route 9W toward Bear Mountain, we passed miles of mothballed liberty ships, comprising some 165 ships of the Naval Reserve Fleet anchored in storage on the Hudson River since 1945. It was an impressive sight to me, reminding me of films I had seen of World War II and the Normandy Beach landings. The mass of ships was a visual exhibit to America's involvement in WWII and a testimony to the industrial capacity of America. Some of these ships were later reactivated for the Korean War, Suez Canal Crisis, and Vietnam War. Today, all the ships have been removed or sold for scrap metal to such countries as Spain.

The "Beast Barracks" Experience

The bus stopped at about noon in front of Grant Hall, where soon I found myself inside Central Area. Within several hours that afternoon, I was given a haircut; assigned a barracks room in North Area; provided a complete set of new uniformed clothing to include underwear, socks shoes, and boots; and undertook a drill lesson on how to stand tall and march in a squad formation. Finally, that afternoon, I found myself standing at Trophy Point around Battle Monument, looking down onto the Hudson River north toward Newburg. Trophy Point overlooks the Hudson River where the "Great Chain" was stretched across to stop the British ships during the Revolutionary War. There are many historic cannons and howitzers there from early wars fought by our nation, to include the Civil War, with West Point graduates as their leaders.

Battle Monument was dedicated in memory of the officers and men of the regular army of the United States who fell in battle during the War of the Rebellion. I could read the names of some of the 2,230 officers and soldiers engraved thereon that had fallen during the Civil War. It was erected by their surviving comrades. The granite structure has a monolithic shaft forty-six feet tall and five feet, six inches in diameter, surmounted by a bronze statue of Lady Fame (Victory).

There, some 752 new male admitted cadets, including myself, were sworn into the academy as the class of 1958 that July 6 of 1954. As a note, some twenty years later, the first class to be sworn in with female cadets was the class of 1980. In 1980, sixty-two female cadets graduated, the first since 1802 when West Point was first founded. Perhaps Kira, my seven-year-old grandchild, Aakash and Christina's daughter, will consider following in her grandfather's footsteps by attending the academy!

In world and national events, some two months earlier, on May 7, 1954, Dien Bien Phu, the French military outpost in Vietnam, had fallen to the Viet Minh Army. On May 17, the USS *Nautilus*, the first Navy nuclear submarine, was commissioned in Groton, Connecticut; and later that same day in 1954, the Supreme Court's unanimous decision in *Brown v. Board of Education of Topeka* banned racial segregation in public schools. All events that were to later impact my active military service after graduating from West Point in unexpected ways.

Cadet Basic Training (commonly known as Beast Barracks) is a six-week process that turns students accepted into West Point from civilians to cadets. Although not explicitly stated, this period of intense physical and mental stress is intended to weed out those that are unwilling or unfit to undergo the demands of military authority and life. In our class, seven new cadets resigned during the summer's Beast Barracks. However, by the end of the first academic year, we lost 151 more classmates because of deficiencies in academics or tactics as well as resignations to include honor code violations. Thereafter, 573 finally graduated in June 1958 and were commissioned in the Army and Air Force. A year later, the US Air Force Academy received academic accreditation and graduated its first class of 207 on June 3, 1959, thus eventually closing the gate for West Point graduates to accept commissions to the Air Force upon graduation.

The US Military Academy as well as the other service academies offer a college education and full four-year scholarships. Tuition, books, board, and medical and dental care are all fully paid for all four years. Graduates of all five academies receive a bachelor of science degree and are commissioned as officers in their respective service branch (Navy, Army, Air Force, Coast Guard, Merchant Marine Academy). In all cases, there is a service obligation of a minimum of five years. In my opinion, many of the cadets in my class that resigned at the conclusion of their first academic year in 1955 did so because they did not want to occur the "obligation" of paying back the US government if they resigned after their second year as cadets their full equivalent college expenses.

These resignations were possibly attributed to the fact that when resignation occurred early at the end of the first-year recoupment of the taxpayer expenses for a cadet is forgiven. The way recoupment works is that if a cadet student attends at least two years at the taxpayers' expense and then does not finish for reasons they could control—especially misconduct or poor performance—they are required to repay the government. If things out of their control cause their departure, including many medical conditions, recoupment can be waived. Upon graduation from West Point, a 1958 graduate was required then to serve in the Armed Services for three years before resigning from the service.

A significant number of my classmates who had were commissioned officers served their obligatory period completing assignments in Europe or Korea and then resigned. Most had attained the rank of captain and had served as platoon and company commanders. Industry picked these officers up because of their leadership skills and habits learned at West Point of honesty and diligence on the job. Such defense firms as Boeing Aircraft, Lockheed Martin, Raytheon, General Dynamics, and many others recruited and hired such former West Point graduates to serve as project and team managers or leaders on their defense contracts. They continue to do so to this very day from various West Point classes.

There were a number of cadets who served in the Armed Forces as enlisted men such as my cadet roommate, Jerry Prohaska, prior to the academy. They had to go through Beast Baracks too because being a cadet has different facets to it than being an enlisted soldier. Cadets in their cow (junior) and firstie (senior) years were assigned the leadership roles during Beast, and together, they and their new cadets train in a number of skills. There were two halves of Beast Barracks, the first of which taught us new cadets how to act, speak, and present ourselves in a soldierly manner, while the second taught us as new cadets military tactics, the basic use of military weapons systems, and other valuable military skills such as repelling, land navigation, marksmanship, and the use of gas masks.

That very first evening, a first classman came into my room and escorted me to his room. He ordered me to stand on my two hands.

That seemed odd. I did not think anyone knew I was a high school all-around state gymnast at Georgia Military Academy. So immediately, I popped into a handstand (being proud of myself). What I did not realize was that Bob Carpenter, class of 1955, was captain of the West Point varsity gymnastics team. He was waiting for me to arrive. Moreover, I did not realize that I would have to stand on my hands against a wall for a long time. Carpenter was testing my mental attitude first but also to see whether or not I had grit as well as being a gifted gymnastic rookie. I passed the test.

During Beast Barracks, we spent time learning how to march on the parade field. I also learned how to polish my black shoes to have a spit shine. I never really mastered the technique—at least not as well as my roommates. As the summer continued, we marched in full combat uniforms out to swim at Delafield Pond, to the USMA Golf Course, and finally to Camp Buckner—each being sequentially longer. I looked forward to Sundays because during Beast Barracks church services for my cadet class were conducted out on Trophy Point and the "mental and physical exercises" were suspended.

My smirks (smiling) often got me into trouble with the upperclassmen. To my amazement, I really found Beast Barracks overall to be exciting and challenging. It helped that I arrived in quite good physical shape and was a good swimmer. My athletic and military training at Georgia Military Academy paid off.

My West Point Roommates and Classmates

After Beast Barracks that first summer was over, I was assigned as a plebe (a freshman student) to Company B, Second Regiment (B-2), where I was housed in the Central Area for some four years. The whole company comprised some one hundred cadets from plebes to firsties all sized to the same height and thus assigned to Company B-2 so that when we marched, we blended in to the sloping parade field to the taller-sized companies in a straight line formation. There was some twenty-two of my class of 1958 in Company B-2 that eventually graduated. My roommates over my four years at

West Point were John Manos, from North Carolina; Jerry Prohaska, from Iowa; and Floyd Spencer, from Texas.

John had attended college before arriving at the academy. He served as our math coach. John was bright. Since he had completed one year of college before being admitted to the academy, he was my tutor in a number of subjects. We were both Hellenes. John breezed through academics plebe year because of his previous freshman attendance. It took me one year just to catch up with John by sheer study.

John graduated as a second lieutenant into the Corps of Engineers with his first assignment being with the Seventy-Eighth Engineer Battalion in Karlsruhe, Germany. After his assignment in Europe, he returned to civilian life to Fayetteville, North Carolina, to become a successful business owner and leader in the then home stereophonic and high-fidelity equipment business. Fayetteville is a city in Cumberland County and is best known as the home of Fort Bragg, a major US Army installation northwest of the city. John's family befriended me in 1959 when John was in Germany and I was assigned to the Eighty-Second Airborne Division at Fort Bragg.

Jerry had been an enlisted man in the Air Force before coming to West Point. Hence, Jerry helped us all with his savvy of military life. He had been assigned in 1953 by the Air Force to the USMA Preparatory School (USMAPS) in Newburgh, New York, to assist him in preparing for the requisite entrance exams. The USMA Preparatory School had a history of being moved quite often. It was relocated from New York to Fort Belvoir, Virginia, and later moved to Fort Monmouth and then again finally moved permanently to West Point, where it is currently located.

Upon graduation in 1958 from West Point, Jerry was commissioned as a second lieutenant and returned to the Air Force to serve in various intelligence and telecommunications assignments. Upon his retirement in 1977, Jerry worked in industry where he was a pioneer in the cellular telephone technology business. While a cadet, Jerry was a member of the Cadet Glee Club and remains active in the West Point Alumni Glee Club, from where he lives in Fauqier County in Virginia.

Floyd came from Texas and was easy-going and had a special humble but firm nature. We both went into the artillery branch at graduation. Floyd was killed in action on January 31, 1968, in Vietnam. The following quotation from Floyd's Silver Star award is typical of his life with me as a roommate and, later, as a friend:

> Major Spencer distinguished himself by gallantry in action on 31 January 1968 while serving as District Senior Advisor, Cu Chi District, Hau Nghia Province, Republic of Vietnam.
>
> On that date, Major Spencer was accompanying a force of one platoon of Regional Forces commanded by the Vietnamese District Chief in an operation to engage and destroy a small enemy force near the Village of Tan Phu Trung. As the unit approached the village, it came under withering automatic weapons fire from well-placed and camouflaged ambush positions.
>
> Seeing his radio operator felled by the enemy fire and left helpless on an open field, Major Spencer dashed through intense enemy fire to the aid of the injured man. Though the focal point of enemy gunners, Major Spencer attempted to pick the man up and move him to safety. While doing so under the concentrated fire of the enemy guns, he was mortally wounded. Major Spencer's conspicuous gallantry in action was in keeping with the highest traditions of the United States Army.

Sunday Spiritual Activities at West Point

While a cadet, I enjoyed attending Eastern Orthodox Church services together with other cadets when the opportunity occurred. On occasion, a visiting Orthodox priest came on Sunday. The Greek Orthodox priests from the parish in nearby Newburg, New York;

Saint Basil Academy in Garrison, New York; or student priests from St. Vladimir's Seminary would come to conduct Orthodox services in the Chapel of Saint Martin of Tours. Saint Martin had served in the military and went on to become the bishop of Tours, France. Saint Martin was known even in his lifetime as a great miracle worker. This chapel is located in the lower level below the main cadet chapel where Protestant services are normally held.

When no Orthodox services were to be conducted on Sunday, I attended Protestant services in the main cadet chapel, which had been dedicated in 1910. The cadet chapel is a large granite structure architecturally reflecting a Gothic medieval fortress towering high above the West Point Plain below. I always enjoyed listening to the vibrant sound of the chapel's famous organ initially installed in 1911 and enlarged with grants thereafter and the cadet choir at these services.

Attendance gave me a chance for a short time to avoid the strenuous unrelenting activities that existed outside. It was a special quiet period, providing me a chance to relax, reflect, and reinvigorate myself—spiritually and psychologically. After graduation, I repeated the sanctuary of the church in many subsequent Army assignments whether it was the chaplain's field tent in Lai Kai, Vietnam, or the Post Episcopal Chapel at Fort Sill, Oklahoma, to sneak away just to meditate in peace and quiet. Today, even here in Tarpon Springs, one may catch me sneaking away to seek the solitude of the small chapel at the Shrine of Saint Michael Taxiarchis at B131 Hope Street near the sponge docks.

A Special Family Visitor

In January of 1955 of my plebe year (freshman college) at West Point, my dad came to visit me. In those years, plebes were not allowed to go home the first year even for Christmas. Dad too had taken the bus from Port Authority in the New York City that Saturday morning. I met my dad at Grant Hall, the academy's cadet visit center, which then also housed the offices of the cadet hostess.

My dad relayed to me that the bus was filled with beautiful college girls whom he overheard were coming to West Point for the weekend for a formal cadet evening dance at Cullum Hall. He hoped that I was not being distracted from my studies by such ladies.

As I found out later, the cadet dates were from Vassar and Bryn Mawr College. They had been dropped off by the bus for the weekend at the historic Thayer Hotel, named after the Father of the Academy, Colonel Sylvanus Thayer.

I was so happy to see my dad who had come to the city for sponge business sales but had taken the time to come up the Hudson River to visit. It was to be his first and last trip to West Point for in my sophomore year, one year after his visit, my dad unexpectedly died at the age of sixty-five and was buried in Cycadia Cemetery in Tarpon Springs on January 25, 1956. To this very date, I have always cherished that one visit.

I am so proud of my dad for he served first and foremost the entire Giallourakis family from Symi, Greece, before himself over many years. Once he arrived in the United States, he never abandoned his Symian family. He made numerous sacrifices for his parents, brothers, and sisters and was so good to my mom, his two sons, Mike and Bill, and his sisters-in-law, Katina, Kaliope, and Ypapanti. He was industrious, hardworking, honest, and respected by all that came in contact with him. We also had fun with each other even while he helped me with my arithmetic. He taught me how to swim at Clearwater Beach. We had watermelon-eating feasts. He often, on frequent evenings, took Mike and me to have ice cream at a special cake parlor.

The Challenges at West Point

Of the four years at West Point, with all its challenges and discoveries, two activities set the stage for my future. The first activity was the diligence and perseverance necessary of molding myself into a national gymnastic champion on the flying rings under the coaching of Tom Maloney, the revered gymnastics coach. Coach Maloney also coached or managed the US Olympic Gymnastics Team for the Moscow, Rome, Helsinki, Tokyo, and Prague Olympic Games. Coach Maloney was responsible for my classmate, Gar O'Quinn, becoming an all-around Olympian in 1960.

Tom Maloney was only the second gymnastics coach in the history of the United States Military Academy at West Point. He enjoyed remarkable successes over a thirty-six-year career. In fact, he retired as Army's most productive coach between 1931 and 1966. Important to include that recruits came to West Point without any commitment to the gymnastics team, but each had to participate in at least one athletic sport. This accounts for the Army gymnastic team consisting mostly of "specialists" of which I was to join the ranks of one such specialist on the flying rings.

One would find me every afternoon at the gymnasium working out on the flying rings. Even in the summer off-season, I would find the flying rings installed between trees at Camp Buckner and at the gyms in other visiting military installations on which to train.

At the end of the rear and forward pendulum swings high near the gymnasium ceiling, I would perform "crosscuts" with my legs releasing the rings from my hands and quickly regrasping them, swinging in the reverse direction. The flying rings taught me the importance of physical training, coordination, timing, prior practice, and confidence to achieve excellence. My high school Golden Gloves experience had been a well-learned lesson in perseverance. It also came in handy during plebe boxing classes as part of the plebe physical training program.

During the winter collegiate season, the main gymnasium stands would fill up to watch the gymnastics competition, especially against Navy, Penn State, Florida State University, and Syracuse. The flying rings competition was a highly attended event. Over several years, I had developed the double somersault dismount at the end of my swinging routine off the flying rings, which caused the weekend cadets' dates to audibly swoon, gasp, and stand in amazement. I had not killed myself.

The second challenging activity was my interest in certain studies. I discovered that I was adept in the social sciences, especially history (world, American, and military), English literature, and economics, but I was also very interested in mathematics and the sciences despite my skepticism of ever mastering mechanics and fluid dynamics. At times, I had wished that perhaps I could have reached the academic status of being a "star man" for distinguished academic achievement as represented by a gold star sewn on each collar of the cadet jacket uniform.

I settled for being ranked high academically in English, military history, and economics. I also did well in my sophomore year in my mathematics courses, especially advanced calculus to include differential equations with "Laplace" and "Fourier Transforms." Little was I to know then that these studies would later form the basis of my studies of graduate electrical engineering, law, and business with their application to federal contract law and intellectual property rights.

As a cadet, I enjoyed combing through the special historical collection of early texts held by the West Point Library where I found the original mathematics texts written in French brought from France in the 1800s and used to teach cadets by Colonel Sylvanus Thayer. The texts were written by such authors as Pierre-Simon Laplace and Jean-Baptiste Joseph Fourier.

Sylvanus Thayer, after first graduating from Dartmouth University, was appointed by President James Monroe in 1807 to attend West Point, which he completed in just one year. He entered the US Army as an officer. In 1815, Sylvanus left for Paris where he spent two years studying mathematics and engineering at the French West Point, École Polytechnique, southwest of Paris. The French engineering school was mentored by Napoleon himself, whom Sylvanus admired. Sylvanus Thayer's assignment, upon his return from France, to West Point in 1817 was sealed. He was appointed by President Monroe as the first superintendent of the academy.

As a plebe, the M1 Garand rifle trigger mechanism whose cross section we had to draft in exact detail was a challenge of the utmost for me. Up on the fourth floor of Washington Hall, the building that also houses the Cadet Dining Hall, was the Department of Military Topography and Graphics (MT&G). Engineering drawing was a must—a prerequisite—in those days for each freshman.

I still remember my associate professor, Air Force Captain Bentley, in drawing and drafting class my plebe year. In as much as my plebe class of some twelve cadets were the "goats" (cadets with low grades with a stubborn refusal to give up) in drawing, we had the privilege of climbing to the fourth floor drafting classroom from the rear entrance of Washington Hall.

For without Captain Bentley's strong hand at my drafting table in guiding my drawing pencil and wrist, I would not have been able to remain at West Point. Moreover, I gained an appreciation for the vast information stored on maps and blueprints, giving a major advantage to one that that understands how to interpret the graphical data. However, it was not until I attended Purdue in the Electrical Engineering Department that the struggle on the fourth floor of Washington Hall some years earlier came in handy and, more importantly, propelled me in my work as patent counsel with the US Patent and Trademark Office for independent inventors and technology firms, various defense laboratories, and as the private counsel to many construction firms.

Cadet Dining in Washington Hall

The cadet mess inside the first floor of Washington Hall with its three wings accommodated the entire Corps of Cadets for three meals daily, each one in simultaneous formal seatings. Covering the entire south wall of the cadet dining hall remains the mural that depicts twenty great battles and twenty great captains of world history, an overwhelming setting for dining for a first-year plebe. The entire corps of cadets was served by a small army of contracted waiters.

As a plebe, I was assigned to one of the Company B-2 tables. I sat at the end of the long table with two other of my plebe classmates when I was assigned to be the "Cold Beverage" corporal, looking directly opposite at the table's commandant, a senior classman at the other end. My classmate, the "Hot Beverage" corporal, sat to my right; and the "Gunner," who normally sliced the dessert, sat on my left. Duties were rotated. As the "hot" and "cold" beverage corporals, we served the coffee, water, and all three plebes held a formal posture during the entire meal unless told to relax by the first class cadet at the other end of the table. We were also the last to serve ourselves after all the upperclassman at the table from firstie (senior) to yearling (sophomore) of whatever food remained.

However, for some reason, my table would be showered by its waiter with extra servings of the main menu item, be it steaks, hamburgers, or chicken. Someone was concerned and ensured that I got enough to eat. As fate would have it, the head cook of the entire mess hall was known as Papa George. Papa George lived in nearby Highland Falls, was Greek, over six feet tall and weighed some two-hundred-plus pounds. He was a towering figure, especially in his white chef's frock and tall cook's hat—well recognized by the entire corps of cadets. It was known that he looked after the few Greek cadets in the corps. Papa George led a large team of cooks in the main kitchen and was responsible for the preparation of all the meals for the cadets to include the pastry.

Being a member of the collegiate gymnastics team, especially plebe year, during the January to April winter season had its advantages too. I was able to travel with the team to various competition events at various colleges and universities such as Temple University at Philadelphia; US Naval Academy at Annapolis; Syracuse University at Syracuse, New York; Penn State at University Park, State College, Pennsylvania; and Florida State University at Tallahassee, to name but a few. However, during the official four-month season, the entire team would be seated in the Cadet Mess Hall together. During that period, we would receive a special athletic menu, which included an abundance of steaks and other special meals specially cooked for us.

My Visit to Annapolis and on the USS *Tarawa*

In my junior (cow) academic year at West Point, I participated in the traditional periodic and semester exchanges by going to the US Naval Academy at Annapolis, the capital of Maryland. Midshipmen in return would be exchanged and come to the Military Academy at

West Point. On my exchange, which was about a week including the weekend, as I remember, I was housed in Bancroft Hall, the dormitory for all the midshipmen, some three thousand plus.

The hall comprises a central rotunda and has some eight wings or decks each of some five stories. It even houses a gym, US Post Office, barbershop, various offices from chaplains to medical services and much more. I recall attending classes that week and spending time just chatting, attending, and comparing math, economics classes, and even midshipmen activities. We also chatted about gymnastics and, especially, about the coming fall football season with the Army-Navy football game to be played in Philadelphia to include our respective academy's prospects for winning.

As exchange guests, we were granted liberty to go down into Annapolis and discover the historic town and even partake in its nighttime activities. As visiting cadets, we were allowed liberty to visit the downtown with my cadet classmates that were also on the exchange. When we returned that first evening to Bancroft Hall, we found ourselves locked out of the main entrance; hence, we entered through the basement of that large dormitory. I had not realized how large the basement of Bancroft Hall was and had no idea on how to find our assigned dormitory room. Having no midshipman accompanying us, we were lost. Eventually, we were saved by an on-duty Navy mechanic from spending the night in the dormitory's basement mechanical room.

Later that summer while on our last training trip as a cow (college junior) before graduation, I had the opportunity to be assigned on an aircraft carrier, the USS *Tarawa*, during my class trip to Norfolk, Virginia. Some other members of my class were assigned to destroyers, cruisers, and battleships. We got some exposure to amphibious operations in as much as the *Tarawa* was the first in a new class of general-purpose amphibious assault ships that combined in one ship type the functions previously performed by four different types: the amphibious assault ship (LPH), the amphibious transport dock (LPD), the amphibious cargo ship (LKA), and the dock landing ship (LSD).

The aircraft carrier had space for some two thousand sailors and Marines; thus, it was capable of landing elements of a Marine Corps battalion landing team and their supporting equipment by landing craft or helicopters or by a combination of both. On that occasion, being on board the carrier was indeed an experience from eating, bunk sleeping to the flight line. Living in close quarters with so many others on the USS *Tarawa* had some similarities to my prior experiences in Bancroft Hall. The USS *Tarawa* was decommissioned in Pearl Harbor on March 31, 2009.

In comparison, President Donald Trump on July 22, 2017, at Naval Station Norfolk, commissioned the Navy's most powerful warship yet: the USS *Gerald Ford*. The nuclear-powered aircraft carrier was rigged with state-of-the-art technology with a capacity for more aircraft and weaponry than ever before from an electromagnetic launch system and advanced arresting gear for faster and more efficient takeoffs and landings. The vessel uses a touch screen navigation display and is equipped with a reactor plant that can power the ship for up to twenty years without refueling with a length of 1,106 feet and able to house 2,600 sailors.

Both the two above cadet experiences gave me a better appreciation of our US Navy that was to extend throughout my Army service down to this very date when I stand in front of Navy, Marines, and Naval civil servants to instruct them on the Federal Acquisition Regulation and the material in the first authored text, which was published by the United States Naval Institute Press in 2008 entitled *Contracting with Uncle Sam*.

The Soup Boy on his Cross-Country Trip

In the summer of June 1957, the beginning of my third year (cow) at West Point, I had decided to visit my brother, Mike, who was undergoing boot camp at Fort Ord located on Monterey Bay off the Pacific Ocean coast of California. At that time, Fort Ord was a major Army basic and advanced training center for infantry. I traveled by bus cross-country to arrive at his barracks only to find him and his entire platoon in bed quarantined therein with the pandemic Asian flu H2N2.

The 1957–58 pandemic was rated a category 2 out of 5 on the Centers for Disease Control and Prevention (CDC) Pandemic Severity Index (PSI). It peaked in the fall of 1957 in the United States. According to the Johns Hopkins School of Public Health, the Asian flu killed almost two million people around the globe, including some 69,800 in the United States. It was most deadly for the elderly. Occupied camps and barracks such as those at Fort Ord had been highly vulnerable.

I traveled daily to the local restaurants and delivered hot chicken soup to his platoon in the barracks for about a week. The soldiers knew me as Mike's brother, the "Soup Boy." As I was writing this paragraph, I could not help but chuckle as I recalled the 1998 football film comedy *Waterboy*, wherein a water boy for a college football team discovers he has a unique tackling ability and becomes a member of the team.

Thereafter, I departed for Travis Air Force Base (AFB) near Sacramento to catch a "space available" flight to New York. En route, I stopped off at Naval Station Treasure Island located in San Francisco Bay. There I discovered that the Navy Noncommissioned Club really had great food and beverages in comparison to the Navy Officer's Club, which that evening was hosting an all-white formal dinner party, requiring formal attire to enter. Later, the desk attendant at the Officer's Bachelor Quarters was kind enough to find me a room at midnight after resting on a sofa directly across from the front check-in desk for several hours. In 1991, the naval station was identified for base closure. The Navy in 2009 made a deal and sold the island with its shuttered facilities to the city of San Francisco to be used for residential and commercial redevelopment.

The very next day, I arrived at Travis AFB located southwest of Sacramento and was walking on the tarmac toward my flight when I no longer could walk. I had contacted the Asiatic flu and was burning up. I was hospitalized at the David Grant USAF Medical Center at Travis AFB. I never have received such wonderful hospital treatment in my life, being attended by numerous nurses who had never met a West Point cadet.

After a week, I was escorted back to the flight line with urgency and placed on the space available Air Force aircraft headed to Stewart International Airport located in New Windsor, New York, some thirty minutes from West Point and sixty miles north of Midtown Manhattan. I was assured of not missing the start of my third year in college. I must add with a bit of guilt that wearing my summer all-white cadet uniform for the entire trip to see Mike served as a must-see attraction and facilitated my extraordinary care. My chicken "Soup Boy" good deed at Fort Ord had been reciprocated.

What I had done at Fort Ord, as I reflect, was really foolish for I did not understand the seriousness of the Asiatic flu at that time. However, that experience has given me a better understanding for the seriousness of what several western African nations (Sierra Leone, Guinea, Liberia) are undergoing with the 2014 Ebola virus epidemic and its threatening spread worldwide. The first patient in the United States that was under treatment in Dallas passed away in September 2014, and two of the nurses who were involved in his treatment contacted the disease but survived—Not to omit a volunteer doctor from New York City who served in Africa treating EBOLA patients and, upon his return, was hospitalized with the Ebola virus.

Doctors Without Borders or Medecins Sans Frontieres (MSF) International began its response to the Ebola outbreak in March 2014, and despite progress made in the fight against the virus, Ebola stubbornly lives on in Guinea, Sierra Leone, and Liberia, where more than 27,678 people have been infected and 11,276 have died. The number of cases in the region has held at around thirty new infections per week, a number that would be considered a disaster in normal circumstances.

Many reports have been calling for change, with many focused on how to improve future responses to outbreaks. As of this writing, the world is working to fully meet the challenges of Ebola—its containment, treatment, and needed vaccine despite global indifference, fear, and fatigue. The job is not done.

As of the writing of this memoir, Doctors Without Borders or Medecins are responding in earnest not to a virus caused epidemic such as Ebola, but rather to the 2017 man-caused chemical attack in Syria, which used nerve agents similar to the nerve agent chemical attack in 2013 previously in Syria, both claiming numerous lives of civilians to include many children. The civilized world cannot turn its back to both virus and natural epidemics but must face the burden of being prepared to respond to man-made causes.

Army Branch Selection

The most important decision I had to make before graduation was what branch of the Army to enter—Infantry, Engineer, Signal Corps, Ordnance, Armor, Artillery, Quartermaster, Transportation, Chemical. Despite the fact that the Air Force Academy had been created since June 1954, a good quarter (139) of my graduating West Point class could and did select the Air Force as pilots. Quotas had been set for each service branch on its projected need for officers and depending on one's academic standing.

Many of my classmates were interested in armor cavalry. They were influenced by General George Patton's WWII reputation and also his son, Major George Patton, who, as an armor officer, served as a Tactical Officer to our class of 1958. The special treatment my class had received from the United States Armor school during summer training at Fort Knox, Kentucky, driving and firing armored vehicles, such as the M1 Abrams Main Battle Tank, was a big influence. These classmates tended to have high academic standings. Then there were those cadets that were star men. They tended to go Corps of Engineers to become involved in construction from bridging, to new building construction to demolitions or Signal Corps to provide communications services. Then there was the mixed group of academic "hives" and those that were allegedly low in academic standing. They chose the Infantry or Artillery branch in emulation of Generals Douglas MacArthur, Dwight Eisenhower, Omar Bradley, Matthew Ridgway, Maxwell Taylor, and Mark Clark.

In the background of the year 1958, there was the interest in Army nuclear weapons and demolitions and the growth of heavy-armored forces and airborne forces in as much as the "Cold War" was at its peak. The Cold War period was from 1950 to 1973, in which the United States and the Soviet Union went through a period of political tension. Despite the lack of actual warfare, the two countries lived in a constant state of fear about the possibility of attack. During this period, people in the United States built bomb shelters and schools practiced attack drills due to a fear of nuclear war.

Such concepts as the internet, which involved packet switching for the transmission of data in small blocks over a channel dedicated to a connection, was not demonstrated until the 1960s with the beginning of ARPANET; artificial intelligence; aerial unmanned attack drones; cloud computing; smartphones; and light helicopter supported versus heavy track armored forces; all had not entered our graduation thinking.

At graduation, I was commissioned a second lieutenant in the US Army. I finally had selected the Field Artillery Branch and was to report for my first assignment to Fort Sill, Oklahoma. I had considered selecting the Corps of Engineers or Infantry branch. However, based upon my experiences in cadet summer training at Fort Sill, Oklahoma, and my military history readings on various battle outcomes, I made the decision to go Artillery. The Iron Curtain had not yet come down, and our artillery was armed with tactical nuclear warheads for its cannons and ground-to-ground short range nuclear missiles.

The use and effects of nuclear weapons on the battlefield interested me. Then after all, Napoleon was an artillery officer. He understood the power and effectiveness of cannon and their ability to pulverize defenses, reduce fortresses and blunt attacks. The guns won Napoleon battles.

I must admit that I was jealous for not being selected to be a cadet captain only achieving the rank of cadet corporal within the Corps of Cadets. I shrugged it off and focused on my academics and gymnastics.

As a cadet corporal my senior (firstie) year at the academy, I was responsible for a squad of some ten cadets (college freshman through juniors) for their training, study, physical fitness, and discipline. Quite different but yet similar to the needs of some thirty boarding grade school students I was during the evening responsible at GMA. Those two embryonic training experiences in leadership ten years later blossomed. While in the Army, I was selected for promotion to the ranks of captain and major. Then I was to be battle tested in 1968 in Lai Kai, Vietnam, at the height of the Tet Offensive, while serving as the executive officer of the Second Battalion, Thirty-Third Artillery (105mm) of the First Infantry Division, involving some six hundred soldiers, both draftees and volunteers.

June Week—Graduation and Commissioning

On that June 4, 1958, at about ten o'clock in the morning, before my graduation parade at three o'clock in the afternoon, my mom, Aunt Ypapanti and her daughter, Kathryn, had arrived in NYC on AMTRAK from Tarpon Springs. They were standing outside the entrance to Penn Station. One cannot imagine the shock that they experienced when I drove up with my polished but used 1955 two-door Pontiac Chieftain and wearing my full cadet white dress uniform. I was to pick them up to go to the Thayer Hotel and graduation parade at West Point.

This was my very first used car that I had purchased for five hundred dollars from a Highland Falls' dealer with a loan from USAA. Later, my three children may have wondered why I never purchased a car for any of them during their high school years and even during or after college times. I considered a car an item that they had to purchase on their own name, merit, and finances.

Sure, I had driven several army trucks and jeeps while at West Point during summer training exercises. I had never driven a car into New York City. For weeks, I had been practicing on the open Buffalo Soldier Field across from the Thayer Hotel on the West Point campus where my car had been parked along with those of the rest of the class of 1958. The week before, I received my first full driver's license from the NY State Police. Some dozen state troopers had descended and tested my class using their official sedans on the West Point reservation and around the parade field.

Needless to say, the drive back to West Point would not have been completed in time to attend the graduation parade had it not been for the courtesy of the New York City Police Department. Due to my all-white uniform, which was recognized, two NYC policemen ensured I safely came down in the correct lane and not on the one-way street from Forty-Second Street to West Side Manhattan at 179th Street at Broadway, Manhattan. We collectively crossed across the Hudson River over the double-decked suspension George Washington Bridge from Washington Heights to Fort Lee in Bergen County, New Jersey, and was safely escorted and released onto the US Highway 9 heading north along the Hudson River.

With graduation over and diploma in hand, I proceeded, as did some 572 other graduated classmates, to change from cadet gray into my Army green service uniform for my commissioning as a second lieutenant. We had graduated some 75 percent of our "entry" class of that June of 1954. The commissioning ceremony was held subsequently that same day in the presence of my mom, Aunt Ypapanti, her daughter Kathryn, from Nassau and two of my cousins, Faye and Helen Mastorides, from Campbell, Ohio. I had paid for my new officer uniforms from my accrued monthly cadet pay over the prior of four years.

As I drove through West Point's main gate that June 4, 1958, I left behind four years of focused study and training, only taking with me the Academy's motto of *Duty, Honor, and Country;* my tennis racket and several books; my new Army service uniforms; and an eagerness to confront new challenges and responsibilities. My dream to make a mark in history was alive!

CHAPTER 4

Breaking-In the Lieutenant

From West Point, I traveled to Nassau in the Bahamas for a short vacation after graduation to visit the Nassau home of my uncle Anthony and aunt Ypapanti and my cousins, Kathryn and Manoli. The local Greek community celebrated with us my college graduation from the United States Military Academy and commissioning into the Army as a lieutenant. Many members of the Greek Orthodox Church of the Annunciation in Nassau remembered the young boy who often visited his beloved uncle Anthony. Vasili (Bill) accompanied him and other relatives for barracuda spear-fishing, just swimming, and/or relaxing at beach evening gatherings to just listening to the grown-ups chat.

Thereafter, I attended the Artillery Basic Course at the US Army Artillery and Missile School at Fort Sill, Oklahoma, and US Army Air Defense School at Fort Bliss, Texas, between August 28, 1958, through January 9, 1959. This was a joint course, which included both field and air defense artillery qualifications, prior to arriving to my first field artillery (mortar and cannon) assignment at Fort Bragg.

The Army had decided that artillery officers would be crossed trained to lead both field artillery and air defense units. The two artillery branch insignias on my uniform lapels at that time were comprised of two crossed cannons with a vertical missile at their intersection. I recall driving my used 1955 four-door Pontiac first to Fort Sill and then Fort Bliss, Texas.

Most of the instruction at Fort Sill was conducted in class-rooms, followed by field exercises involving forward observer spotting of targets (tanks, personnel, fortified trenches) previously positioned to create the Fort Sill Artillery Target Ranges. We conducted our spotting from distant dug-in positions from which we would adjust the howitzer air and ground bursts adjusting their detonations and impacts until we ultimately destroyed the target. We also took turns as gunners firing the howitzers from the battery locations where we also had the opportunity to assume the position of fire direction officers (FDOs). As FDOs, we computed the range to the various targets, fuze burst timing, howitzer elevation settings, and any associated powder types for the guns and type of ammunition to be fired in response to my classmates acting as the forward observers.

At Fort Bliss, we were instructed in radar systems and airborne target acquisition, to include identification of aircraft friend or foe (IFF) procedures, followed by radar tracking and missile firing. We first received classroom training and then assumed various positions at an anti-aircraft missile battery learning how to fire Basic HAWK air defense missiles at simulated aircraft targets. It was here that I first got introduced as a second lieutenant to the HAWK missile system built by Raytheon Corporation with which I got deeply involved when I became the Improved HAWK (IHAWK) System project manager on the Army Staff in the Office of the Chief of Research and Development at the Pentagon some ten years later.

It was also at Fort Sill and Bliss that I was trained in Army nuclear weaponry from the employment and target effects of artillery nuclear warheads for the eight-inch (203mm) howitzer to rocket and intermediate missile nuclear warheads. The assembly, safety and security of Army nuclear weapons were taught. This training several years later was instrumental in my assignment as the battalion commander of an Honest John Rocket (Nuclear) Battalion located in Aschaffenburg, Germany, and later when I was assigned on the staff of deputy chief of staff for operations in Heidelberg at United States Army, Europe, and Seventh Army (HQ USAREUR and Seventh Army).

Fort Bliss and the nearby city of El Paso, Texas, not to exclude Juarez just across the Rio Grande in Mexico, were collectively lonely places for a bachelor second lieutenant student at Christmas time when the courses were suspended. Moreover, my salary as a second lieutenant was quite meager. Fort Bliss was a one- or two-minute drive to the official Ciudad Juarez—American border crossing by cab; however, the extended Fort Bliss Military reservation bordered on the Rio Grande River with Mexico. Crossing cards were easy to obtain in either direction despite the Rio Grande River and selected border fencing. Even to this day, Ciudad Juarez remains a major trade and transportation hub into El Paso. After a few daytime weekend shopping visits, I had no interest to travel across the border to nearby Juarez, Mexico, for its night clubs.

The current controversy related to the construction and payment of a "wall" running the entire distance of the United States-Texas border and other United States border states with Mexico proposed by the President Donald Trump administration continues as this book proceeds into printing 2018.

Parachute Training

After Fort Bliss and before arriving at Fort Bragg, North Carolina, for my first assignment, I was sent to undergo parachute training at Fort Benning, Georgia. Becoming a parachutist was a must-have qualification for an Artillery officer who was to be assigned to the Eighty-Second Airborne Division.

The Fort Benning Parachute Training Jump Towers were originally constructed as part of an amusement ride at the 1939 World's Fair in New York City. The US Army saw value in them as platforms from which to train paratroopers (known as jump towers). Three were purchased by the US government after the World Fair, disassembled, moved to Fort Benning and re-erected with an addition to their height. Each of three jump towers stood some 256 feet high with a distance of 134 feet from tip to tip of their massive arms.

For training, we were hauled up to the tip of an arm by cable, then released to descend by parachute.

I must admit that the high parachute tower exercises in which a lift would take us harnessed in an open parachute to the top were almost like being at a major circus with thrill rides. As one approached the top, one would become unhooked to slowly drift downward so one could learn to perform a proper parachute body landing. An incorrect body landing could cause a broken ankle or leg. These exercises progressed to eventual parachute drops from AF troop carriers (C119, C130) from 1250 feet flying from Lawson Army Air Field located on Fort Benning.

The Covetted Ranger Tab—The Ranger Assessment Phase

The second "must have" qualification was to earn and wear the ranger tab. Hence, training followed at Ranger school also conducted at Fort Benning in three phases.

First, the Ranger Assessment Phase (RAP) was conducted in two parts. The first part was conducted at Camp Rogers in the Harmony Church area of Fort Benning. This phase consisted of Ranger Physical Fitness Tests involving push-ups, sit-ups, five-mile runs and chin-ups, combat water survival tests with lots of swimming, a twelve-mile march with boots and a loaded back pack, and day and night navigation tests. This phase was overall designed to assess and develop the necessary physical and mental skills to complete combat missions and the remainder of Ranger school successfully.

The second part of RAP was obstacle courses and long ruck marches as a major part of the physical fitness requirements. However, the fundamentals of patrolling and small-unit tactics were the focus of this part of the Benning phase. Graded field exercises included ambush and reconnaissance patrols, close-quarters combat, airborne operations, and air assault operations. We then demonstrated our expertise through a series of cadre and student-led tactical patrol operations. Combination night and day land navigation testing took place requiring us to navigate using only a map and compass to reach a predetermined number of Military Grid Reference System coordinate locations.

The second phase of RAP started with a twelve-mile forced, tactical march with full gear from Camp Rogers to Camp Darby, which had to be completed in some three hours. The emphasis at Camp Darby was on the instruction in and execution of Squad Combat Operations. The phase included fast-paced instruction on troop-leading procedures, principles of patrolling, demolitions, field craft, and basic battle drills focused toward squad ambush and reconnaissance missions. We received instruction on airborne and air assault operations, demolitions, environmental, and "field craft" training. We executed the infamous "Darby Queen" obstacle course and learned the fundamentals of patrolling, warning and operations orders, and communications.

While at Camp Rogers, the Combat Water Survival Assessment was conducted at Victory Pond (a Water Confidence Test). This test consisted of three events that test the ranger student's ability to overcome any fear of heights or water. We had to calmly walk across a log suspended thirty-five feet above the pond, then transition to a rope crawl before plunging into the water. Each student then jumped into the pond and ditched their rifle and load-bearing equipment while submerged. Finally, we had climbed a ladder to the top of a seventy-foot tower and traversed down to the water on a pulley attached to a suspended cable, subsequently plunging into the pond. This was labelled the slide for life, which had to performed calmly without any type of safety harness.

Students that failed to negotiate an obstacle (through fear, hesitation, or by not completing it correctly) were dropped from the course. I must admit that the "slide for life" test was a bit more "accelerating" than my first double somersaults off the flying rings into a circus-type trapeze catch net at the West Point gym.

The Covetted Ranger Tab—The Mountain Phase

The second phase of Ranger school was the mountain phase at the remote Camp Merrill near Dahlonega, Georgia, which lasted some twenty days and nights. Its object was to teach students to operate in small units while sustaining themselves and their subordinates in the adverse conditions of the mountains. The rugged terrain, adverse weather, hunger, and sleep deprivation were the biggest causes of emotional stress encountered. We ate, slept, and operated in these conditions for three weeks, usually eating no more than several meals ready to eat (MRE) per day.

During this phase, we received instruction on military mountaineering tasks as well as techniques for employing squads and platoons for continuous combat patrol operations in a mountainous environment. We took turns and developed our ability to command and control a platoon-sized patrol through planning, preparing, and executing a variety of combat patrol missions. In addition to combat operations, we received mountaineering training. During the field training exercise (FTX), we executed a mission requiring mountaineering skills.

The Covetted Ranger Tab—The Swamp Phase

The Swamp phase was the third and final phase of Ranger school. It was conducted at Camp James E. Rudder (auxiliary field no. 6), Eglin Air Force Base, located in the swamps of the Florida Panhandle. The Florida phase taught small-boat operations, ship-to-shore operations, stream-crossing techniques, and skills needed to survive and operate in a jungle and swamp environment. This phase lasted some sixteen days and nights and tested the patrolling and leadership techniques of every prospective ranger. This phase continued to develop our combat arms functional skills to be capable of operating effectively under conditions of extreme mental and physical stress.

This was accomplished through exercises in extended platoon-level patrol operations in a swamp environment. This phase of training further developed our ability to lead small units on airborne, air assault, small boat, ship-to-shore, and dismounted combat patrol operations in a low-intensity combat environment against a well-trained, sophisticated enemy.

I distinctly recall our frequent all-night training combat patrols. In particular, on one evening, I had been picked at random to lead the patrol from a returning mission, wading in swamp water chest high. Concurrently, the lane grader scoring our patrol's performance, simulated that one of our ranger students in the patrol had been wounded and would have to be carried by our patrol. Hence, we were carrying home on our shoulders our very own simulated wounded classmate while struggling to navigate undetected by enemy forces with map and compass in hand on the trail through the swampy areas with its snakes and sink holes.

The simulated wounded classmate turned out to be my very own West Point class of 1958, Vijit (Sammy) Sookmark. Sammy had graduated from the USMA as an exchange student from Thailand. Sammy later rose through the ranks to become a key general officer in the Royal Thai Army and later a defense minister of Thailand. One good thing about Sammy was that he was light. It sure helped us those early-morning hours through the swamps as we carried him.

After some six hours, we arrived safely back to our base camp—exhausted but happy that we had found our way back. That morning never before had my appetite been better. We could smell the scrambled eggs and bacon strips and sausage emanating from our mess hall as we stumbled into our base camp.

At the end of the last swamp exercise, having met graduation requirements, we spent several days cleaning our weapons and equipment before returning to Fort Benning for graduation. In a ceremony at Victory Pond, the black-and-gold Ranger tab was pinned to our left upper shoulder of the left sleeve of the military uniform. The Ranger tab is permanently worn above the soldier's unit patch. Wearing the tab is permitted for the remainder of a soldier's military career. The cloth version of the tab is worn on the Army combat uniform and class-A dress uniform of the US Army; a smaller metal version is worn on the new Army service uniform. The first two female soldiers, Captain Kristen Griest and First Lieutenant Shaye Haver, to join and graduate in the previous all-male classes attending Ranger school occurred on August 19, 2015.

Soldiers, officers, and noncommissioned officers covet to this day the wearing of the Parachute badge and yellow Ranger patch as marks of endurance, skill, and perseverance—grit. In today's Army, only more coveted is the service patch worn by those soldiers that reflect past combat duty in Vietnam, Iraq, or Afghanistan. By my experience, soldiers in times of peace become restless as they serve in a peacetime training, preparing for eventual commitment into combat.

My First Troop Assignments

In May 1959, having completed all my artillery officer, parachute, and ranger training courses, almost a year after graduation from West Point, I finally arrived at Fort Bragg. I was assigned to my actual first unit assignment, the Mortar Battery of the Second Airborne Battle Group, 501st Infantry with the Eighty-Second Airborne Division. I first served as the fire direction officer of the Airborne Battle Group and then commander of a platoon in its Mortar Battery.

At the Airborne Battle Group fire direction center though, I came into my own. My math studies at West Point and the Fort Sill Artillery Basic Course were instrumental in my swift ability to master the fires of massing artillery fires using both 4.2 mm mortars and 105 mm howitzers. A skill that was later to be used employing 105 mm and 155 mm howitzers and 8-inch gun batteries to inflict heavy casualties onto jungle routes and even the tunnels of the North Vietnamese, who had infiltrated down through the Cambodian border into South Vietnam.

Thereafter, it was at Fort Bragg in November 1959, being assigned as platoon commander, that I met Master Sergeant McMullen, my assigned 4.2 mm mortar platoon sergeant. He was a seasoned platoon master sergeant. He took me under his wing. I must admit that I was overwhelmed. I had all the academic credentials, Fort Sill artillery basic course graduate, ranger tab, parachute badge, and all; but no troop leadership experience in peacetime or wartime. I was not yet a combat veteran. Master Sergeant McMullen's presence, a Korean veteran, helped me to transition to the active real army and develop my troop leadership skills.

Over a two-year period, I soon led my platoon (a stick) out of the jump door of the C-123 AF Aircraft flying at some 1,200 feet above the ground at an air speed of about 150 mph for our weekly parachute jumps. Some were conducted in the daylight and others at night. I often led the daily early-morning physical training (PT) runs from the barracks. I trained my platoon under the watchful eye of Master Sergeant McMullen. He had become my mentor.

During my service in the Army, I completed some thirty-four jumps, including some with combat equipment, and attended jumpmaster's school, followed by being awarded the Senior Parachutist badge. Soon, my assignment with the Eighty-Second Airborne Division was going to end for I was to be assigned to a unit from Fort Bragg, which was to be moved and stationed in the Pacific Theater of Operations.

CHAPTER 5

My Pacific Cruise

One cannot imagine our excitement as the chartered two multicar troop trains with several thousand soldiers in early April 1960 moved from the Fort Bragg, North Carolina, rail station for their cross-country trip west across the central United States to the Oakland Army Terminal outside of San Francisco, California.

I was assigned to the Mortar Battery, Second Airborne Battle Group, 503d Infantry Combat Team and further assigned as the assistant adjutant (S-1) of the Airborne Battle Group Combat Team. The combat team was assigned to the Twenty-Fifth Infantry Division of the Pacific Command with duty station on Okinawa as a quick reaction force.

This was to be my first experience in serving as a staff officer where my writing skills came into good use. Some eighteen years had passed since we liberated Okinawa, the "Rock," from the Japanese. Vietnam had not yet become the US focus with boots on the ground.

Except for a small advance party that was flown to Okinawa, the entire combat team was on board two very long trains. We were told that the USS *General J. C. Breckinridge* would be waiting to take us on a seventeen-day "cruise" across the Pacific Ocean to our new station in Camp Sukiran, Okinawa.

I had never been on a cruise ship, much less a troop ship, and in my mind must admit that I was quite excited especially since I would get to see the Pacific Ocean. On Okinawa were stationed thousands

Marines of the Third Marine Division. The division had preceded us from Japan in 1955 and was stationed on the northern part of Okinawa at Camp Buchner (Renamed Butler).

The trains were quite long carrying some two thousand parachutists. It was the second time that I had crossed our country. The first occurred while I was a cadet to visit my brother at Fort Ord. However, this time it was in a train in lieu of a Greyhound bus. I was overwhelmed again with the grandeur of our geography and the animal life (deer, moose, horses, and cattle) observed from our window seat. Daily, the trains would stop, and the combat team would dismount for exercise and then reboard.

We arrived at Oakland Army Ship terminal outside San Francisco. This huge Army terminal was on the Oakland waterfront just south of the eastern entrance to the San Francisco-Oakland Bay Bridge. Oakland Army Base was the home to the largest military port complex in the world during the Vietnam era. Operations then were handled by the Military Ocean Terminal Bay Area (MOTBA), a subordinate command of Military Traffic Management Command-Western Area (MTMCWA). Over 37 million tons of cargo passed through MOTBA. The terminal was finally closed on September 30, 1999, and its functions transferred as part of consolidation and economy measures directed by Congress.

Duties Onboard Troop Ship

As we embarked onto the USS *Breckenridge*, I was summoned by the combat team's executive officer, Lt. Col. Chester B. McCoid, and assigned several missions for the cruise editor for the ship paper to be published daily, unit message and correspondence assistant, courts and boards officer, and mess officer. As a first lieutenant, I undertook those duties without hesitation despite their overwhelming scope.

Court-martials were to be conducted in the "brig" of the ship. The brig is a temporary confinement area or prison onboard Navy ships. I was to inspect the Navy dining room daily where the troops ate in shifts standing. The daily troop newspaper had to carry key news stories and ship gossip. I performed, among other duties, those that an assistant adjutant was assigned.

I must admit that I learned quite a bit about the USS *Breckenridge* and was grateful to my small assigned Army enlisted staff and, especially, the Navy supporting staff too. A positive aspect was that since quite a few of the senior combat team's staff officers and commanders were flown to Okinawa as part of the advance team, my ship duties got me to be well known by the majority of the troops.

One of my frustrations was to set up the court martial room in the ship's brig area. The brig walls were constructed of steel plates, which served also as the integral part of the forward ship's hull. Hence, it was almost impossible to hang a US flag on the wall behind the president of the court-martial as directed. The assigned president of the court-martial, a major, eventually was satisfied with a small American flag on a tiny stand on his table.

It was in that brig that several special court-martials were conducted involving a number of enlisted men that had deserted during the process of embarkation in Oakland. They had been apprehended by the Military Police in the San Francisco area before the USS *Breckinridge* had sailed for Okinawa.

Needing to get my hair cut after the second week afloat, I submitted myself to the ship's barbershop. I sat in the barber's chair and told the Navy barber, "Cut it short." Thereafter, I fell dead asleep from exhaustion. When I woke, to my shock and amazement, my head had been given a bald shaven haircut. I wore my headgear several days during the cruise daily until, at last, one day, Lt. Col. McCoid ordered me to remove my headgear suspecting that I was hiding something! Needless to say to my chagrin, I had to bare my shining bald head exposed to all the smirking soldiers in as much as even an officer was not allowed to wear his military cap indoors and, especially, as the mess officer in the ship's dining hall.

The final insult to pride though came when we were unloading at Naha, the principal port in southern Okinawa. As I walked down the plank to get off the ship, none of the Okinawan service women, who had lined up at the foot of the offloading ramp, wanted to do my laundry. They thought that I was a sacred monk.

The voyage to Okinawa had crystallized in the minds of my superiors that here was a lieutenant that had proven that he was competent to run court and boards, knew how to write well—both a product of his West Point education. I was stigmatized and directed to remain as assistant adjutant for twelve months before being released to return to my artillery battery.

This was the beginning of subsequent assignments to the senior staffs of major commands and their commanders in the years to come as their executive officer (special assistant) to handle their calendars, personal and official correspondence, visitors, and any necessary sensitive matters from carrying high-level orders and directions to other commanding officers in the chain of command. Little did I know that as I would be serving these high-ranking general officers in a professional manner, I was to become their bearers of bad news as well. In many instances, my performance of duty created jealousies and personal enemies of senior officers and even my peers.

The Novice Assistant Adjutant

My desk was in an adjacent room to that of the Combat Team's adjutant. As the assistant adjutant, I read all the incoming paper messages. The facsimile machines, smartphones, the internet, or computers had not come of age. The message room had radios, typewriters, radio teletype terminals, and lithograph machines used for reproduction. The encrypted voice radio message and written message transmitted by teletype were the principal means of communications. Moreover, I still had the responsibility of administering the setup of all court martials and various disciplinary boards. In essence, I was the right arm of Major Chester M. Clark II, the Battle group's adjutant, and its executive officer, Lieutenant Colonel Chester B. McCoid.

While in the adjutant staff position on one training jump onto Corregidor Drop Zone on Okinawa in May 17, 1961, to keep up my parachute proficiency, I had a parachute malfunction. It involved my reserve parachute getting also tangled with the main partially opened parachute, known as a "Mae West" or inversion-reserve malfunction. I was lucky. I hit the ground quite hard and lay there. Soon, a crowd had surrounded me. For quite a while, I lay still with my eyes closed until I realized I was still alive, not paralyzed, and had no broken bones.

To fill my evenings, I received the opportunity and taught evening courses in college level mathematics for the University of Maryland Extension Division in Okinawa to soldiers and civil service personnel. I yearned to be back in the field parachuting into the Pacific Ocean or traveling to the Korean Demilitarized Zone (DMZ) where the annual artillery range live firing proficiency exercises were conducted.

In my spare time, when I was not in my office at headquarters or later when I was assigned with my unit while on Okinawa, I played lots of tennis. As a bachelor and without a cook, periodically I would visit some of my class of 1958 West Point classmates that were married and had been given family housing on Okinawa. Jack and Margaret Downing would befriend me often in their home with a wonderful cooked meal.

My neighbor in the Bachelor Officer's Quarters (BOQ) where I resided, when not in the field, was also a bachelor and former Catholic priest, but also a great cook. He was a civil servant schoolteacher with the DoD Dependents' Overseas Schools for the minor dependents of soldiers and DoD civilian personnel stationed on Okinawa. He would periodically invite me to join him for supper.

On June 4, 1961, I was promoted from second to first lieutenant. I yearned to be sent to the artillery battery deep in my heart but suppressed any show of gloom or depression because I was not down with the troops. I wanted and needed to be assigned directly to a troop howitzer artillery unit rather than being a staff officer. Outwardly, I displayed a sincere and cheerful attitude to do a good job and hoped that the Command group would recognize that a lieutenant should be down with soldiers in lieu in a business-type office environment. After a year with the Command group, I got my wish.

Graduating to a 105MM Howitzer Airborne Artillery Battery

On July 13, 1961, I was released from being the assistant adjutant of the Combat Team and assigned down to be assistant executive officer and, later, executive officer of Battery C, (105mm Howitzer) 319 Artillery Regiment, Second Airborne Battle Group, 503rd Infantry Combat Team. I had been graduated from having another 4.2 millimeter mortar battery assignment into a 105mm howitzer unit.

As executive officer, I led the battery's artillerymen in their morning daily runs and thereafter followed up with bayonet training exercises before breaking for showers and breakfast. The remainder of the daily training schedule varied with frequent parachute jumps from helicopters onto various portions of northern Okinawa to parachute drops onto the Pacific Ocean, which I found very exciting.

Training classes in fire direction gunnery; chemical, biological, and radiological (CBR) defense training exercises wearing protective clothing and masks; rifle firing training on the ranges; and howitzer maintenance periods were but some training I conducted or oversaw. I spent quite a bit of my week in the motor pool with my unit supervising the conduct of vehicular maintenance.

Live Fire Training on the Demilitarized Zone (DMZ) in Korea

My Artillery Battery was flown from Okinawa to Seoul, South Korea, on August 23, 1961, for its annual live fire exercises. As we approached the Han River in Seoul, when the pilot was at the release point, the green light came on, and I led my stick of soldiers out of the plane's jump door.

It was a daylight jump where we were to join our howitzers and vehicles, which had been pre-positioned. Then we were to drive through Seoul to US Camp Casey near the demilitarized zone (DMZ), some forty miles from Seoul for our annual battery firing tests. The parachute jump was itself impressive and reassured the South Korean population of America's commitment to them. It also was not lost on the North Koreans.

I landed in the middle of a large hole joining a giant watermelon growing therein within a melon farm located at the edge of the Han River. The river was being used for irrigation. Soon, I was surrounded by several Korean children who, before I could get up, were rolling up my parachute for me. Although unexpected, unprepared, I had some rations and candy that I shared with them. I was soaked and discovered that the watermelon hole was quite well irrigated and contained lots of "organic" fertilizer just by the smell of my uniform. My mission was to lead the convoy of artillery vehicles with its soldiers to Camp Casey through Seoul.

We found our vehicles in the immediate vicinity of the jump zone. The Battery convoy comprised of its howitzers and trucks was indeed a sight to see, stringing some twenty plus loaded vehicles from a quarter-ton trucks (jeeps) to 2 1/2-ton trucks. As battery executive officer, my jeep was in the lead. We now had to traverse through the city of Seoul northward toward the DMZ and Camp Casey. I had radio communications with elements of the convoy and a paper map covered in plastic in the event of rain. All the vehicles had their windshields folded down.

I had not, in my planning, considered the demographics of Seoul being focused primarily on the parachute aspects of jumping inside a major city. By 1960, Seoul's population was some 2.5 million with a population density of nine thousand people per square kilometer due to Korea's dramatic industrialization and economic development. The population of Seoul in 2016 was estimated at 10.29 million, although this is just the population of the Special City, which has a density of about 17,000 people per square kilometer (45,000/square mile). The sprawling metropolitan area is much larger at 25.6 million. Before long, I realized that in our movement through Seoul, we had really been going around in circles. This was the time that I recalled also wishing that I had paid more attention to map reading in the Department of Topography and Graphics at West Point. In those days, there were no mobile iPhones or androids to be able to run the software for a Google Maps APP or mobile Global Positioning System (GPS). Despite being embarrassed, I stopped the convoy and passed the word down the chain of vehicles to the troops to take lunch. We had preloaded Meals Ready to Eat (MREs).

In the interim, just for such an event, I promptly, using our VRC-12 VHF radio, notified the MPs from Camp Casey who sent an escort. We were escorted to Camp Casey. I learned on that occasion that moving a military convoy in "peacetime" through a major mega foreign city, especially such as Seoul, one needs an escort service to ensure traversing it can occur in an optimum manner.

Camp Casey remains staffed by soldiers of the Second Infantry Division (2ID), known as the "Warrior" Division, as of the writing of this book. The division's mission, along with our Republic of Korea ally and other coalition forces serving side by side, remains to assist in deterring North Korean aggression. The 2ID has a unique force structure and fighting capability not found anywhere else in the US Army or on the Korean peninsula. The Second Infantry Division was formed in 1917 and served in WWI, WWII, the Korean War, and the Global War on Terrorism. Camp Casey spans 3,500 acres (14 km2) and is occupied by 6,300 military personnel and 2,500 civilians. There are plans for the relocation of most of the Second Infantry Division to Camp Humphreys, which are underway with the latest estimate for completion being 2019.

Being at Camp Casey was, indeed, a valuable military experience, especially being able to see across the DMZ into North Korea. The battery live firing was excellent for our battery's proficiency and unit esprit. We returned back to Okinawa a much better unit. Under an agreement with the South Korean military, one US Army brigade will remain at Camp Casey, right near the DMZ, after the Yongsan garrison has closed

Exercise "Sky Soldier" in Taiwan

While assigned with the 319th Artillery, 503rd Infantry Combat Team, I was attached for seven weeks to the controller staff for the joint and combined exercise "Sky Soldier," executive group and advance party. I assisted in the planning and coordination with the Nationalist Chinese Group for a field training exercise in 1961, which took place in Taiwan (Republic of China). Taiwan historically was called Formosa, from Portuguese: meaning, "beautiful island." To put this exercise in perspective, one needs to recall that Japan had invaded China during WWII under the pretext of the ongoing civil war, which began with the Chinese Revolution of 1911 between the Nationalist forces and those of the Communists. After the defeat of Japan in 1945, the Chinese civil war of the 1920s resumed. In 1949, the Communist forces under the leadership of Mao Zedung defeated the Nationalist Party or Kuomintang (KMT) forces of Chiang Kai Shek and declared the creation of the People's Republic of China. Chiang's forces, with the assistance of the United States, retreated to the island of Taiwan, taking over that government to establish the Republic of China. Each side now was divided by some one hundred miles of the South China Sea. This was an obstacle that could not be overcome by either side in pursuit of forcing its will on the other.

The United States, to this date, adheres to a One China Policy so not to provoke the People's Republic of China (Beijing) to undertake military action to remove the governing body of the island of Taiwan. The government of the Republic of China claimed to be the legitimate government of all China, seated in Taiwan. In Beijing, the People's Republic of China claimed the same. The positions have not changed.

In the following decades, the countries of the West, especially the United States and Europe, recognized the government in Taiwan as sovereign over all of China, while the communist countries, led by the Soviet Union, recognized the People's Republic as the only legitimate China. Up until 1971, the government in Taipei represented China in the United Nations. In 1971, the General Assembly recognized the communist People's Republic as representing China. Taiwan lost its UN membership.

The field training exercise was planned to be a combined exercise between our 503rd Airborne Infantry Combat Team and that of the Chinese Nationalists' Airborne Division. We parachuted with the

Combat team's advance party just outside Kaohsiung, then a small town located in southern-western Taiwan and facing the Taiwan Strait in the South China Sea. Since 1961, Kaohsiung has grown from a small trading village into today a global city.

My mission as the exercise's adjutant controller and additional duty as the Combat Team's public information officer (PIO) was to parachute with the advance party on that September 21, 1961, and link up with the civilian US and Taiwanese news media teams on the ground. The prepositioned multitude of Asiatic newspaper reporters with their photographers, to include those from the American media such as the *Stars & Stripes*, were located on the ground waiting to cover and photograph aircraft dropping both the US and National Chinese Forces for the combined exercise.

Before the main party jump commenced, we had joined the news media on a small bridge strategically overlooking the drop zone. It was indeed a sight to witness when the armada of aircraft commenced their flyovers, dropping hundreds of parachutists. Across the Taiwan Strait, no doubt the People's Republic of China took notice of this combined US Nationalist Chinese exercise. The number of very favorable press releases that were eventually printed about the 503rd Infantry Combat Team far exceeded normal expectations in an exercise of "Sky Soldier's" scope.

Later that week, we were invited by the commander and staff of the Chinese Airborne Division to supper in a special military-owned entertainment home facility. I accompanied the group executive officer who was to represent the combat team. We all sat around a large circular table and celebrated the success of the parachute drop. A multitude of courses were placed sequentially onto a centered lazy susan mahogany turntable (rotating tray), allowing for the self-sharing of dishes easily among the two US and six Chinese diners.

To not offend our hosts, I learned on the spot how to use chop sticks through a variety of courses, eaten from the same bowl before me. However, I was saved by our executive officer who handled the multitude of alcoholic beverage toasts of sake (rice wine or *Nihonshu*) from the Chinese airborne officers. In return, I did my duty to get my boss to bed safely.

Most of the Chinese parachutists in their division had left their families behind in the rush to be evacuated by the US Navy from the mainland or be annihilated with their backs to the Taiwan Strait as the Communist had surrounded the Nationalist Army. Once on Taiwan, as the years went by from 1949 to the very date I chatted with the officers, they had integrated into the then Formosan society. They had started new families from scratch since there was little hope of returning to the China Mainland. The average age of our soldiers in the US combat team I estimated was about twenty years old whereas the Nationalist Chinese airborne soldier and officer was well in his late thirties or early forties in 1961—an experienced but "old" fighting unit by US soldier age standards.

WWII Memories of Bataan and Corregidor in the Philippines

While on Okinawa, a group of us parachuted from a C-130 aircraft on February 17, 1961, onto the Clark Air Base Drop Zone in the Philippines outside Manila to visit the island of Corregidor located in Manila Bay. This was done in celebration of the anniversary of the airborne and amphibious assault on Japanese-held fortress Corregidor Island on February 16, 1945, by our then 503rd Combat Team. Corregidor, also known as the Rock, was a key bastion of the Allies during the war.

When the Japanese invaded the Philippines in December 1941, the military force under the command of General Douglas MacArthur carried out a delaying action at Bataan. Corregidor Island became the headquarters of the Allied forces and also the seat of the Philippine Commonwealth Government. The walk through parts of the "Malinta" tunnel with its thick walls was eerie. Yet it felt holy-like ground by just imaging the constant bombardment by the Japanese air force, which the Malinta tunnel withstood filled with American soldiers.

Although Bataan fell on April 9, 1942, the Philippine and American forces held out at Corregidor for twenty-seven days against great odds. On May 6, 1942, their rations depleted, the Allied forces were forced to surrender Corregidor to the Japanese. It was two years and ten months later in March 1945 when the Allied forces under the command of General MacArthur recaptured Corregidor, making good his promise to return to the Philippines. The Rock was recaptured by the airborne assault of the 503rd Parachute Infantry Regimental Combat Team. After twelve days of heavy fighting, Fortress Corregidor was returned to US control, allowing the American flag to be raised over the island once again. Six thousand Japanese surrendered on Corregidor.

The guns of Corregidor have been silent for over seventy years and the ruins of buildings, structures, and tunnels in the island still tell a moving story of a war that had claimed so many lives.

Two USMA Professors Coin Tossing

Despite all the training activity, I must admit that I was starting to get lonely and the prospect of combat action was not in the near horizon. Unbeknown to me, I was noted while a cadet (junior and senior years—1957–58) by the professors of the Electricity Department and Social Sciences and targeted to become an assistant professor in their respective departments.

Back at West Point in January 1962 at a dean's department heads meeting, the coin toss had been won by Colonel Cutler, the professor of the Electricity Department in lieu of the professor from the Social Science Department. They both wanted me as an instructor to return to West Point based upon my cadet academic record and recorded faculty observations when I was a student in their departments. The coin toss between these two department heads was to result in my early return from my artillery assignment on Okinawa in 1962 to attend Purdue University for a master of science degree in electrical engineering.

In March 1962, after some two years on Okinawa, I received orders from the department of the Army to immediately leave

Okinawa and return to the United States to attend graduate school at Purdue University with assignment to teach at West Point in the Electricity Department starting in mid-August 1964.

Inwardly, I was bored on Okinawa. How much tennis could one play and how many more parachute jumps while waiting for Vietnam deployment? There would be time for Vietnam for it was just starting to boil. Reluctantly, I accepted to attend graduate school in electrical engineering despite the fact my heart and talent were for graduate study in history and economics.

While still at Purdue, on March 26, 1963, the 173rd Airborne Brigade (separate) was assigned to the regular army and activated on Okinawa. In 1965, when I was in my first year of teaching at West Point, it was the first US Army ground combat unit committed to the war in Vietnam. Combat elements of the 173rd Airborne Brigade included the First, Second, Third, and Fourth Battalions, 503rd Infantry; the Third Battalion, 319th Airborne Artillery; Company D, 16th Armor; Troop E, 17th Cavalry; and the 335th Aviation Company.

CHAPTER 6

Romance—From the Cornhuskers, Boilermakers, to the Black Knights

Instead of returning directly from Okinawa to the United States by flying east to San Francisco, I decided to travel "west" to New York City and continue to Purdue University at Lafayette, Indiana, by traveling using the weekly special American embassy flights, which stopped at the capitals of Thailand, India, Saudi Arabia, Turkey, and finally landing at Rhein Main Air Force Base, Germany. I had an ulterior motive. When I arrived at Rhein Main Air Force Base, I would take a "break" to visit nearby Zurich!

The German high-speed train I boarded traveled south toward Switzerland from Frankfurt that early March day of 1962. While viewing the passing landscape, my thoughts wondered back to that early beautiful clear evening on the West Point plain before the cadet barracks that graduation June week for the class of 1957. The plain is a large plateau upon which the Corps of Cadets periodically marches in parade before visiting foreign dignitaries such as the king of Jordan and Prince Rainer III, the sovereign of Monaco with wife, Grace Kelley. Parades were included during June week graduations and those for Army fans before lunch tailgate parties and kickoffs for fall football games at West Point.

The plain is used to drill and develop marching training for the corps in the event it is called upon to march in the next presidential inauguration in Washington or even NYC on St. Patrick's Day. So it was on January 20, 2017, when the US Military Academy West Point cadets marched down Pennsylvania Avenue during the Fifty-Eighth Presidential Inaugural Parade, following the inauguration of President Donald Trump on January 20, 2017, in Washington, DC.

Going back in time to that West Point June graduation week in 1957, the plain's perimeter road lamps were just lit. I was standing nervously on the corner of the barracks just before the entrance to Washington Hall. In the distance, one could see the lights at Trophy Point and its Lady Fame statute on the top. Nearby on the plain were the illuminated statutes of General George Washington mounted on his horse and Colonel Sylvanus Thayer, the Father of West Point.

My presence at that corner was to honor my commitment to a class of 1957 first classman who was to graduate in several days. I was then a college junior, or a "cow," under cadet language having passed the plebe and yearling years and soon even cow year to become a firstie, the college senior designation.

The commitment was to entertain the graduating first classman's parents and, more particularly, his sister, Antonia, for the evening. I owed "Chris" Christ John Poulos (class of 1957) for his overwatch over me while I was a plebe and for his guidance and academic help the past three years. Chris had also served as the organizer of all the Orthodox cadets (Greek, Russian, et. al.) at West Point for attendance at the weekly Orthodox church services at Saint Martin's Chapel at the main Protestant chapel. This evening was the 1957 USMA graduation class "ball," and my mission was to entertain the family while the senior attended his graduation ball with his date.

I performed my commitment by taking Chris's sister to the junior dance that was ongoing concurrently in a separate gym ballroom. I was saved by the use of the formal dance card, which I used to sign up in advance my best cadet friends to dance. Dance formal cards once signed were to be honored. Chris's sister was amazed to be befriended for numerous dances by so many suitors. Hence, the evening passed swiftly. I must admit that my classmates, or for that matter myself, did not realize that they were signing up for a thirteen-year-old; however, they did their duty. I followed up with the subsequent multiple payback favors that had to be fulfilled and strained classmate relations that had to be smoothed.

What I did not realize at that time was that Chris used the evening to plant the "seed" of curiosity in me to perhaps check in the years that were to pass as to how his sister, Antonia, had matured. He did succeed.

Checking on a Past Date in Switzerland

As the train from Frankfurt finally rolled into the Zurich Haupt Bahnhof (Zurich Central Station), a curious Army first lieutenant was to meet Antonia again. Antonia was now a graduating eighteen-year-old senior high school foreign exchange student under the American Field Service Program in Switzerland on her senior year where she was studying German among other subjects. Thereafter, she was to matriculate and graduate from the University of Nebraska in Lincoln with a BS in art and education on August 6, 1965.

In an indirect way, westward from Okinawa rather than heading directly east to San Francisco, I was en route around the world to Frankfurt with a short excursion to Zurich. Then the trip was to continue to Dover, Delaware, and onto to Fort Sill and Fort Bliss for the Artillery Officer Career Course. Thereafter, I was scheduled to proceed to Lafayette, Indiana, to attend Purdue University with assignment at West Point in the Electricity Department to teach Electrical Engineering as an associate professor.

A concurrent pressing reason was also to pay my belated respect to Antonia, for the untimely death of Chris, her brother, some four years earlier. Chris was killed in a crash in his fighter jet trainer on June 11, 1958, over the skies of Ponca City, Oklahoma, in 1958, one year after his June 1957 graduation. Chris chose the Air Force, thinking of the future and his beloved country. For basic flight training, Chris was assigned to Graham Air Force Base, Marianna, Florida. Being able to choose his next base because he was among the top officers, Chris chose Vance Air Force Base, Oklahoma. On September 3, 1958, Christ was to receive his pilot's wings. On June

11, 1958, Christ went to Illinois on a routine training flight with his flight instructor, Lt. Robert E. Irons. This was to be their last flight. However, on their way back, they hit a storm where God reached out with his mighty hand and called them to his legions. The plane crashed into a farmhouse, taking also the life of Mrs. Harman, five miles northeast of Ponca City, Oklahoma.

In the class of 1957 "Howitzer" yearbook, one may read, "Chris shall be remembered for his quiet, friendly, and helpful manner." Arch Jarrell, editor of a Grand Island newspaper said, "Even though his life was short, he achieved and left us more to think about than many who live a long life." The time had come to honor Chris's memory.

Never before had a teenager worked so hard from his early teens and thereafter through high school after classes. Every afternoon, seven days per week, Chris would report to the local bait-and-tackle store in downtown Grand Island to work in its basement. He tended and sold freshwater minnows and other live fresh water baits from various tanks and drawers to include fishing tackle. He earned some five dollars per week, which he presented to his mom to aid in their family's finances. His dad, John, had had a stroke and was unable to work. Chris had given up playing any varsity or intramural sports, but he used his free time in that basement to study. This dedication to work and study resulted in exceptional academic grades. He was designated the valedictorian of his high school class and also received the principal senatorial appointment from Nebraska to attend West Point.

As I stepped off the train in Zurich, I was intercepted by Antonia's Swiss parents and the senior high school student herself. My curiosity had brought me more than halfway around the world from Okinawa in one of our weekly US embassy flights. My flight had stopped overnight or for several days as the courier flight to service multiple US embassies. For Manila, we stopped at Clark Air Base in the Philippines for four days; then Bangkok, Thailand, for a week; New Delhi, India, overnight; Dhahran, Saudi Arabia, for five days; Ankara, Turkey, for two days; and finally to Frankfurt Air Base, Germany. I was a space-available passenger and was lucky not to get bumped, although I had to hang out a number of days at the various embassy stops, which allowed me time to obtain necessary entry visas and to conduct some wonderful sightseeing tours.

For several days, Antonia took me on a tour of Zurich, a global city founded by the Romans and the primary center of the Protestant Reformation. Moreover, Zurich was then and remains a world financial center and is one of the wealthiest cities in Europe. We walked on the old cobbled streets visiting more than several chocolate stores and delicatessens but, primarily, just hung out with each other chatting, laughing, and reflecting on what we had each accomplished.

We were like two young children discovering each other. By evening, we sat around the Swiss family table having supper together. At my last family supper before departing, her Swiss dad told me that I would one day marry Antonia just by the look in our eyes.

After several days, I was escorted by the senior high school exchange student who accompanied me on the train as far as Basil, Switzerland, before turning back to Zurich. Thereafter, I continued my trip to Frankfurt and Rheine Main Airbase and then onto Dover Air Force Base, Delaware.

It was on that escorted ride that I realized that the thirteen-year-old, now eighteen, had grown more than I had imagined. In the coming fall, she would soon be a first year college student. It was on that train ride to Basil that I received my first kiss. The stage had been set for a true fairy tale love story.

Interim Return to Fort Bliss and Fort Sill for Career Course

My first stop before heading for Purdue University, when arriving back in the United States, was to attend the seven-month Artillery Officer Career Course, which was a joint course conducted for the first part at the US Army Artillery and Missile School at Fort Sill, Oklahoma, and ended with the second part at the US Army Air Defense School at Fort Bliss, Texas. My key elective was counterinsurgency.

At graduation, I was assigned a Prefix Five designation as a trained Nuclear Weapons Employment specialist. This latter designation became critical in later years when I was assigned to command a nuclear missile battalion and served on the US Army Europe Operations Staff stationed in Heidelburg during the Cold War period. While I was attending the Artillery Officer Career Course, I was promoted to the rank of captain on October 26, 1962. The career course having ended in November 2, 1962, I was temporarily assigned to the Army Air Defense School for some forty days as an electrical engineer instructor in the Missile Science Division.

In early January 1963, I decided to drive from Fort Bliss, Texas, en route to Purdue stopping off in Grand Island, Nebraska, to visit. In preparing for my trip, I visited Juarez across the Rio Grande to pick up a leather cow hide purse for Antonia. It was fun to negotiate with the Mexican shopkeeper. I felt that such cowhide purses would be rare up in Nebraska.

My Drive to the Cornhusker State to Meet the Family

As I drove through Oklahoma and into Nebraska that early winter, I noticed many pasture fields in addition to corn and wheat fields plus numerous storage barns. I started to have second thoughts about the uniqueness of the leather purse. I had not really studied my geography. There were just lots of cows and cattle. More importantly, I did not realize that the further north I drove through Oklahoma, the more snow and ice were being encountered.

I finally arrived in Grand Island late at night just in time to slide into the parking lot of the first hotel in town whose lights were on. My car's gas gauge had been showing an empty tank. The innkeeper showed me to my room where I crashed for the evening. The next morning, I woke to find the snow was at least two feet high. My car was buried. I asked the guest desk manager where was I located with respect to Antonia's family home. I became ecstatic when I was told that the home was just down at the end of the block.

Antonia, now a college freshman, had come home for the weekend to be with me. Her dad and mom were so happy to see me and embraced me with such warmth. I slept in Chris' vacant bedroom.

Antonia's dad, John Bacopoulos, who earlier had shortened his name to Poulos, lived and worked in Grand Island, Nebraska. He was the owner and operator of a hat-cleaning and shoe-shining store. John was born in Gastooni Elias, near Patras, Greece, and the only one from his family to migrate to America first to Chicago and then Grand Island where he had an uncle who was working on the railroads.

Antonia's mother, Emorfia, was born on October 13, 1915, in Allissa, Turkey, a suburb of Alsar Kolonia, of Constantinople (modern Instanbul) to her parents, Adam and Despina Alexiadis. She was a Greek Christian child living in Turkey during WWI and the Greco-Turkish War of 1912–1922. This era is known as the Great Disaster. Thousands of Christian Greeks were annihilated by the Turks by the end of 1922. A criminal genocide occurred almost as large as that of the Christian Armenian population living in Turkey in 1915. Emorfia's father had fought against the Ottoman Turks and was killed. Her mother eventually died in Turkey due to malnutrition and the absence of medical care.

Emorfia survived in a temporary refugee camp despite absence of both parents. At the age of some four years old, in 1919, she was rescued when US Navy destroyers loaded her and other Greek refugees, comprising thousands of other young Greek children living in Turkey from the port of Smyrna and transported them to Athens. The children were placed in crowded orphanages from which they were transferred into Red Cross Camps. Emorfia never saw her mom again. She remained in a Red Cross refugee camp from age four to around nine years old by then forgetting her last name. Emorfia recalls in her diary letter that her head was shaved as protection against lice.

Finally, in 1924, Emorfia was adopted by Efthalia Lagas, an elderly lady, and lived happily with her stepmother for nine years at Leonedio in the province of Kynourias, in Arcadia, Peloponnese, in Eastern Greece. In 1933, when Emorfia was some seventeen years old, her stepmother, Efthalia, died. However, Gus Lagas, her stepmother's son, living in Kansas City, went through the process and sponsored her to come to the United States to live with his family. He felt obligated because Emorfia had brought great happiness to his widowed mother in a difficult period of Greece's history. As Emorfia grew as a teenager, she had performed the duties of a health aide and housekeeper for his mother.

The major impediment to obtaining a visa at that time was the Immigration Act of February 5, 1917, which made it inadmissible to the United States persons likely to become public charges and Section 2 (f) of the Immigration Act of 1924 prohibited the issuance of visas to persons who are known to be, or who there is reason to believe, are inadmissible under any of the excluding provisions of the immigration laws.

Gus Lagas had two daughters of his own—Ethel, then fifteen, and Helen, thirteen years old, yet he considered Emorfia to be an immediate relative, as his very own adopted sister. By letter on January 18, 1934, he promised the Honorable Edwin A. Pitt, the American consulate general, in Athens that if Emorfia, his stepsister, was allowed to come to America, he would continue to take care of Emorfia financially. Gus Lagas was a successful drugstore owner. Emorfia had no property or any other means of support in Greece. She also would have a better chance to marry in America since she had no dowry. In early 1935, finally, Emorfia was admitted with a US visa under the allocated Turkish nationality authorized quotas for such citizens into the United States at the age of nineteen. She was still being considered a Turkish citizen.

The plight of refugees fleeing from ruthless regimes and ISIS, assembled in Red Cross Camps around the Mediterranean region such as the Greek Islands from such countries as Syria, Afghanistan, Iraq, and other Muslim countries seeking safety and wanting to come to Germany, other Western European countries, and the United States continues unabated even in the year of 2018. ISIS stands for the Islamic State of Iraq and Syria or Islamic State in Iraq and al-Sham. This dangerous offshoot of al-Qaeda is responsible for thousands of deaths in the Syrian civil war and has taken credit for terrorist acts in Iraq.

Such relocation is even more frustrating because of serious terrorist activities causing borders into the United States and other Western European countries such as England to be tightly patrolled. Moreover, immigration laws and presidential orders, such as that issued by President Donald Trump in March 16, 2017, restricted refugees from the six Muslim countries of Iran, Libya, Somalia, Sudan, Syria, and Yemen from entering the United States for ninety days even for humanitarian reasons have become serious barriers. In addition, the nation's refugee program was suspended for 120 days. The United States will not be accepting more than fifty thousand refugees in a year, down from the 110,000 cap set by the Obama administration.

Later in 1935, it was at the American Hellenic Educational Progressive Association (AHEPA) Convention in Omaha, Nebraska, that Emorfia Lagas was introduced to John Bacopoulos whose last name was shortened to Poulos. AHEPA, as a fraternal organization, was founded on July 26, 1922, in Atlanta, Georgia. One of its primary missions is to assist Greek immigrants be assimilated into American society. John met Gus's qualification for any prospective groom to marry his adopted daughter—John owned and operated his own cleaning shop (hat cleaning, shoe shining, etc.) business and owned a small home. On May 2, 1935, at the age of twenty, an arranged marriage occurred to her husband, John Poulos, who was some ten years older.

Their home at 115 Sycamore Street in Grand Island was small but neat. Antonia's mom was a real cook and even had a wine cellar with numerous wooden kegs or barrells in the basement of homemade wines. John and Emorfia were well known in Grand Island for the home garden they planted annually in the spring to produce for the entire winter pickles, stewed tomatoes, and enough canned vegetables to last the family a winter. During the Great Depression, they exchanged the grown parsley with the local Safeway grocery store in return for butter. The entire family was frugal and industrious.

The Great Depression (1929–39) was the deepest and longest-lasting economic downturn in the history of the Western industrialized world, thereafter triggering the rise of Adolf Hitler and

World War II. In the United States, the Great Depression began soon after the stock market crash of October 1929, which sent Wall Street into a panic and wiped out millions of investors.

That Sunday afternoon her dad, mom, and I escorted Antonia to the Greyhound bus stop to catch her ride back to the University of Nebraska at Lincoln. I loaded her suitcase into the lower compartment of the bus, and just before she mounted the bus, I handed Antonia my West Point tie clasp. I told her that I wanted to marry her. She was thrilled and said she too wanted to marry me, accepting the tie clasp with the one condition—she had to finish college because she had promised Chris.

Her mom and dad were overwhelmed but happy. I recognized how brave Antonia's mom, Emorfia, must have been, but acknowledging in an unspoken manner, that I was replacing her beloved Chris in her heart. There was a risk that her new "second son" too could also be lost as he served in the Army. The National Liberation Front (NLF), also called the Viet Cong, had been established in South Vietnam back on December 20, 1960. Vietnam was starting to heat up, but not in the headlines.

Even to this very day as I am writing, I am still realizing more than ever what unselfish, essential contributions Emorfia played in my life and that of Antonia and her grandchildren— Cosmas, Stamie, and Christina—in the years that were to follow as mother-in-law, grandmother, and mom to Antonia not to mention nanny, housekeeper, and consultant to all of us.

The tie clasp was the substitute for an engagement ring. The West Point '58 miniature engagement ring was delivered that summer in June 7, 1963, at an engagement ceremony in Antonia's home, followed by a tea for family and friends at the local Holiday Inn when I returned from Purdue University in Lafayette, Indiana, to Grand Island with my mom, Stamatia, for a short break before summer graduate classes.

Graduate Study at Purdue University

I arrived at West Lafayette, Indiana, that winter on January 5, 1963, and was assigned a two-bedroom apartment in a building housing graduate married students. My West Point classmate of 1958, Herbert C. Puscheck, and his wife, Betty, who had preceded me at Purdue occupied the apartment below me. Soon I was embroiled in first taking undergraduate EE courses that summer, and by fall, I was taking graduate EE and nuclear engineering courses.

My widowed mom had come up from Tarpon Springs to Purdue to be with me for a year in the spring of my first graduate year. It was at that time that Antonia also came to Purdue to visit with me and my mom during her college breaks. Mom, Antonia, and Betty Puscheck became friends and spent some time together while Herb and I attended classes.

Having Mom with me at Purdue was great. She ensured that I had cooked meals before leaving in the morning for classes and waiting for me in the late evenings when I returned from the Purdue Engineering Library. It was also at Purdue that my cousin, Emmanuel (Manoli) Alexiou, then a student in Canada, came to visit me. He had a painful ingrown toenail that we assisted him in alleviating its pain.

I would not have been able to move so rapidly had it not been for my academic adviser who supported the military students, advice from Herb Puschek, and coaching by the naval enlisted men that were concurrently attending Purdue as part of Admiral Hyman Rickover's nuclear submarine crew training program.

Basically, many members of the crew of each fielded, commissioned nuclear submarine were to have their undergraduate degrees in EE or nuclear engineering. Rank among us was secondary in importance. The naval enlisted students who had already been at Purdue the prior year were interested in tutoring me as we studied together in the same section of the Siegesmund Engineering Library located in the Potter Engineering Center.

The most exciting aspect of the Purdue curricula for electrical engineers was the introduction of the use of semiconductors—the transistor was then a new phenomenon destined to eradicate the vacuum tube radio amplifier and the vacuum diode for the rectification of power. The new solid state laboratory classes were long but full of excitement as we learned for the first time the distinct voltage-current relationships of the transistor, thermistor, and solid state diodes. In contrast, high-energy power laboratory was built around understanding the "classic" use of transformers to amplify voltages and to adjust high currents to deliver stable electrical power to various users for running machinery and lighting systems.

An Army in the field to this very day uses lots of generators and transformers to generate power to operate its engineer equipment such as lighting within fortifications and operations centers; weapons systems such as air defense missile systems; communications hubs, mobile hospitals; mess halls; and radars to mention but a few power needs. The recent events during Hurricane Irma (category 5 storm, 165 mph winds) which on September 6, 2017, passed north of Puerto Rico, en route through the western part of the full Florida peninsula, dramatically revealed the presence of a neglected, unprepared power electrical power generation grid, causing more than 1 million residents of Puerto Rico to lose power not to mention loss of homes. As of this writing, some three hundred days after Irma, Puerto Rico still has a major part of its US population and facilities without electrical power.

The transformers (coils) we used in the labs at Purdue were bulky just to handle in setting up power circuitry, which would allow us to control the high currents (amperes) and voltage during power measurement classes. Some of the transformers were air-cooled while others were water cooled. From these laboratories, we learned and compared the difference between the new technology in solid state engineering and the standard old, but necessary, technology for electrical power engineering quite quickly.

We also had our firsthand experience with large-scale computers. The Purdue student computer center housed a large IBM system. We would in the evenings do our homework and before midnight take our deck of "punch" cards with our handwritten high-level programming language (Fortran) programs thereon to be compiled into assembly language and then be converted to machine code and run over night. In the morning, we would pick up our cards and the hardcopy printout reflecting lots of errors. So the cycle would be repeated until we achieved an acceptable running source program that would provide correct solutions to an assigned classroom problem as the variables were adjusted.

It was also at Purdue that I discovered the power of remote teaching using TV-made presentations. Such teaching lent itself well to mathematics and EE circuit analysis. At Purdue, I had quite a few TV classes and grasped the importance of TV as a medium to teach mathematics and engineering effectively to individual students remotely or in a classroom. Problems could be solved on a blackboard that students could more easily follow televised than if in a lecture hall or classroom. The computer and overhead power point projector-amplifier had not come to the campus as yet. We had to be satisfied with overhead projectors and plastic flip charts-vu-graphs.

By August 10, 1964, I had completed the academic course work for my master in electrical engineering (MSEE) degree with a minor in nuclear engineering from Purdue, just in time to report to teach at West Point in the "Juice" Department on September of 1964.

The MSE degree was indeed gained in a usually short time. My orders allowed me no more than eighteen months to finish my graduate work, receive my master degree, and report ready to teach. In fact, I arrived in mid-August just in time to attend New Instructors training course in the Electricity Department.

Over that same period of time, Antonia was matriculated at the University of Nebraska in Lincoln, studying just as hard during the normal academic year and summer schools to finish college in three years with her major in art and German language. Her goal was to finish as quickly as possible so that we could get married.

Teaching at West Point

When I arrived at West Point, I was assigned a bachelor's officer's quarter in the basement lower second floor of Cullum Hall adjacent to the West Point Officer's Club and within walking distance to my classroom in Bartlett Hall.

Cullum Hall was dedicated in 1900 having been built in the Greek Revival Style of Milford granite by Architect Stanford White. It was then and to this date remains the site of cadet social events, military ceremonies, and lectures. The structure had been built against the mountainside high above the Hudson River and the Parade Plain itself. The hall was built to serve as the memorial repository to honor deceased graduates through portraits, sculptures, and plaques. Cullum Hall houses the grand ballroom upstairs, the triumph of the building. The main first floor contains the Pershing Room, which opens onto the terrace overlooking the Hudson River. This room was rededicated in 2014 as the West Point Memorial Room. It contains the nameplates of graduates killed in our nation's wars and honors those graduates who receive the Medal of Honor.

On many a Saturday evening, I would lie in my bed and listen to the live music flowing down to my basement room from the grand ballroom above me. Cadet "hops" (dances) were frequently held in Cullum Hall. My room was indeed quite small having only one window, a single bed, and small study table and refrigerator located on a floor with a community bathroom. In fact, as I reflect, it was smaller in size to my grandson Orry's single room at Stanford University at Palo Alto, which I had visited in February of 2014. As of the final writing of this text, Orry Despo graduated from Stanford University on June 18, 2017, with a bachelor of science degree in mathematical and computational science with university distinction.

My room's single window allowed me to gaze the vista of the frequent barge traffic coming down to New York City or that going up the Hudson River to Albany. The Hudson River was amazing to watch. Directly across the Hudson River, one could see the academic buildings and dormitory of St. Basil Academy in Garrison, New York, then an Orthodox Teaching School for Greek teachers and now a home serving children in need.

Down the hallway, most of the other rooms were occupied by old graduates that traveled to West Point primarily for the football season. These graduates daily would visit the gymnasium and the various athletic fields to watch the teams practicing. Cullum Hall was on the east end of the plain where several practice football fields, baseball and soccer fields were immaculately maintained for use each afternoon. Moreover, the area directly across Cullum Hall had the West Point tennis courts and the West Point library.

Cullum Hall was then a perfect, economical destination for senior widowed graduates and retirees to hangout for several months in the fall and just before Christmas capturing all the fall athletic home coming games. I soon became friends with several and chuckled as on frequent occasions I would be shown their pedometers strapped to their feet accounting for the distance of their walks. In today's time, they would be wearing an Apple wristwatch or Fitbit Blaze smart black fitness watch and carry an Apple iPhone.

My biggest frustration, however, was with the control of the steam-heating system, which was in the lower boiler room of the building. The old graduates would invariably go to the boiler room and adjust the heating system boilers to suit their body blood temperature levels, thus causing all the rooms to be either too hot or cold. This would go on all through many an evening until the Corp of Engineers padlocked the door to the boiler room. The boiler room controlled the heating of not only Cullum Hall, but several other adjacent buildings to include the officers' club. After my departure, the two basement floors of BOQ rooms were converted to offices and club rooms.

Every weekday morning especially, during the academic year, I would wake up early and have breakfast at the West Point Officer's Club before heading to my classroom to teach. I particularly enjoyed having breakfast on Monday mornings with other bachelor instructors and, in particular, Major Norman Schwarzkopf (class of 1956).

After earning his master's degree in mechanical engineering from the University of Southern California, Norman Schwarzkopf returned to West Point where he instructed cadets for two years in the Department of Mechanical Engineering. Norman taught in the same building as myself. Norman would bring me up to date on his weekend trips to the city, which I must admit were more exciting than my bachelor weekend trips to the West Point gym and cadet chapel on Sunday.

I had great respect for Norman as a contemporary instructor. We often chatted about Vietnam and were both eager to experience combat first hand. On August 2 and 4, 1964, the North Vietnamese had attacked two US destroyers sitting in international waters in the Gulf of Tonkin. On August 7, 1964, in response to the Gulf of Tonkin incident, the US Congress passed the Gulf of Tonkin Resolution. By March 2, 1965, a sustained US aerial bombing campaign of North Vietnam began labeled, Operation Rolling Thunder. The bombing campaign was designed to interdict North Vietnamese transportation routes in the southern part of North Vietnam and slow infiltration of personnel and supplies into South Vietnam. The first US combat troops had arrived in Vietnam on March 8, 1965.

Norman and I were concerned that we would be left out of the fight. Norman was an infantryman. I was an artilleryman. We both received our respective branch combat assignments to South Vietnam when we left teaching at West Point—Norman in 1966 and I in 1967. I had been promoted to the rank of major on May 18, 1966. A year later, I arrived in Saigon at Tan Son Nhut US Air Force Base on June 8, 1967.

I have been honored to have taught at West Point together with Norman. I salute him for he went on, some twenty four years later, to become four-star General H. Norman Schwarzkopf, the commander in the Persian Gulf War of 1991 of some half million men. He successfully led Operation *Desert Storm* gaining the freedom of Kuwait and destruction of Saddam Hussein's forces. By April 1, 2003, Bagdad had come under American control.

Norman died in Tampa, Florida, on December 27, 2012, at the age of seventy-eight. He was laid to rest at the West Point Cemetery on February 28, 2013, returning to his beloved alma mater to be laid among many prior graduates who had dedicated their lives in war and peace to service to America, such as Lieutenant General Winfield Scott, commander of the US Army during the Civil War (1861–65); General Lucius Clay, father of the Berlin Airlift (1948–49); General

William Westmoreland, commander in Vietnam (1964–68), and many others.

The EE or "Juice" Department at West Point was the department that presented every junior cadet's (cow's) most dreaded hurdle to graduation. Electricity in those years was not an elective course. It was a prerequisite to graduation. For me, it was an exciting time to teach at West Point in the Electricity Department. The two semester course curriculum in electricity had been primarily focused on the generation of electrical power (generators), radios, and conduct of circuit analysis. Radio technology was central with the associated teaching of vacuum tubes for amplification. Command, Control, and Communications could not be exercised on the battlefield in those years without knowledge of radios and teletypewriters at VHF (Very High Frequencies), UHF (Ultra High Frequencies), and SHF (super high microwave frequencies). Computers had not been deployed as yet much less the use of the internet.

I set out to teach students the new solid state devices that were replacing the vacuum tube technology—the transistor, used closed circuit TV to teach circuit analysis in a series of TV lectures, and conducted lecture hall demonstrations that were exciting. I taught "Juice" with a fervor, as if Socrates, relishing the new solid state electronics and computers. It was there that the cows (college cadet juniors) pinned on me the nickname the Galloping Greek, only to have these student graduates (USMA classes of 1963, '64, '65) remind me of that nickname but later as officers in the field.

Colonel Elliot C. Cutler, the professor and head of the Department of Electricity in his letter of August 1967 stated:

> I doubt that this Department has ever had an instructor who prepared his lessons with greater care or greater imagination than you gave to the task … As a result of your outstanding work, you were selected for the position of Assistant Professor, in which you displayed great energy and organizing ability.

The Era of Computers and Cadet Initiation

IBM was a great help. IBM was located up the Central Hudson River Valley at Poughkeepsie, New York, just some twenty minutes from West Point. We took our classes on field trips to the IBM mainframe plant at Poughkeepsie to see and be briefed by the IBM staff on the large frame computers being assembled and the ongoing software development and testing for each system depending on the buyer's needs. It was uplifting for the cadets in 1965–67 to walk the assembly floor, which had the semblance of a "stationary" automobile assembly line. The class would stop at each station to read overhead the name of the firm purchasing the large mainframe—the who's who of banks, Wall Street, industry, universities to US government agencies. Today, Fortune 500 companies still use IBM mainframes or have migrated to IBM's "cloud data services" for cognitive computing to make sense of "big data" and to execute daily business transactions in a cost effective manner.

IBM operated on a four hundred-acre site, which, in 2010, housed its newest manufacturing facility, which produces IBM's line of System z mainframe computers and high-end power systems servers that manage business operations from critical banking transactions to internet workloads to the most demanding emerging new applications for clients worldwide. The manufacturing facility in Poughkeepsie continues to reflect IBM innovation in the design, testing, and assembly of its mainframes and high-end servers.

Although I could not match the onsite IBM tour experience, I undertook to bring to all the cadets and West Point faculty in 1967 the latest artillery computer system to be fielded—the M18:FADAC (Field Artillery Digital Automatic Computer), an all-transistorized general purpose digital computer manufactured by Autonetics' division of North American Aviation, which later became part of the Boeing company. FADAC was first fielded in 1960 and was the first semiconductor-based digital electronics field-artillery computer.

The M18 allowed fire direction officers to compute range to targets, to include taking into consideration recent meteorological data inputs for weather conditions, to provide accurate elevation, azimuth settings, type of projectile, necessary powder charge to reach a target for 105 and 155mm howitzers and 8-inch guns rather than using manuals, slide rules, and protractors.

To that end, we arranged for a series of seminars for all interested students and faculty at the academy. Each of the seminars was carefully tailored for the particular audience to which it was presented. Qualified enlisted instructors had come from Fort Sill, Oklahoma, and programming and technical experts came from Frankford Arsenal, Ohio. Eventually improved cannon program tapes for the M18 gun direction computer, FADAC, were issued to units in Vietnam during the summer of 1968.

It was during that assignment at West Point that I became friends with Alan Salisbury, my 1958 classmate, who also joined the EE Department to teach, having completed his master degree in computer science from Stanford University. Alan was a Signal Corps officer who went on some seven years later to return to Stanford to complete his doctorate degree with his dissertation in computers. I also had the privilege of being assigned with Alan to Fort Monmouth, New Jersey, with the Army Communications-Electronics Command. There we worked in different professional assignments.

We annually shared a beach house each summer for several years at Long Beach Island, New Jersey, near Barnegat Light where our children played together and derived memorable times. In the years thereafter, Alan commanded various Army computer agencies and had a major impact on the adoption and use of computer systems throughout the Army. He retired as a major general in our Army.

Our cherished friendship continues to this day with Alan, Florence, and their children, Barbara and Kathy, to include their families joining Christina, my daughter, and her family annually for Thanksgiving parties in Virginia and Washington DC.

Exchanging Vows

In the summer of 1965, I returned to Grand Island for my marriage to Antonia John Poulos. Antonia had completed all her requirements for her BS to include a major in German language, from the University of Nebraska, except for a literature research paper on the works of Johann Wolfgang von Goethe(1749–1832). She was allowed to submit the research paper in the fall of 1965.

Goethe was a German poet, novelist, playwright, courtier, and natural philosopher, one of the greatest figures in Western literature. His most famous work is the poetic drama in two parts, *Faust*. With the concurrence of the University of Nebraska, a professor from the USMA English Department, as a professional courtesy, had agreed to be her adviser for her paper.

The wedding was held on June 13, 1965, three days after Antonia had completed her final exams at the University of Nebraska, in the Holy Trinity Greek Orthodox Church of Grand Island. Rev. James Kyriakakis performed the double-ring ceremony. Several days before the wedding, my uncle Tony from Nassau had arrived. He had flown to Miami with my cousins, Manoli and Kathryn, then drove to Tarpon Springs and picked up my mom and Irene Arfaras. They arrived in Grand Island in a crowded station wagon. The trip for all five was a first. Uncle Anthony was my best man. Kathryn was our matron of honor. Irene was one of the bridesmaids. My cousin, Manoli, and brother, Michael, comprised the wedding party's groomsmen along with Eddie and Dean Cero, Antonia's cousins from Wichita, Kansas, who had joined us.

Emorfia and John had converted the basement of the house into a bachelors' suite, which all the men occupied except my uncle, my mom, and Kathryn who shared the upstairs bedrooms. The wedding reception was held at the Holiday Inn. All the wine was homemade by Antonia's mom, Emorfia. She had aged fresh grapes into wine in several special large wooden barrels in that very basement over some three years in preparation for our wedding. Emorfia had also prepared all the Greek pasties for the some two hundred guests that attended the wedding reception at the Holiday Inn.

We were two young adults wanting to get our lives started together. Saying our farewells, we left early after the reception-dinner and several dances. Mr. Gibbs, Antonia's childhood neighbor, had his car ready. He was thrilled to be our chauffeur. He took us to the Grand Island Train Station on time. We made the last train for Lincoln to catch the first plane the next day to Miami and then to Nassau. We remained overnight in Lincoln and also remained in Miami overnight at airport hotels before arriving in Nassau.

Honeymoon Couple Stranded on Paradise Island

Aunt Ypapanti had one of her hotel rooms at the Gleneagles specially decorated and set aside for Antonia and me. In Nassau, Uncle Anthony and my aunt Ypapanti hosted a second wedding reception for us, including cake and beautiful wedding ice sculptures. It was attended by the small but closely knit Nassau Greek community. Many remembered me as a small boy spear-fishing with my uncle Anthony. They were now curious to see me in my Army white dress uniform and, especially, to meet the new bride who had won the heart of a former eligible bachelor.

While in Nassau, we would take the boat taxi over to Paradise Island to swim and picnic daily. In those years, the car and walking bridge from East Bay Road over to Paradise Beach had not been built or had the Atlantis Resort with its casino and its luxurious Aura night club or the Cove Atlantis Resort arrived. Paradise Island and its beaches were indeed pristine and beautiful—secluded beaches, lots of sea and animal wildlife and trees loaded with ripe coconuts. Perfect place for a honeymooning couple. Each day the taxi boat driver would know to come back to pick us up for the return trip to the mainland at six o'clock in the early evening.

To our dismay, that particular day, the taxi ferry failed to return. There were no payphones on the island. Cell phones had not yet become of age. My uncle Anthony realized there was a problem and, in the late evening, sent a special boat that found and extracted us from Paradise Island.

The Married Couple Arrives at West Point

Antonia was thrilled to finally arrive at West Point. Since no quarters were available on post, we were placed on a waiting list for military housing. In the interim, we rented an upstairs one-bedroom apartment just outside the West Point main gate in Highland Falls from a Greek couple who owned a large apartment home within walking distance of the main gate.

The second floor rental was an efficiency unit with a small bedroom. The combined living room and kitchen were crowded, especially since Antonia used the area to sew her clothes, both day and evening dresses. We had purchased a table size but very heavy-duty used Singer (German made) sewing machine. Antonia had been taught by her mom how to make various type dresses using patterns. She was the best dressed Army junior officer's wife at West Point.

The apartment had an unscreened balcony with a laundry pulley, allowing washed clothing hung on a line to be lowered down to ground level, just above the parked cars, to dry. Antonia was happy to use the pulley to hang her washed clothes to dry. Moreover, the landlady allowed Antonia to use her washer and attached manual wringer. There was no electric dryer. So Antonia would use the laundry pulley to draw the wet washed clothes, attached with cloth pins, out to the sun and back.

Antonia was re-energized while we waited to receive on post housing. She completed her research paper on *Goethe* and received her college diploma from the University of Nebraska. Then she turned around and walked several blocks into Ladycliff College located in Highland Falls across from our apartment. She matriculated, taking her first course in French. Ladycliff College on the Hudson River, outside the main gate of West Point, had opened its doors in 1933, by the Sisters of Saint Francis. The college received its charter from the board of regents of the University of New York. The college interested young women and their families for its ideal location, a liberal education, social activities, and religious activities. It was at Ladycliff that Antonia also met a number of student Army wives whose husbands were also on the West Point faculty from with whom new friendships sprang.

Being neighbors with West Point was a drawing card for this Catholic women's college ahead even then of the Seven Sister Colleges of Smith, Bryn Mawr, Barnard, Vassar, Mount Holyoke, Radcliffe, and Wellesley. Ladycliff closed its doors at the end of the 1980 academic year for financial reasons. The academy acquired the property using it to this day as the location of the academy's museum, Visitor's Information Center, and Guest Temporary Visiting Quarters known as the Five Star Inn.

On her spare time, Antonia would be found at the West Point Post craft shop, spinning her clay pots on one of the potter's wheels and then placing them in the kilns. One day I had found her being challenged in as much as several of her pots, which she had labored over, had blown up while being baked in the kiln—the pieces were not fully dry or they had air bubbles in their clay. Those that had survived thereafter, she would paint designs thereon in color for further processing.

Soon she was teaching Post officers and their wives to include cadets on how to make clay pottery using a potter's wheel. She conducted her first art show of clay pottery and oil paintings at the West Point Library, selling her works that one Sunday. On that occasion, I was able to convince Antonia to not sell a few selected pieces, which to this very day can be found in my home here in Tarpon Springs.

Antonia loved West Point's rolling hills and mountains along the Hudson River. She participated in all the activities of the Officers' Wives Club. We owned a beat-up Ford Falcon, which one could hear a block away and sometimes would roll backward on a hill before going forward. Antonia learned to drive and passed her first driver's test receiving her New York license.

Due to the size of the academy's military faculty and the supporting enlisted staff, there were many dependent young children living on post of school age. Hence, at West Point, there was a Domestic Dependent Elementary and Secondary School (DDESS) for PreK-8 grades within the DoD Education Activity (DoDEA), operating under the direction, authority, and control of the Undersecretary of Defense for Personnel and Readiness.

Antonia was instrumental in finding a position for Kathryn Alexiou, my cousin, from Nassau who had recently completed college as a teacher. Kathryn qualified on her own for the position as the kindergarten teacher and joined us at West Point for an academic year. In as much as our apartment in Highland Falls was too small, Kathryn lived in an apartment off post in the nearby neighboring town to West Point of Cornwall-on-Hudson near the slopes of Storm King Mountain on the west side overlooking the Hudson River. It was also at that period that my mom and her sister Ypapanti, Kathryn's mom, and Manoli, her brother, visited us.

By the end of the first year in Highland Falls, a townhouse came available on post in the Grey Ghost Area of the military reservation. Grey Ghost was a neighborhood that offered two-bedroom townhomes to officer service members teaching at West Point. Features included fully equipped kitchens, central air, garages, and washer/dryer hookups. Grey Ghost was conveniently located close to the post hospital, West Point grade schools, and the community center.

We were both elated since many of our neighbors were also from the class of 1958.

More importantly, Antonia was expecting our first daughter, Stamie, who was born soon thereafter on June 26, 1966, in the cadet hospital. Her delivery was handled by an experienced Army sergeant first class delivery nurse. Being a toddler, we enjoyed each evening playing with Stamie on the living room rug before her bedtime as she rolled and later crawled to and from Antonia and me.

It was at Grey Ghost that Antonia entertained cadets on frequent occasions. To this day, I remember those delightful suppers when all the baked turkey was consumed, leaving no leftovers, which we were expecting due to our budget. West Point provided a wonderful time to relax and focus on my new family. The last two years of my assignment when I was first married allowed us to enjoy chatting with my classmates who were also instructors at the same time in various staff and teaching assignments. They and their wives were growing their families too. Attending the home football games at

Michie Stadium to watch the Black Knights was always exciting especially when Army won.

We attended the Cadet Chapel, the Greek Orthodox Church services at the Basil Academy Chapel in Garrison, New York, and St. Nicholas Greek Orthodox Church in Newburgh. It was such precious family downtime. Also, it was during this faculty assignment at West Point that all the Orthodox cadets (Russian, Greek, Romanian, et. al.), and I met with Archbishop Iakovos, of the Greek Orthodox Archdiocese of North and South America at the First Class Club located below Trophy Point. At his request, the archbishop, due to his foresight, wanted to discuss and explore the construction of an Orthodox chapel similar to the existing Cadet Catholic Chapel. The location of such a similar liturgical chapel serving the needs of the faculty and cadets of the various "Orthodox" branches of the Armed Forces at West Point was a dream that to this day remains elusive. The Jewish chapel and synagogue was completed and furnished in 1984.

Looming in the horizon, Antonia and I well knew that I was destined to be assigned soon for duty in South Vietnam. US combat troops had been in Vietnam since early 1965. It was now 1967.

CHAPTER 7

The Rubber Plantation

Setting the World Stage

Japan had, in 1940, invaded Vietnam, which was colonized by the French. With the defeat of Japan at the end of WWII, Ho Chi Minh in September 2, 1945, declared an independent Vietnam, called the Democratic Republic of Vietnam. In May 7, 1954, the French, who had colonized Vietnam for some one hundred years, were defeated at the Battle of Dien Bien Phu. Soon after, in July 21, 1954, the Geneva Accords created a cease-fire for the peaceful withdrawal of the French from Vietnam and provided a temporary boundary between North and South Vietnam at the seventeenth parallel.

On October 26, 1955, South Vietnam declared itself the Republic of Vietnam, with newly elected Ngo Dinh Diem as president. Subsequently, on December 20, 1960, the National Liberation Front (NLF), also called the Viet Cong, was established in South Vietnam.

As a refresher, the events, thereafter over nine years, leading up to the US intervention and eventual American withdrawal from South Vietnam, are summarized at table 7-1 below.

Table 7-1. Chronology of US Involvement in Vietnam

August 2–4, 1964 North Vietnam attacks US destroyers sitting in the Gulf of Tonkin.

August 7, 1964 Gulf of Tonkin Resolution by Congress, gives president authority to increase US military presence.

March 2, 1965 US bombing campaign of North Vietnam, Operation Rolling Thunder, begins.

March 8, 1965 First US combat troops arrive in Vietnam.

January 30, 1968 North Vietnamese join with Viet Cong located in the south to launch "Tet Offensive," attacking South Vietnamese cities and towns.

March 16, 1968 US soldiers kill Vietnamese civilians in town of Mai Lai.

December 1968 US troops in Vietnam reach over five hundred thousand.

July 1969 President Nixon orders first US troop withdrawals from Vietnam.

April 30, 1970 President Nixon announces that US troops will attack enemy locations in Cambodia. News sparks nationwide protests, especially on college campuses.

June 13, 1971 The classified Pentagon papers titled "United States-Vietnam, 1945–1967: A Study Prepared by the Department of Defense" were released by Daniel Ellsberg who had worked on the study and were published in the *New York Times*. The papers revealed that the United States secretly enlarged the scale of the Vietnam War also into Cambodia, Laos, and coastal raids into North Vietnam. The *New York Times* said that the Pentagon Papers had demonstrated, among other things, that the Johnson Administration "systematically lied, not only to the public but also to Congress."

March 1972	North Vietnamese cross demilitarized zone (DMZ) at seventeenth parallel to attack South Vietnam.
January 27, 1973	Paris Peace Accords are signed that provide cease-fire.
March 29, 1973	Last US troops are withdrawn from Vietnam.
March 1975	North Vietnam launches assault on South Vietnam.
April 30, 1975	South Vietnam surrenders to communists.
July 2, 1976	Vietnam unified as communist country, the Socialist Republic of Vietnam.

The South Vietnam Challenge

Early in July 1967, Antonia, Stamie, and I departed from West Point for Fort Sill, Oklahoma, where I attended the two-week Senior Field Artillery Officer's Course at the US Army Artillery and Missile School. This schooling was completed as required en route to my assignment with the First Infantry Division, South Vietnam. Thereafter, Antonia, with Stamie, went to live in Grand Island, Nebraska, so that Antonia would be with her parents, and I flew on to San Francisco and Saigon.

Upon arrival at Da Nang US Air Force Base outside Saigon (now Ho Chi Minh City), I was driven to Di An, some ten to fifteen miles from Saigon, the main base camp and headquarters for the First Infantry Division, the Big Red One. Thereafter, I was ferried by helicopter to the helipad used by the Second Battalion, Thirty-Third Artillery, First Infantry Division Artillery, at its base camp in Lai Khe.

Lai Khe was an abandoned Michelin Rubber Plantation positioned along the main north-south highway (QL 13, also known as Thunder Road), due northwest of Saigon. Some of the other units co-located at Lai Khe were the Third Brigade of the First Infantry Division and Company A, 227th Assault Helicopter Battalion, and First Calvary Division(Airmobile). With the combat units located there, Lai Khe provided a shield from enemy forces marching onto Saigon from the nearby Cambodian border.

Later that first evening, overhead I heard for the first time the *woosh* of an incoming unmanned, unguided rocket followed soon thereafter by an air explosion. The intelligence folks had stated that their sound was similar to the V-2 rockets that the Germans flew over England during World War II.

As the battalion executive officer with the rank of major, I was expected to handle all the logistics, general administration, personnel and material readiness fields. I had to ensure that the artillery battalion was able to maintain around-the-clock operational readiness. This translated that soldiers had to be adequately fed, howitzers had to be able to shoot, trucks were properly serviced, rifles worked, ammunition had to be readily available, and lastly, our medical teams proficient.

During my tour in Vietnam, I served two battalion commanders as their deputy. The first for five months was Lieutenant Colonel Arthur D. Wells who had been already battle tested when I arrived and, later, the second for seven months, Robert L. Schweizer, who had come in country for the first time. This was their one-year combat command at the battalion level, the requisite stepping stone to Artillery Group Command for the rank of colonel. I was loyal to both and ensured they were free to concentrate on the combat operations of the battalion. In addition, I had the duties of being the base commander and coordinator during counterinsurgency operations within Lai Khe.

I was appointed as the material readiness officer too. In addition, I supervised the procedures and operations of all the staff officers such as the adjutant, operations officer, intelligence officer, supply officer, chaplain, and medics. Despite being near the enemy, I was amazed still at the amount of paperwork that the battalion was required to keep.

During my year in Vietnam, I met my assignments and more despite the challenges of the constant personnel change of soldiers (officers and enlisted) due to the one-year tour limitation for all armed forces members in country; the requirement for air resupply of units in the field for supplies, ammunition, and meals; and the extended periods of time that the firing batteries were in forward base camps away from Lai Khe. We even had Command Maintenance Management Inspections (CMMI) conducted by the staff from the First Infantry Division Headquarters to assess the combat readiness of the artillery batteries in the battalion. One of our units received the highest score in the First Infantry Division administered CMMI.

As each evening would come at the battalion headquarters, I completed what was essential in my field office and moved to assist at the underground battalion fire direction center.

Since my first artillery assignment with the Eighty-Second Airborne Division in Fort Bragg, as a second lieutenant, was that of a fire direction officer, I spent many a night in the battalion fire direction center over-watching operations through the evening and early dawn hours. We got pretty good at night, directing the batteries from the firing of illumination rounds with air bursts to light up the countryside, as requested by the infantry commanders through our assigned artillery forward observers in close proximity of the enemy, to the use of high explosive projectiles to include phosphorous shells.

Once activity had subsided, I would leave the underground artillery command center and retire to an underground bunker built under the canopies of the French-planted rubber trees of the now-abandoned plantation. The tall rubber trees with their extensive canopies served to cause the incoming rocket's fuze to trigger the Viet Cong rocket payload of high explosives. The premature explosion drastically reduced the effectiveness of the explosives against the intended American targets. The explosion would cause what was primarily a rainfall of harmless, ineffective metal fragments.

What was more frightening was that enemy "sappers" would use the cover of darkness to infiltrate our defensive perimeter position to cause havoc by setting demolitions to any facility that the sapper team could find to destroy. Americans called them "sappers," from the French *saper*, a word meaning to "undermine or weaken, typically by digging." In military usage, the term was originally applied to French soldiers who dug narrow trenches, or "saps," toward an enemy fort to provide a somewhat-protected channel for moving men and artillery closer to the fort in preparation for an assault. In Vietnam, however, American troops used the name primarily for North Vietnamese Army and Viet Cong units that broke through defensive lines using tactics more akin to raids by commandos than to the work of engineers, tossing satchels with explosives of any facility and inflicting terror to US troops in their Quonset huts or dugouts who were sleeping.

Hence, daily when I walked around in the late evening checking on our perimeter's sentinels, I was apprehensive and properly armed to encounter such a sapper team, which lacked the current password. I repeatedly left my command center and bunker at night to ensure that the fighting effectiveness and security of the battalion perimeter were maintained.

On January 30, 1968, the North Vietnamese joined forces with the Viet Cong in South Vietnam to launch a coordinated attack on approximately one hundred South Vietnamese cities and towns. Lai Khe was not spared.

At approximately three o'clock in the morning on January 31, 1968, the enemy initiated an intense mortar and rocket attack onto Lai Khe, which was followed throughout the day by continuous barrages. I recognized that the base ammunition supply point was a prime target for a ground assault as well as mortar attack. The base ammunition supply point stored not only our battalion's artillery projectiles but numerous other munitions for use by armored, infantry, attack helicopter units, and engineer units operating out of Lai Khe. This initial attack was not able to penetrate our defenses to cause any material damage or serious troop casualties.

Again on February 8, 1968, at approximately six fifteen in the morning, the camp was subjected to a second hostile rocket attack, which, on this occasion, started a fire in the main ammunition supply area. I went immediately to the supply point to ensure the physical security of the area was intact. The fire was spreading rapidly and causing low-order detonations of high explosive, illumination, and white phosphorous munitions.

Despite the danger of shrapnel from the exploding munitions and incoming rounds, we were able to supervise the guard of that sector and checked the safety of the personnel under my command. We moved through the impact area to investigate casualties and the damage to government equipment and assisted in organizing an effective firefighting operation. We moved throughout the entire ammunition supply area to ensure that flying shrapnel and debris from the exploding munitions had not ignited additional fires.

The aggressive actions of our team repelled the determined enemy attacks and preserved vital weapon assets. The chain reaction destruction of the supply point would have seriously limited the fighting effectiveness and efficiency of the battalion and other combat units during the attack, not to mention the loss of human lives.

We had averted a major disaster at Lai Khe. However, overall, due to the Tet Offensive, the US and South Vietnamese forces sustained heavy losses before finally repelling the communist assault. The Tet Offensive played an important role in weakening US public support for the war in Vietnam.

The Artillery Forward Air Observer

During my one year at Lai Khe, combat operations found me serving as the battalion's airborne helicopter forward air observer, directing the firepower of the guns (howitzers) of not only our battalion, but the collective firepower of the First Infantry Division's other three artillery battalions that happened to be in range to also reach the selected enemy targets.

In Vietnam, infantry operations tended to be fragmented, and the guns had to disperse in order to support them. This was a violation of the time-proven principle that artillery is effective primarily when fired in mass, but during the Vietnam War, the enemy rarely presented massed targets for American artillery.

We used the two-seat OH-6A, Light Observation Helicopter, called the Loach or Cayuse, built by the Hughes Aircraft Company. This light helicopter was known for its speed, agility, and ability to achieve high altitudes swiftly, so essential to surviving anti-aircraft enemy ground weapon fire and missiles.

My assigned pilot would pick me up from the helipad for each mission. Normally, the Loach, or when armed, *Killer Egg,* which was armed with the M27 Armament Subsytem carried a M134 7.62 mm mini-gun on the left side of the helicopter plus had three tubes for 2.75-inch rockets on the right side. The pilot would confirm that both our seats were bulletproofed with armored plates. We would be flying at tree-top level. The risk of enemy flak was high, and there was no sense in getting wounded by a bullet into one's buttock.

On one occasion, while serving as an air observer, even with the thick jungle foliage and tall trees, I spotted that enemy soldiers were moving below us. My pilot initially lifted the Loach as high in altitude as possible to be out of range of anti-aircraft fire or a ground-to-air missile. As my pilot skillfully kept "darting" between low- and high-flight environments, I was able to bring in to bear the heavy artillery high-explosive rounds. We used delayed or concrete piercing fuzing to allow for penetration of the thick tree canopy and ground foliage from the firing howitzer batteries of the battalion with Time on Target (TOT) fire direction techniques. Time On Target (TOT) is the military coordination of artillery fire by many weapons so that all the munitions arrive at the target at precisely the same time.

Despite the fact that I saw no dead enemy, I knew from the rising smoke that we had definitely destroyed a key enemy underground storage site, resupply route actually occupied by significant North Vietnamese, Viet Cong forces, or a combination of both.

As early as 1965, the North Vietnamese used areas of Cambodia and Laos near the borders of South Vietnam as sanctuaries in which to stock supplies and conduct training without interference. It was in these countries that the North Vietnamese built the famous Ho Chi Minh Trail as their principal supply route to the south. The trail was a vast system of improved roads and trails, many of which could be used year-round. By late 1968, the North Vietnamese were moving most of their supplies by truck, pipeline, and river barge.

This transportation system terminated at depots within and adjacent to South Vietnam. Because for political reasons these base areas were inviolate, they provided sanctuaries to which the North Vietnamese and Viet Cong units could retire periodically from combat in South Vietnam, train and refit, and return to combat. In the late 1960s, as the free world forces extended their operations into the enemy base areas in South Vietnam, the enemy regular forces expanded the bases and depots across the borders in Cambodia and Laos. Enemy combat units in South Vietnam received supplies from these depots by a simpler but highly organized system of distribution that made use of small boats, pack animals, and porters.

The range of our artillery weapons was extended by the helicopter airlift of our howitzers, which were able to be moved to forward operating fire bases, bringing them within the range and reach of the eastern Cambodian border. The coalition government of Laos had an arrangement with North Vietnamese sympathizers that did not permit it to object to Viet Cong and North Vietnamese operations in Laos, through Cambodia and into South Vietnam.

With our heavy continuous, regardless of weather, bombardment, we intercepted and destroyed some of the multitude of underground tunnels and pathways of the enemy movement of supplies and North Vietnamese Army and Viet Cong guerilla troops day and night into South Vietnam from the extensions of the Ho Chi Minh Trail into South Vietnam. Our decentralized forward artillery fire bases would be withdrawn after a short period of time over several days or a week in many cases to prevent them from being overrun once their mission was completed or they were reinforced with our infantry units to be able to sustain attack to remain for longer periods of time in a forward base camp.

From the period of February 9 to June 11, 1968, I participated in more than twenty-five helicopter artillery aerial missions over hostile territory in support of these counterinsurgency operations. Afterward, I then better understood why the Air Force, which also significantly participated on such aerial missions, was authorized to use Agent Orange, which contained chemical dioxin and other similar chemical agents to defoliate such thick jungle, eliminating forest cover and even the crops that fed enemy troops. The defoliation program increased the effectiveness of the bombing campaign on the Ho Chi Minh Trail.

The US program of defoliation, codenamed Operation Ranch Hand, sprayed more than nineteen million gallons of herbicides over 4.5 million acres of land in Vietnam from 1961 to 1972. It was later revealed to cause serious health issues—including tumors, birth defects, rashes, psychological symptoms, and cancer among returning US servicemen and their families as well as among the Vietnamese population.

I am haunted to this very day by the fact that the consequences of just that action had such far-reaching health issues for so many people both in Vietnam and for those American veterans that returned home in those years and whose effects are felt to this very day. The military benefit was not worth the cost to the health of so many humans then and to this day.

My hardest duty was to brief newly arrived second lieutenants assigned as forward observers, knowing that the odds were high that some would be killed in action. These second lieutenants were basically drafted or volunteered from ROTC colleges or Officer Candidates School (OCS). They had completed the Artillery Basic Course at Fort Sill, Oklahoma, the home of the Artillery. Most had received added training and practical exercises in the field on exercises directing and controlling artillery fires at Fort Sill. They were then assigned overseas to South Vietnam for their first artillery assignment. Each forward artillery observer was assigned by me to a vacancy with a specific infantry captain company commander. I would spend quite a bit of time briefing each officer before he left by helicopter with his radio operator to join his assigned infantry company commander in a forward base camp.

To the infantry company commander, the artillery forward observer with his radio operator was the most critical team partner. With that forward observer's presence, side by side accompanying the company commander, there was the assurance that artillery support was immediately at hand in a firefight and even close air support from USAF fighters and bombers.

The most difficult part of my assignment was to visit the combat field morgues and hospitals to identify my battalion soldiers' remains and to start the process for their return home and family notification.

The soldiers in my battalion were comprised of both volunteers and draftees. From 1965 until 1973, men were drafted to fill vacancies in the armed forces for Vietnam, which could not be filled through voluntary means. During the Vietnam War, about two-thirds of American troops volunteered. The rest were selected for military service through the drafts. In the beginning of the war, the names of all American men in draft age were collected by the Selective Service. When someone's name was called, he had to report to his local draft board, which was made up of various community members, so that they could begin to be evaluated. Local draft broads had the total power to decide who had to go and who would stay.

Most soldiers drafted during the Vietnam War were men from poor and working-class families. Few came from upper-classes families. Many soldiers came from rural towns and farming communities. Many tried to avoid or delay their military service and there were some legal ways to do that. Men who had physical problems, were attending college, or were needed at home to support their families might be granted deferments by their local draft boards. Many draft-age men that received deferments were from wealthy and educated families. After Vietnam, prominent political figures who were accused of avoiding the draft due to student deferments included Bill Clinton and Dick Cheney. Some other Americans fled to other countries to avoid the draft. These people were derogatorily referred as draft dodgers—a popular term during the Vietnam war. The public believed that US draft policies were unfair.

As anti-war protests increased in the United States during the late 1960s, the draft became a target of much criticism. In 1964, many students burnt their draft cards. In the early 1970s, draft resistance reached its peak. Such disturbing national news events reached us at Lai Khe.

In 1973, the draft ended and the United States converted to an All-Volunteer Army. In 1977, on his first day in office, President Carter offered a full pardon to any draft dodgers who requested one. However, the obligation for registration continues today as a hedge against underestimating the number of servicemen needed in a future crisis under the Selective Service System. Almost all male

US citizens, and male immigrants, who are eighteen through twenty-five, are required today to register with Selective Service (www.sss.gov/). Colleges ask their male students at matriculation to complete a special form confirming their registrations.

While I was in Vietnam, I wrote almost daily to Antonia, who was back in Grand Island. I did not have a smartphone or use of the internet. Stamie, as a toddler, was the love of her grandparents, John and Emorfia. Antonia taught in the very elementary school that she was a former student in Grand Island. It was Antonia's first public school teaching assignment.

During their stay, John, my father-in-law, died on April 1, 1968, due to kidney failure and was interned next to his son, Chris. I was not able to attend his funeral. Midway through my tour in Vietnam, I took my rest and recuperation (R&R) leave out of country, in lieu of Australia as many did, in Hawaii. Antonia and Stamie joined me for a week of relaxation before returning back to South Vietnam to complete my tour. It was great reuniting with my family, but difficult when it came time to say our goodbyes once again.

Dining in the Field

However, it must be stated that, in Vietnam, the Armed Forces supported themselves in the field and in its bases of operations such as Lai Khe and Di An. I recall distinctly that the battalion had its own uniformed mechanics, medical staff, guards, and cooks. At the battalion headquarters, we had set up a field tents were the headquarters' soldiers and those from the artillery batteries when in base camp would be able to eat three meals seated at tables with table clothes under cover of a tent.

Moreover, for those soldiers that were in forward fire bases near enemy contact, our uniformed cooks would prepare and send warm freshly cooked meals in "mermite" thermos food containers that would keep the food warm or cold, as appropriate, by helicopter to the forward bases. I ensured that my battalion's soldiers were fed well even under combat conditions when permitted.

The battalion mess sergeant, on one occasion, actually took a team of his staff in a two and one half–ton truck and returned to Saigon Port. He reported to me that at Saigon Port, he had found many unclaimed refrigeration units sitting on the docks. He picked up a new refrigerator along with its generator unit that was sitting on the docks awaiting delivery. When the truck returned to Lai Khe, along with the gasoline generator for the refrigeration unit, I can to this day hear the cheers of the soldiers as the truck arrived. The bonus inside the refrigeration unit was the numerous cartons of canned Coca Cola and Pepsi.

In contrast to Vietnam, in Iraq and Afghanistan some forty years later, the use of support contractors (US civilians and third country parties), from 2008 to 2011 far outnumbered the war fighters. In Vietnam, there was not a proliferation of government support services contractors such as KBR, Blackwater, DynCorp International, IAP, and others to provide services from construction, security guards to convoys, food preparation services and more, replacing uniformed soldiers (boots on the ground) as experienced in the subsequent Iraq and Afghanistan wars.

In these latter wars, the war fighters in uniform had been shrunk and their uniformed support echelons had been eliminated from the Army's force structure. Support contractors were the prevailing answer to the reduced force structure creating cries that the Army had lost its internal ability and expertise from deploying Information Technology (IT) systems to managing large-scale support contractors.

Information technology (IT) is the application of computers to store, study, retrieve, transmit, and manipulate data, or information, often in the context of a business or other enterprise. IT is considered a subset of information and communications technology (ICT). This loss of "inherent" federal technical and management expertise in-house capability in the management of major defense systems; computer software designs, development, and verification and validation testing of various systems; and other large defense programs led to cost overruns and lengthy development times. This absence was dramatically reflected in the technical problems that arose on the government's 2013 fielding of the contractor dependent website

for national healthcare known as the Affordable Care Act (https://
www.healthcare.gov/) managed by the US Centers for Medicare and
Medicaid Services in Baltimore, Maryland. As of the writing of this
memoir, the Affordable Care Act is under controversial congressional
review intended to lead to its revision, repeal, and/or replacement.
The congressional outcome remains highly controversial under the
presidency of President Donald Trump.

In retrospect, I now reflect how eager I was to go to combat.
I had chosen West Point at seventeen years old because I was willing to go to war only imagined and glorified in movies and books.
Although I had studied and prepared for that event, the exhilaration
was amazing despite the personal peril and the ultimate sacrifice that
may be extracted from one. I was perhaps guilty of wanting to prove
myself under fire and played down and suppressed the personal danger to myself and discounted the risk to my newlywed wife and first
infant daughter. It is not so much a thirst for glory as a professional
impulse. When you are a soldier, if the game is to be played, you
want to be on the ground "over there."

Despite studying military art and history in the classroom, it
did not take long for me to first-hand understand that war is not
glorious or to be romanticized. I quickly realized that war is serious,
deadly, destructive, and that soldiers depend on each other, die for
each other, and are expecting sound leadership.

It is now some fifty years since the war in Vietnam where
540,000 US soldiers were committed and some 40,934 were reported
as killed in action (KIA) aside from those lost due to wounds, missing in action, and other categories, thus far outnumbering those
committed and lost combined in Iraq and Afghanistan.

In 1954, the French left Vietnam only to be replaced by
Americans who, in the eyes of many North and South Vietnamese,
were considered still imperialists. Whether the subsequent American
intervention is to be considered worth the effort to American security is a subject that will continue to be debated for years to come by
many common American citizens, historians, and politicians.

As I reflect on that period of my service, my thoughts are that
it was not worth the price we paid in human life. In fact, it did not

teach us a lesson. America stepped into two subsequent conflicts, Iraq and Afghanistan, which were wars that were not overall winnable, forgetting the lessons of Korea, the experiences of the French in Vietnam, and even that of the Russians in Afghanistan.

I doubt if our underground fire direction center and other facilities built by the US Engineers at Lai Khe have any current use today but rather sit empty and dilapidated, if not caved in, among the many shrapnel "scared" rubber trees of Lai Khe.

A similar fate occurred in numerous projects from new hospitals, schools to police stations in Iraq and Afghanistan that represent the waste and abuse for "unsustainable" projects built and financed by the United States as reported by the "Final Report to Congress, Commission on Wartime Contracting in Iraq and Afghanistan" in 2011, chapter 8.

As this memoir is about to go to press for publication, I am deeply concerned about America's repeat involving now after sixteen years when some hundred thousand American soldiers fought in Afghanistan to remove the Taliban.

President Donald Trump, now the third US president to be involved, announced on August 21, 2017, that the current residual American force of 8,400 soldiers would be increased by some 4,000 additional troops to provide training and advisory services to the Afghan forces and to conduct counter-terrorism operations against the Taliban and other insurgent terrorists groups. This action would be bringing the total to some 12,400 US troops on the ground plus the needed support forces for them. Such expanding role in a conflict was once considered futile and not to be undertaken from the past lessons of Vietnam, Iraq, and Afghanistan.

CHAPTER 8

Traversing the Pentagon Rings

Leavenworth Studies for Pentagon Duty

As the plane lifted off that July 1968 from Tan Son Nhut US Air Force Air Base, Saigon, I breathed a sigh of relief. I had realized that I had not been fair to my newlywed wife and first child, leaving so soon to serve in South Vietnam. I felt a sense of guilt. Somehow, Antonia could sense the importance of my serving in South Vietnam to fulfill my professional duty and ego, but quietly had suppressed her inner emotions. Chris, her brother, was killed during his USAF flight training in his jet just over one year after his West Point graduation. The prospect of a similar fate to her husband must have been extremely difficult to her and her family, despite their efforts to disguise inner feelings.

Arriving at Leavenworth, Kansas, on July 5, 1968, I soon got consumed with the courses at the US Army Command and General Staff College—a twelve-month career-required stop in Leavenworth en route to my staff assignment in the Pentagon. As electives at Leavenworth, I studied German and Operations Research and System Analysis. The various Army career schools, as similarly found in the other military services, prepare one for assignments with greater responsibilities.

However, their values lie even more so with the friendships and exchanges with classmates from all the services to include Judge

Advocate General (JAG) Corps, Air Force, Navy, and even foreign exchange officer students. Antonia and I, especially, got to know several field grade officers from the Greek Army, which we would have never had the opportunity to really get to know and to establish lasting friendships.

It was here that we created a special friendship with Robert and Stacey Poydasheff. Bob was a JAG officer with great wit. He had attended and was a graduate of the Citadel, the Military College of South Carolina, located in Charleston. Stacey and Antonia became close friends, especially because Bob and Stacey were being assigned to the Washington, DC, area too. We met at the Leavenworth Army Commissary during our weekly families' food run. Bob and Stacey later had baptized our son, Cosmas at the Saint Katherine Greek Orthodox Church in Falls Church, Virginia. Bob, currently, is in the private practice of law in Columbus, Georgia, which is nearby Fort Benning.

Moreover, my school assignment at Leavenworth was a good break for Antonia and me, giving us the opportunity to really get to know each other and to enjoy our first daughter, Stamie, who was some three years old at that time. Antonia's young cousins, Dean and Eddie Cero, lived at nearby Kansas City, less than an hour drive from Leavenworth. Eddie and Dean were Ethyl Lagas's children. Their grandfather, Gus Lagas, had sponsored Antonia's mom, Emorfia, to come to America as a young woman from Leonideon, Greece, after Gus's mother who had adopted Emorfia died. Emorfia and Ethyl and her sister Helen had lived together in Gus Lagas's home and were like sisters being of similar ages. We spent a number of weekends getting to better know each other. Especially enticing was that the Ethyl's husband, John Cero, operated a homemade gourmet candy and ice cream shop, Cero's Candies, reknown since 1885 as the best ice cream and chocolate candy store in Kansas City.

Life in the Communities of the District of Columbia

From Leavenworth, on June 8, 1969, we arrived in the Washington, DC, area in our car to our amazement of the continuous traffic exiting the District of Columbia at about 4:00 p.m. on that week day on US Highway 95. I must admit that we were all overwhelmed by not only the traffic but the spread of the DC area on the Potomac River bounded south by Virginia and to the north by Maryland. This was our first visit to the District of Columbia and to the communities adjacent to this major metropolis. Our stay at a nearby motel in Alexandria taught us that the noise of the traffic in and out of DC does not stop at midnight.

We had selected a single two-story family house to rent in Alexandria, Virginia, close to the Pentagon. I was to be assigned to the Army general staff in the Office of the Chief of Research and Development (OCRD). The corner stop for the commuter bus to the Pentagon was just a block away from our home's front doorsteps—definitely a plus!

The assignment to the Washington area became a wonderful family opportunity. First and foremost because Antonia's mom, Emorfia, now a widow, had joined us from Grand Island, Nebraska, in our single two-story rented home. Antonia and three-year-old Stamie had stayed with Grandmother (Yiayia) Emorfia in Grand Island, Nebraska, the previous one year that I served in Vietnam. Emorfia loved Stamie, our first daughter, and became more than her nanny. Emorfia took over the responsibilities of running the home and became our mentor, opening up opportunities for which to this day I wish I had appreciated more at that period of my career.

Grandmother Emorfia's presence in our home allowed Antonia to be free to teach art in the Alexandria public school system—an opportunity she took.

Washington provided Antonia's "enlightenment" period. Antonia accepted that I left in the morning for the Pentagon bus stop at about 6:00 a.m. and did not return home until late in the evening for supper some six days a week. I did, however, make time each daily for a physical workout in the Pentagon gym—a big plus! Washington was Antonia's turn to attend graduate school. So Antonia attended during the day George Washington University. After two years, Antonia earned her master of fine arts degree in painting.

Moreover, she became the choir director of the nearby newly built Saint Katherine Greek Orthodox Church at Fall Church, Virginia. Her leadership in the choir and as an organist created a host of new family friendships to include that with Bill and Leoni Nelsen to include Leoni's sisters, Zula and Nina.

Most important, on October 2, 1970, Antonia brought great excitement to us and all our friends because of the birth of Cosmas, our first son, who was named after my beloved father, Cosmas. I was in a conference that morning at the Pentagon when I got the message from Grandmother (Yiayia) Emorfia that they were heading to the hospital. Excusing myself, I grabbed my hat and ran to the Pentagon parking lot. When I arrived, what excitement on that particular October 2, 1970, in the delivery room at DeWitt Army Hospital at Fort Belvoir, Virginia. Antonia had at least four in-training delivery nurses plus doctor still helping her. Antonia later told me that her delivery was extravagant in comparison to the Spartan delivery by one Army sergeant nurse at the West Point Hospital for Stamie. Yiayia Emorfia and I were standing by and were overwhelmed when we saw it was a boy—Cosmas.

The District of Columbia with its universities, museums, national monuments, and art galleries provided a period of excitement and scholarship for Antonia, which she fully grasped. One afternoon in the spring of 1971, while a graduate student in the Master in Fine Arts (MFA) program at George Washington University, Antonia left class to attend spontaneously an ongoing Vietnam anti-war rally at the Washington Monument.

Antonia had taken along her easel, canvas, and paint brushes to the Washington Monument to capture the fervor of the event in art form, which she included in her art graduate thesis portfolio. Today, that oil painting hangs in my daughter Christina's home in Washington, DC, Christina currently works as a civil service attorney in the Residence and Naturalization Division, Office of Policy and Strategy, US Citizenship and Immigration Services, Department of Homeland Security in DC. Her first assignment in immigration was as a White House fellow upon completion of Seton Hall Law School assigned in Congresswoman Sheila Jackson Lee's Washington Office of the Eighteenth District, Texas. The White House Fellows Program continues to this day. The fellows typically spend a year as full-time paid assistants to senior White House staff, the vice president, cabinet secretaries, and other top-ranking government officials.

The anti-war rally was triggered by the release of the Pentagon papers entitled "Report of the Office of the Secretary of Defense Vietnam Task Force" (1969, comprising forty-seven volumes) to the *New York Times*. Portions of the papers revealed that five presidential administrations had all misled the public about the degree of US involvement in Vietnam. The papers, with their supporting voluminous classified documents, reflected President Truman's decision to provide military aid to France during its struggle against the communist-led Viet Minh to President Johnson's plans to escalate the war in Vietnam as early as 1964. He had claimed the opposite during that year's presidential election.

The IHAWK Missile System Staff Action Officer

At the Pentagon, I found myself assigned as an Army general staff officer in the High Altitude, Air Defense, and Missiles Division of the Office of the Chief of Research and Development (OCRD). I wondered why an Air Defense career officer had not been assigned this position. However, I was fortunate to have attended twice the Air Defense School in Fort Bliss, was a combat artillery officer trained both in artillery and missiles at Fort Sill, and had been trained as nuclear weapons officer.

In particular, I was assigned as the action officer for the Improved HAWK (IHAWK) Air Defense System and Self-Propelled HAWK Program that were entering production by the Raytheon Corporation in New Bedford, Massachusetts. IHAWK was the follow-up air defense program to improve the effectiveness and reliability of "basic" HAWK, which had been developed in the 1950 and deployed with the US Army and Marine Corp some twenty years. First article testing of the new first production IHAWK units off the assembly line was to be conducted at White Sands Missile Range in New Mexico.

Concurrently, it was also during this assignment that I was also assigned as an assistant project officer for the development, limited production, and testing of the AN/TSQ-73 along with my duties on IHAWK. I supported Lieutenant Colonel Kenneth Evans working in the same Pentagon office. The system was contracted to be built by Litton Systems Inc. The Missile Minder AN/TSQ-73 was a command and control system (computer system) with special software. It was transported in an air-conditioned shelter by truck. It was designed to perform fire direction functions for IHAWK and patriot units to include the capability for identification of friend or foe (IFF) aircraft to prevent accidental attack. It had two data link capabilities: ATDL-1 to link with Army Air Defense fire units and TADIL-B to link with an Air Force control and reporting center (CRC) or other higher units.

I soon realized, to be effective in the Pentagon, one had to know how to obtain approvals on written staff papers from the responsible officials—military general officers and senior civil service servants in the Senior Executive Service—from different departments, especially for funding, fielding, and deployment readiness. These officials are mostly career permanent civil service employees and are not politically appointed that could be dismissed.

The Senior Executive Service (SES) is comprised of the men and women charged with leading the continuing transformation of government. These leaders possess executive skills and share a broad perspective of government. Such members of the SES serve in the key positions just below the top presidential appointees. SES members are the major link between these appointees and the rest of the permanent civil service federal work force. They are the key for our government's continuity from one administration in office to the next one. They operate and oversee nearly every government activity in the federal executive agencies. The SES is a key factor to the success of any newly elected president and his/her appointed officials. President Donald Trump elected in November 2016 and subsequently inaugurated as the forty-fifth president of the United States on January 20, 2017, will be a beneficiary of the efforts of the SES.

My interests fell in the Office of the Assistant Chief of Staff for Force Development (ACSFOR), Army Comptroller, Army Assistant Deputy Chief of Staff for Operations (DCSOPS), Chief Scientist of the Army, and Army Directorate for Program Analysis and Evaluation under the Army Chief of Staff to name but some of the key Army staff decision offices and agencies. We were also fortunate to have good relations with the staff at the Office of the Secretary of Defense within the Office of Program Analysis and Evaluation (PA&E) which was replaced by the Director of Cost Assessment and Program Evaluation (CAPE). Without this latter office staff's support, it would have been impossible to have obtained approvals for a major Army program such as IHAWK.

To find offices, I soon learned how to navigate the Pentagon. The sprawling single structure fully occupied during WWII consists of five concentric rings connected by ten corridors that run, like spokes, from the inner ring to the outer. Interior courtyards separate the rings.

Quickly, I learned how to study, research, visit the field, research centers, and contractors' plants to be current and, thus, be effective in briefing senior Pentagon staff officers. Gaining their confidence, I soon obtained repeatedly their initials on key staff papers; thus, Iwas able to move staff papers quickly through the Army and DoD Staffs for crucial funding program approvals. My superiors and contemporaries were amazed. Shortly after my arrival in the Pentagon, I was promoted to lieutenant colonel on October 7, 1969, by then Lieutenant General Austin W. Betts, the chief of the Office of Research and Development (OCRD).

My main concern became whether or not the new IHAWK missile was really ready for initial production and limited deployment. In the horizon, at stake were significant foreign military sale opportunities for the Raytheon Company, in Western Europe and especially in the Middle East. To that end, I dug in to learn the entire system starting with Basic HAWK; studying all the reports available on IHAWK;

visiting multiple times the Raytheon Corporation Headquarters and related production facilities in the Bedford, Massachusetts, area; visiting the Harry Diamond Laboratories (HDL) in nearby Adlphi, Maryland, which had been involved in the design and independent testing of the radar fuze on board the missile; and visiting the initial production field-testing facility at White Sands, New Mexico. I had become the most knowledgeable person in the Pentagon on the Improved HAWK system.

Conceptually, the IHAWK system operates as follows: The IHAWK system comprises a series of computer-controlled ground-based radars and missile launchers that each mount three missiles onto their rails. A group of radars (pulse, continuous-wave, high-power illuminator Doppler, range-only radars) detect, acquire a target, track, and illuminate the target with radio frequency (RF) energy. An information coordination center is responsible for confirming whether or not the flying aircraft or target is friend or foe. The illuminator Doppler radar also provides missile guidance for the launched missile to the vicinity of the target; whereat the radar warhead fuze on board, the IHAWK missile timely explodes its warhead. The explosion releases metal fragments in a kill zone adequate to intercept and destroy the incoming enemy target being aircraft or incoming missile.

Soon, it became clear by missile testing that the missile's warhead proximity fuze designed by Raytheon was not working properly, either causing the onboard warhead to explode prematurely or too late. It was a difficult time since both Raytheon and Army proponents wanted to allow the air defense missile to enter full production, which, in my opinion, was not ready. I had become the stumbling block to the production of the entire missile system.

With the help of the Harry Diamond Laboratories' (HDL) experts on radar fuzing, Raytheon was directed to make fixes to the radar proximity fuze and to submit the new missile to a "core" test program at White Sands Missile Range. The prime interests of the Army were foremost, those being to succeeding to timely deploy a reliable, improved air defense missile system and minimizing cost overruns. Only recently has the Department of Defense taken a strong position that the cost of new major weapons system can be delivered economically, minimizing cost overruns, forcing long-time defense firms such a Lockheed Martin, Boeing, and Raytheon to control and reduce program costs. This new atmosphere was demonstrated in 2017 when the cost of the F-35 Joint Strike Fighter program even found itself in President Trump's crosshairs on several occasions. President Trump called for a review of whether a modified version of the older F/A-18 aircraft could replace the Navy's costly F-35 variant, thus forcing Lockheed Martin to reduce the costs of the new F-35 below $100 million per plane.

During World War II, Harry Diamond at the National Bureau of Standards (NBS) led the efforts directed to a new type of fuze. The fuze was a proximity or variable time fuze that could detonate a munition during a close encounter with an air target (air plane or missile) or at some distance above the ground. No longer would anti-aircraft gunners expend countless rounds trying to hit a moving aircraft. No longer could an enemy wait out an artillery barrage safely in a trench or foxhole. The War Department later described inventor Harry Diamond's proximity fuze as "one of the outstanding scientific developments of World War II … second only to the atomic bomb in military importance." In 1992, Harry Diamond Laboratories was one of seven Army laboratories merged to form the new Army Research Laboratory (ARL). HDL's laboratories and offices at Adelphi, Maryland, served as the new entity's headquarters. ARL is part of the US Army Research and Engineering Command(RDECOM).

Sufficient warheads would be fired at live airborne unmanned drones to confirm that the entire IHAWK system from radars to missiles were ready for production. The designed test program, with success and failure clearly defined therein, was approved by the Program Analysis and Evaluation Office of the Army in the Pentagon, which supported the undersigned and concurred by the DoD Office of Program Analysis and Evaluation. Raytheon, despite its vocal supporters inside the Army and outside, submitted its missile system to the White Sands Test program. The delay in production was well worth the resources expended by the Army and Raytheon.

The "core" test program proved to be successful, allowing the missile system to move to its production and deployment. The results of the missile test program were briefed to congressional committees. These briefings resulted in the congressional appropriation of adequate funds for the production and fielding of the IHAWK system. IHAWK provided the ability to engage and destroy fixed-wing aircraft, helicopters, unmanned aerial vehicles (UAV), cruise missiles and could provide anti-tactical ballistic missile (ATBM) capability against short-range ballistic missiles.

The IHAWK itself was removed from the US Army inventory in the 1980s and replaced by the M1M-104 Patriot Missile System and also from the US Marine Corps in 2002, which was replaced by the man-portable short-range F1M-92 Stinger. The IHAWK air and missile defense system still remains fielded with many international customers, with more than four hundred fire units and nineteen thousand plus missiles and has more than eighty combat kills by allies. The system can acquire targets beyond one hundred kilometers and engage targets in excess of thirty-five kilometers in range and ten kilometers in altitude.

The Israeli Iron Dome Air Defense Anti-Missile System, which protects the airspace above Israeli cities against the multiple rockets fired from Gaza by Hamas militant forces, once again demonstrated its viability in the summer of 2014. This system is similar to that of the IHAWK system. Iron Dome deploys multiple firing batteries comprised of radars, launchers with loaded missiles, command, and control systems around the periphery of an Israeli city. The system was built by the Israeli Defense Industry (Rafael Advanced Defense Systems) with the financial aid of the United States in exchange for the sharing of technical data, proprietary data. In addition, the Raytheon Company has a working relationship with Rafael.

The proper use and training of such air defense systems are critical to be effective and just, as importantly, not to have casualties from friendly fire or major catastrophes with the loss of human life, as occurred in July 2014 with the downing of Malaysia flight MH17 over Ukrainian airspace. In that instant, some 298 innocent Dutch and Australian civilian passengers, including children and crew members onboard, died by the exploded shrapnel from a Russian SA-11 missile fired from its Buk radar-guided missile launcher. The SA-11 is a large truck mounted high-performance missile system similar to the US Standard Missile— a very scarce and expensive piece of equipment.

The Ukrainian crisis started with the seizure of Crimea. Vladimir Putin had sent Russian troops into the Crimean peninsula aimed "to ensure proper conditions for the people of Crimea to be able to freely express their will," while Ukraine and other nations argued that such intervention was a violation of Ukraine's sovereignty. It had escalated to the fighting by the Ukrainian army against the Russian-supported faction in eastern Ukraine. These Soviet sympathizers had been armed with Soviet weapons and massing of Russian troops on Ukraine's eastern border. In response, NATO and the United States imposed a series of economic sanctions against Soviet firms. Historians may have recorded that perhaps mid-July 2014 was the beginning of Cold War II.

Military Assistant to Army Chief Scientist

After two years as the IHAWK program manager, in July 1971, I was re-assigned to be the military assistant to the chief scientist of the Army and Director of Army Research. Doctor Marvin Lasser was a member of the Senior Executive Service. His offices were housed also in the Office of the Chief of Research and Development. Dr. Lasser, before being appointed to his position in 1966, had been the director of research at Philco Corporation in Philadelphia. Philco was a leading developer and manufacturer of radios, batteries, and heating and air-conditioning systems. The firm was later purchased by the Ford Motor Company in 1961.

Dr. Lasser's Pentagon Army job included responsibility for a billion-dollar budget and supervision of thirty-seven Army laboratories. I was not only Dr. Lasser's planner and administrative assistant, but his technical and scientific assistant. This assignment was dynamic and interesting in as much as we focused on the ongoing high technology at that time involving high-energy lasers, night-vision systems, forward-looking infrared radiometers (FLIR); fire and forget missiles, tube launched optically tracked wireless (TOW) guided missiles, weapons embedded computer systems, and R&D Laboratory management.

His interests extended even to the use of dogs to be trained to detect mines and booby traps for deployment with their handlers to Vietnam. Our small office always had a steady stream of industry representatives coming in to discuss their companies' ongoing technology projects and seeking the chief scientist's ear.

On just one typical afternoon, I was asked to accompany Dr. Lasser and to brief the possible use of an Army airborne laser weapon system to the chief of staff of the Army. I recall being in the chief of staff's office and discussing the issues related to the heavy weight of the power supply requirement for such a powerful laser. Such a system could be able to destroy an enemy helicopter or incoming missile warhead.

It was an exciting time for me. I had the opportunity to understand better the partnership role of the US Defense Industrial Base for R&D on new military weapons systems. The use of lasers by the Army was as exciting then as big data, cloud computing, cyber security, handheld i-phones, robotics, miniaturization, advanced manufacturing, disaggregated networked systems, or artificial intelligence, are today for the future of our Armed Services.

On another afternoon, I was instructed to proceed to Fort Detrick, Maryland, to inspect and report back to Dr. Lasser on the mine and booby trap detection dog R&D program on going at that installation. The funded program for deployment to Vietnam was being conducted by the veterinarians of the US Army Medical Research and Material Command. A congressional inquiry had been received by the Army due to concerns by members of Congress from constituents of possible mistreatment of the dogs at Fort Detrick, Maryland.

A congressional reply was required from the Army. I had little experience with animals and the only dog I was familiar with was a bull dog, Marika, which my dad used to protect the family car from its theft. I recall as small boy that one morning when we had awoken, the car had been stolen and so was Marika.

I arrived at Fort Detrick, which is a short distance from the Pentagon, with an open mind and a lot to learn. The research project's veterinarians were quite respectful and gave me a tour of their facility and the training program, which involved the use of only German shepherds. Behavioral science techniques were used commencing with first selecting from a large pool of German shepherds only those with a "happy and playful" disposition to enter the program. Once that was done, then behavioral lanes were used to alter the dog's behaviors to the mine and booby trap environment that would be found in Vietnam. Those dogs that were not selected were transferred to the Military Working Dog (MWD) Training Center at Lackland Air Force Base in Texas for training as police dogs along with their handlers. I found no mistreatment of the dogs and so reported back to the chief scientist and in my subsequent written report to Congress. This program was successful in Vietnam.

On retiring from federal service in 1983, Dr. Lasser and his son Bob formed Imperium Inc., a Beltsville-based company where he developed an ultrasound camera for medical and industrial use. Marvin Elliot Lasser was born in Brooklyn. He served in the Army in the Philippines during World War II and graduated from Brooklyn College in 1949. In 1954, he received a doctorate in physics at Syracuse University. Dr. Lasser passed on December 20, 2013, at the age of eighty-seven.

My service in the Pentagon gave me the opportunity to be involved in the major development and fielding of a major air defense weapon system, IHAWK. It allowed me to get a firsthand experience in major Defense budget, planning, testing, production, and fielding of a weapons system. I had learned how to swiftly and efficiently coordinate matters through the Army and DoD staffs while at the same time walking the corridors to various congressional staff offices across the Potomac River to justify and seal the availability of budgeted funding.

I learned that there can be no success on the battlefield without the cooperation of our industry team members. American industry is a key member of our national defense. Our government laboratories, such as the Army Research Laboratory, are key partners essential to provide our government internal expertise for the proper management of large projects and resolution of major technical issues. We should never lose that "inherent" capability in government found in our very own military and civil service laboratories to be able to conduct research, manage complex weapons and enterprise developments and systems—both hardware and software.

CHAPTER 9

Cold War Command

My next assignment in climbing the ladder to promotion was to command an "artillery howitzer battalion," which typically was comprised of three artillery firing batteries each with six howitzers. One needed such a troop command to be promoted to colonel. The Artillery Personnel Desk in Virginia had discussed my next assignment, which was to be in Europe. Vietnam was being closed down, so a second tour to command an artillery battalion the Pacific Theater was foreclosed. The last US troops were withdrawn in March 1973 from Vietnam. Hence, I received written orders in 1972 to command a 105 mm Howitzer Artillery Battalion stationed in Augsburg, Germany. I was excited to be selected for my first command as a newly minted lieutenant colonel by the Artillery Branch.

It was imperative to command a howitzer artillery battalion to be promoted to colonel. The infantry needed to have a battalion's howitzers pounding targets and rolling in front as it progressed. To clear the way or to provide shielding protective fire or to deliver time on target (TOT) fire massing, every artillery piece was needed to reach a target to prevent an enemy breach in a defensive perimeter. You could not do this with missiles, helicopters or jet aircraft in all types of adverse weather.

When I arrived at Frankfurt Air Force Base that late summer of 1972 with my family in tow, I was notified that the airborne artillery battalion that I had been scheduled to command was reassigned by

US Army Europe out of Heidelberg to another qualified officer. The reason was the need to balance the ratio of minority officers in command slots in comparison to other American nationalities. In essence, the bottom line was that I was without a command. I refused to be sent to another staff position. I had been there the past three years in the Pentagon—enough was enough. I was on the phone with the assignment personnel office in Falls Church, Virginia.

My new instructions from Washington were to remain at the Officer's Club Officer Quarters until a command assignment could be found. At that point in time, I arranged to have Antonia with our then children, Stamie and Cosmas, join my mother-in-law, Emorfia, in Leonidio, Greece, for the summer and fall. While I waited at the club, I once again played lots of tennis and went swimming, similar to my extra-curriculum activities in Okinawa.

Command of an Artillery Missile (Nuclear) Battalion

The only battalion command that was available after some thirty days of hanging out at the officer's club was an artillery missile battalion. In 1972, I was being tested. I was assigned as commander of the Third Missile Battalion, Twenty-First Artillery (Honest John M50 [Nuclear] Rocket), which was part of the Seventy-Second Artillery Group of the VII Army Corps Artillery located at Peden Barracks in Wertheim, Germany. The Honest John Rocket consisted of a truck-mounted, unguided, and solid-fueled rocket, transported in three separate containers with the capability of mounting high explosive as well as low-yield nuclear warheads.

I reported to two group commanders during my some nineteen-month command period from March 25, 1972, through December 5, 1973—Colonel Donald E. Sampson initially for some fifteen months, followed by Colonel John E. Baker for the remaining five months. The battalion had a headquarters battery and three Honest John missile (nuclear) batteries, totaling approximately four hundred soldiers. The battalion's barracks were Fiori, an ex-Wehrmacht installation, in Aschaffenburg, Germany. I was also assigned as the installation coordinator of the Fiori Barracks, which also housed the First Battalion, Fourth Infantry (Mechanized), Third Brigade of the Third Infantry Division and two separate companies. Then Colonel George B. Price (now brigadier general retired) was the commander of the Third Brigade and community commander of the military community of Aschaffenburg of which Fiore Barracks was one of several former German *kasernes* under his authority. His sister was the opera diva Leontyne Price of whom he was proud and often would mention her name. Leontyne Price was the first African-American singer to perform opera on television. At the age of fifty-seven, she made her final stage performance at the Metropolitan Opera in 1985. Colonel Price passed at the age of eighty-five on March 17, 2010.

Concurrently, I was designated as the commander of the special (nuclear) weapons storage facility located at the outskirts of Aschaffenburg. The special weapons storage facility was similar to a prison with guard towers, sandbags, heavy-built storage bunkers, multiple barbed-wire barriers, and night lighting but without inmates. It was, in essence, a mini Fort Knox. It stored Army artillery nuclear warheads for ground missiles, rockets, howitzers, and engineer demolitions. The facility required twenty-four hours seven days a week guarding by the soldiers of my battalion. In addition to my battalion's onsite armed guards, a "standby" company-sized quick reaction force was rotated among the six infantry battalions and one engineer battalion stationed in Aschaffenburg in the event of a threatened or actual attack of the storage site or its breach by terrorists. The presence of these nuclear weapons was an equalizer during the Cold War, since the Russians had numerical soldier superiority. The realistic threat posed by the presence of these nuclear weapons equalized the two forces.

The first US Army units had received their rockets and Honest John battalions were deployed in Europe since the spring of 1954. Developed at Redstone Arsenal, Alabama, Honest John was a large but simple fin-stabilized, unguided artillery rocket weighing 5820 pounds in its initial M-31 nuclear-armed version. Mounted on the back of a truck, it was aimed in much the same way as a cannon and then fired up an elevated ramp, igniting four small spin rockets as it cleared. The rocket had an official range of 15.4 miles with a twenty-kiloton nuclear warhead but was also capable of carrying a 1,500-pound conventional warhead.

This rocket system was being replaced by the MGM-52 Lance Missile System; hence, my assigned unit would not be receiving new soldiers trained in the Honest John as shortages occurred in the requisite military occupational specialties (MOS). (Note: The Lance system was itself replaced by MGM-140 ATACMS, which was initially intended to likewise have a nuclear capability during the Cold War.) Our battalion was not scheduled to be converted to the Lance Missile System. Moreover, the enlisted soldiers in my battalion knew that their rockets were absolescent and that their MOS would no longer be needed. The non-commissioned officers and junior officers would have the same unspoken thoughts.

As historians have noted, the US Army during and after Vietnam had fallen into decay into a combined volunteer and conscript force rife with racial antagonisms, drug abuse, and disciplinary failures. Soldiers were disillusioned, the uniform seemed tarnished in a nation that no longer cared, and once-proud traditions had given way to progress measured by the infamous "body counts" of Vietnam.

The conflict in South Vietnam had caused a serious decline in discipline and competence especially to our Army forces in Europe. Moreover, Defense budget cuts, lack of training, and drug usage had caused the overall readiness of US Army Europe to seriously decline. The best officer and enlisted talent had been sent to South Vietnam and the forces in Europe had been overlooked.

I was part of the new effort of bringing those forces back up to full readiness, discipline, and high morale with assigned combat experienced officers and noncommissioned officers who were taken more seriously than those without combat experience. The assignment was accepted, recognizing that it was that command or another staff position in Europe. The deck of cards had been stacked against me before I even started. Even if I was a successful battalion commander, the experience had not been with an artillery howitzer unit with which the Army won battles. I was to be commanding an absolescent tac-

155

tical nuclear rocket battalion with volunteers and conscripted troops that in many instances went to Germany to avoid Vietnam. They had no interest in being in the Army. For many, their tours of duty were almost over. They could care less about soldiering. I was handed a herculean mission of maintaining this battalion operational. The added burden of the nuclear weapons storage site was to be found heavy weight for all.

The change of command was conducted by Lt. Col. Virgil D. Dietrich on December 6 at two o'clock in the afternoon who passed on the colors to me as its new battalion commander. Later at the reception immediately following the short ceremony at Fiori Kaserne at the Aschaffenburg Officer's Club, we exchanged his experiences, giving me some insights on activities during his tenure. Concurrently, I also assumed the duties of commander of the entire Fiore Kaserne, which also housed infantry units.

It was late afternoon after the reception; and I was escorted thereafter to my office. I could sense by premonition that I would be tested soon as the "new" commander.

That late afternoon, a soldier, quite tall and muscular, appeared in front of my desk without any formal announcement as was the required normal courtesy. My sergeant major or executive officer were unavailable for some unexplained reason. No knock on the office door. No salute as an expected courtesy. I was initially taken by shock, surprise, and just sat in my chair staring at a very tall, large African-American soldier towering over my desk.

The enlisted soldier finally introduced himself and informed me that he was the unofficial leader of the battalion and Kaserne itself. All the enlisted men in the battalion did exactly as he instructed them or else. He, furthermore, informed me in a threatening manner that I would have to follow his orders. I must admit that I was taken aback. We had no such leadership issues in Vietnam. I was unprepared for such a welcome and remained in a controlled state of shock but silent, unexpressed anger.

After the enlisted soldier completed his introduction and announcements, I stood up cautiously and, without any emotion, informed him that it had been a long day and I was retiring to my government quarters for the evening. I took my hat and left my office, feeling that this battalion had an unofficial command structure and a serious readiness posture in light of its nuclear capability and special warheads. An unofficial element had overridden the existing chain of command comprised of its officers and noncommissioned officers. The latter were ineffective. The battalion harbored serious racial tensions. Drug availability in the Kaserne or from nearby German neighborhood with its use in the barracks was to be found to just be the icing on the cake. It was now time to act.

Act 1

I exited Fiori Kaserne on foot and stopped the first Military Police vehicle in my path. I instructed the Military Police Patrol to proceed to the Fiori Kaserne and promptly apprehend the individual soldier and lock him in the brigade community jail pending a court martial for threatening an officer with bodily harm and insubordination. Colonel Price, the community commander, was notified by me of my actions. Throughout my tenure as battalion commander and Fiori Kaserne leader, I must say that Colonel George Price fully supported my actions. This was Act 1 to assuming my battalion's command. A much more symbolic act than passing the colors at the change of command ceremony. In a few hours, I was notified by the Provost Marshall that they had apprehended the individual and that he was locked up in the Military Police (MP) jail.

Act 2

Early the next morning, I returned to my office and took control of my battalion and Fiori Kaserne. I asked my executive officer and sergeant major to call an immediate morning battalion formation after breakfast. I could sense at the morning battalion formation that the troops realized that their new battalion commander was the boss! My service ribbons and combat badge from Vietnam were recognized. None of the officers, noncommissioned officers, or enlisted men had served in that theater or under wartime conditions. The jailing by the MPs of the threatening soldier had spread through the night throughout Fiori Kaserne to both artillery, engineer, and infantry soldiers alike. I could sense that there was a sigh of relief from the troops that the bodily threats to each of them had been lifted with the jailing of the underground leader whose supporters faded in the ranks.

The soldiers in my rocket battalion had no interest to be in Germany in as much as they were by and large draftees. Many, however, even had college degrees. Being assigned to the US Army Europe saved them from an assignment in Vietnam. Moreover, their morale was even more lowered by the fact that the Honest John Rocket system was outdated and was being replaced by the LANCE Missile system in the future.

Hence, with the help of my assigned sergeant major, we initiated a program to first clean up the barracks of drugs by frequent inspections, removal of the kaleidoscopes hung on the ceilings for drug parties, and removal of curtains from each room used to hide the conduct of drug orgies at night. GI cleanup parties served their purpose for several continuous days.

Concurrently, I visited the battalion dining room and reinstated the assigned mess sergeant who had wrongfully been removed. He had been shoved aside and had been on the sideline doing nothing. His duties had been assigned to another noncommissioned officer who was not qualified or had the proper rank. Meals soon thereafter dramatically improved, followed by morale. Soldiers need to be fed well, a lesson from my days at Lai Khe in Vietnam. The commander visiting the mess hall of one's unit and eating there frequently sends a message to the mess staff and soldiers that its commander cares.

Act 3

After a week, I received an unexpected small sealed envelope with three stars on its exterior—the signature symbol of a letter or

note from a three-star lieutenant general. Upon opening the envelope, I noticed it was from the Seventh Corps commander himself. He had been made aware of the soldier that was in jail and his
upcoming court martial. He requested that I give the drafted soldier
from Brooklyn who only had less than three months a chance to
receive an honorable discharge from the Army. I was taken aback,
but complied.

After discussing options with my sergeant major, the senior noncommissioned officer in the battalion whose advice was always valuable, I visited the Army-Air Force Post Exchange in Aschaffenburg.
It was located close to the Fiori Kaserne. I chatted with the manager
who was a German citizen working for the US Army. He agreed to
provide housing for the soldier in an existing apartment adjoining
the third floor of the exchange and gainfully have him work at the
post exchange unpacking supplies, labeling products, and other useful work as needed in operating the exchange. The soldier would
wear civilian clothes. In essence, we had created a retraining program
for the soldier, which would prepare him for his return to civilian life.

Once having received the manager's agreement, I went to the
jail and had a face-to-face meeting with the soldier. I relayed to him
the request intervening on his behalf that I had received. I offered to
withdraw all court martial charges if he agreed to work at the post
exchange, wear civilian clothes, and not enter Fiori Barracks or any
other barracks until his discharge from the Army date came. He had
less than seventy-five days left to go. He would receive an honorable
discharge. He wholeheartedly agreed and was transported and placed
into the hands of the post exchange manager by the Military Police.
I soon thereafter sent a short note back to the three-star general to
bring him up to date.

Less than two months passed and I was again writing a short
note to the three-star general sadly informing him that I had failed
to retrain his soldier of interest. The soldier had been apprehended
by the Military Police and was now in jail for burglary of the post
exchange. He was caught trading on the German open market new
American TVs and other household items he had stolen from the
post exchange in the evenings.

Act 4

We instituted a series of training and firing exercises taking the entire battalion out of the Fiori Kaserne to the field at the Grafenwoehr Training Area repeatedly. Grafenwoehr was established for the Royal Bavarian Army in 1907. The first artillery round was fired at the base on June 30, 1910. The base trained troops for the two world wars and the Cold War. The Grafenwoehr training area still remains a major US Army installation spread over 223 square kilometers in Bavaria, Germany. Today, this training area is the largest NATO training facility in Europe. With facilities such as simulation centers, classrooms, and other training resources, the base offers training to the US Army, NATO staff elements, allied units, and service component forces and leaders.

As of this writing, the Efficient Basing-Grafenwoehr (EBG) initiative was initiated by the US Army Europe (USAREUR), formerly the Seventh Army, and involved the relocation of USAREUR command and control HQ and six battalion units to a consolidated complex in East Camp Grafenwoehr. The EBG provides operational readiness and operational control through the consolidation of troops in a single installation.

My soldiers responded to the active training cycle in lieu of just training in the barracks area. It was good for all to go to the field and conduct live firing of the rockets and training exercises. Morale responded with the energized training program and firm discipline as required. However, I could discern that there were some resistant elements especially within my officers' ranks to my programs.

Since we were a nuclear-capable unit, we were subject to unannounced technical proficiency inspections (TPI) by a team of nuclear experts. Within several months of my command assumption, such an inspection occurred. One of the key matters inspected was the ability by each rocket battery to properly assemble and arm a nuclear warhead to the Honest John Rocket. On this particular occasion, I was standing by and following the procedure by one of the battery nuclear arming teams as it was being tested. After all, I had been trained and qualified as a prefix 5, nuclear weapons specialist.

The first lieutenant leading the team was noted by me to be purposely making errors so that the battalion would fail the Technical Proficiency Inspection (TPI). Such a failure would be a red mark on the reputation of the entire battalion and its commander.

I intervened by calling for a time-out, which was approved by the inspectors. I privately met with the lieutenant on the spot and relieved him of all his duties. Thereafter, I had his battery commander assign his backup on the arming team, a sergeant first class, to continue the weapon arming exercise. The sergeant first class and his team then completed the warhead arming satisfactorily and the battery and entire battalion passed the TPI—a must accomplishment for a nuclear proficient unit.

That lieutenant earlier had been identified to me as resisting my training improvements and morale efforts. Rumors had come to me that he had intended to cause his rocket battery and in turn the entire battalion to fail the TPI so that perhaps I would get relieved as its commander. My training at Fort Bliss and Fort Sill on tactical nuclear weapons and as a nuclear weapons special weapons officer had paid off. The lieutenant was ordered to return to his quarters and to be prepared to move his family and be reassigned out of my battalion.

The matter was reported promptly by me to my group commander who considered my actions too harsh. However, he had no choice because either the lieutenant had to go or I would have to be relieved. I considered the training and handling of nuclear warheads of the highest priority. The lieutenant was reassigned within twenty-four hours from the battalion and out of Aschaffenburg. The Seventh Corps Artillery commander and even the Seventh Corps commander, based upon my reputation and record from the Pentagon, had shielded me from a relief by my group commander who disagreed with my manner of command.

Based upon my experience, training is key to maintaining the readiness and morale of a peacetime army. This principle remains true today as we have disengaged our large on-the-ground fighting forces from Iraq and Afghanistan and returned those main forces stateside. In that regard, training funds are crucial for the conduct of field training exercises near camps and stations, joint exercises involving Army, Navy, AF, and Marine forces in amphibious and heliborne exercises and especially those that require live fire exercises to sustain readiness. Training munitions are essential for live firing exercises of the various weapons from tank rounds, anti-tank rockets, demolitions, to fire and forget missiles to name a few.

Fuel is required for airborne units to maintain paratrooper jump status readiness and efficiency not to mention for the movement of armed vehicles and helicopters and operation of generators in field training exercises. Moreover, the budgeting and funding for the periodic conduct of NATO exercises and those with the armed forces of various countries with whom we have treaties are crucial.

The Special Weapons Storage Site

As darkness would come in the evening or in the early morning hours, I would travel daily to visit the special nuclear weapons site that I had been assigned as its commander as one of my major additional duties. My battalion's artillery men provided the twenty-four-hour guards for the security of the weapons storage site. This was the era that the United States had Army nuclear munitions storage sites in multiple locations such as Germany, Greece, and Turkey backing up the NATO forces along the Iron Curtain.

The Iron Curtain was a phrase made famous by Winston Churchill who coined the phrase to describe the line separating the Soviet-dominated Eastern Europe from the sovereign nations of the west. It was literally a guarded barrier that millions of people could not cross. In essence, they were imprisoned in their home countries. But by 1988, reformers inside the Hungarian government decided to open their border to the west and allow Hungarians to leave for Austria. The next year, they began allowing East Germans on Hungarian soil to leave for Austria as well.

Finally, on November 11, 1989, the Berlin Wall came down.

In 1973, our Honest John battalion's rockets had nuclear warheads stored at the storage site as well as the nuclear weapons projectiles for eight-inch guns among other artillery weapons, and for engineer nuclear weapons demolitions, which in time of war could be used to destroy the Rhine River crossings in the event of a Soviet Union counterattack across the Iron Curtain.

My unannounced visits in the late evenings to the special weapon site provided to my soldiers proof that the guard mission was a key mission and appreciated by the Army. I would chat with the guards, personally inspect their weapons and ammunition and alert them to the fact of any newly received intelligence indicating the possibility of a sneak attack threat by a rogue group or Soviet-trained clandestine element. We often received realistic threats ascribed to the German terrorist group Baader-Meinhof Gang, which could be encountered, whose intent was to penetrate the weapon storage site's igloos to place demolitions and cause their destruction; or attempt to steal a nuclear warhead. In that regard, we always ran simulated drills to ensure that the guards and standby reaction forces were not complacent and always prepared by reacting in a timely and responsive manner to an actual attack at the special weapons storage site.

It was during this assignment that the Ninth Engineer Battalion commander visited me on one Friday morning. We discussed his battalion's mission in support of the assigned "reaction" forces for the defense of the Special Weapons Site. We discussed the terrorists' recent threats from intelligence I had received on possible attacks against the special weapons storage site and plans for reinforcing the physical perimeter security of the nuclear weapons site.

On Sunday, just after midnight, as commander of the Special Weapons Site, I called an emergency alert, which triggered the deployment of his entire Engineer Battalion to include its bull dozers and other heavy construction equipment. Colonel Price, the commander of the Third Infantry Brigade in Aschaffenburg and my superiors at the Seventy-Second Artillery Group and VII Corps Artillery Headquarters were notified. I considered the terrorist threat to the special weapon site too real.

The Engineer Battalion was given the mission of fully deploying its some three hundred soldiers to the nuclear weapons site. Their immediate mission was to concurrently design and build the immediate construction of an extensive defensive moat with obstacles around the entire weapons storage site plus to construct a second complete barrier fence with guard towers. The concurrent "design and build" work was to take place until completed with no other interfering activity.

My orders took precedence over any other duties that engineer battalion had to perform for at least some sixty days or until the construction project was completed. The new engineer works reinforced the defenses of the special weapon storage site. My superiors considered the improvements to the special weapons site to be a major sound upgrade in security. They too could not afford to have a nuclear warhead stolen on their watch. Both the Engineer Battalion commander and I had done our duty.

Since the entire Engineer Battalion had been committed to the urgent construction project, it also avoided a barracks major "spit and polish" inspector general's inspection. Needless to say, I was extremely popular with the engineer troops and, especially, their commander who only had a few days left before rotating back to the United States for a new assignment. He received a special commendation for the completion of a highly sensitive construction project mission!

CHAPTER 10

The Horse Holder

The Army in Europe was under the spotlight now that Vietnam was over and focus was redirected to what type of US land forces should be stationed in Western Europe. The Cold War was ongoing. The reorganization and reduction of current forces and restationing of newly organized forces to meet threat objectives had high priority. Cost cutting in the US defense budget was triggered in the aftermath of the Vietnam withdrawal by US forces.

After my nineteen months as a battalion commander in Aschaffenburg, I was assigned on December 6, 1973, through July 2, 1975, to the Office of Deputy Chief of Staff for Operations (ODCSOPS), Seventh Army Europe, Headquarters, Heidelberg, initially as the Chief of the Doctrine, Test and Evaluation Branch and later as executive officer, followed by Operations Staff Officer for the permanent stationing of Brigade 75.

My initial assignment for four months at ODCSOPS was to develop a new Air Space Management Doctrine. I supervised general staff officers, senior operations research analysts and staff assistants in the branch. My desk was located in the front office. We coordinated joint and combined evaluations of new material and tactical doctrine to determine the potential for employment in US Army Europe. The expanded use of helicopter forces in a mix of heavy armor forces was being implemented in light of lessons learned from Vietnam. We formulated options such as proposed new Air Space Management

Doctrine, which were presented and approved by Maj. Gen. Edward "Shy" Myers for presentation to the Commander-in-Chief (CINC) US Army Europe.

One of my greatest challenges was to serve two major generals. For Maj. Gen. Edward "Shy" Meyer, Deputy Chief of Staff for Operations (G3) for the US Army in Heidelberg, Germany, I was a key staff officer in his inner circle. Upon General Myer's re-assignment, I served Maj. Gen. Clay T. Buckingham, the new DCSOPS. I was the office manager for these general officers supervising the administrative staff to include the European Army's Office of Military History. I often spoke and acted for these DCSOPS in all matters pertaining to administration, management and much more—handling numerous sensitive matters.

In July 1974, Turkish forces invaded and captured some three per cent of Cyprus before a United Nations ceasefire was declared. More than one quarter of the population of Cyprus was expelled from the occupied northern part of the island where Greek Cypriots constituted 80 percent of the population. The Turkish invasion ended in the partition of Cyprus along the UN-monitored Green Line, which still divides Cyprus.

I recall being on the staff in the USAEUR Operations War Room in Heidelberg during the Greek-Turkish faceoff in Cyprus. Our intelligence team had calculated that due to petroleum shortages the Greek Air Force and Army was in no logistical position to wage any type of serious threat to the Turkish army's activities in Cyprus. The faceoff led to our decision to remove the stored US Army nuclear weapons from the US guarded special storage sites in Greece and Turkey. The directed removals were managed from the war room in Heidelberg. US naval helicopters were used to lift and transport the nuclear warheads in sling nets to our aircraft carriers in the Mediterranean one evening that summer in 1974. My experience from my recent assignment at Aschaffenburg as commander of the special weapons site at that location was valuable to the USAEUR staff.

On January 1, 1975, I was assigned to an ad hoc group in the ODCSOPS to develop the plans for the stationing of Brigade 75 in

Europe. This required the development of detailed studies and analysis on the opening and closure of USAEUR kasernes, restationing of units throughout USAEUR, and manpower and base development planning. There were many variables that affected the design and development of an extremely complex stationing action, causing conflicting issues to arise among the team with whom I worked.

Finally, we developed the basis for a negotiated exchange of major Army and Air Force facilities in Germany. In doing this work, I was given many controversial actions that pertained to personnel and facility realignments. I recall distinctly traveling to Munich with written orders to meet with a general officer, the commander of the Army-Air Force Post Exchange Facilities, to personally inform him that he was to promptly shutter his facilities. That order was consistent with the ongoing closing down of Munich and eventual removal all US forces stationed throughout the Munich area to include the Army General Hospital. Needless to say, he was extremely unhappy and I am sure he remembers that meeting even to this very date.

My staff actions during this last assignment caused the DCSOPS, General Clay T. Buckingham, in his written comments as the reviewer of my last performance evaluation to write:

> In spite of the ... problems ..., I believe that LTC Giallourakis should be promoted to Colonel at the next opportunity. He is another Admiral Rickover. (Clay T. Buckingham, Major General, GS, Deputy Chief of Staff, Operations)

Germany's Oldest and Most Romantic City

Heidelberg itself was a refreshing assignment for an Army wife. Especially because of its cultural and art center, Antonia was thrilled to have the opportunity to live in the city. Antonia had studied German and was fully fluent. We received housing when we arrived in Heidelberg. Grandmother Emorfia, Antonia's mother, was with us. Often I would look out of our second floor apartment and see my son, Cosmas, and daughter, Stamie, playing at the swing set with Grandmother Emorfia.

Antonia enjoyed visiting Heidelberg and, especially, its numerous museums and art galleries. She renewed her interest in oil paintings and participated in a show with her new portfolio of Heidelberg canvas landscape scenes at the Heidelberg Officer's Club. Her creative, talented spirit in oil paintings focused on historic sites in the city of Heidelberg. As the art show opened to the public, all of Antonia's oil paintings of various Heidelberg landscapes were purchased at once by just one buyer to adorn his home before anyone else had a chance to buy even one.

Antonia was a most frugal wife, taking her queue from her parents. While in Germany for three years, Antonia and I saved as much of her teaching and my military salaries as possible so that eventually, when we returned to the United States, we could purchase or build a new home. In the years 1970–1976, interest rates on certificates of deposits in the US banks catering to the overseas military were approaching 10 percent per annum with Treasury Bills in excess of 5 percent—a far cry in 2013–2018 when ten-year US Treasury yields had been fluctuation between only 1.3 and 2.5 percent.

I knew that I would soon need to make a decision as to whether or not to continue service, retire, or change professions. I was thirty-nine years old. I had served to the best of my ability the soldiers for whom I had been given responsibility in time of war and peace, served in the Pentagon as the special assistant to the chief scientist of the US Army, was the project manager for the Improved HAWK Air Defense Missile System built by the Raytheon Company, and served several general officers of major commands as their adjutant and executive officer.

Generals sought me out to be their "horse holder." "Horse holder" was the name given to that person whom the general officer or senior executive service principal confides in; who drafts letters for such high-ranking individuals—in essence their personal secretary and "gate keeper" for access; delivers personally command critical messages; and other tasks that at times create bad feelings towards the "messenger." Such "Horse Holders," who in many instances are General Officers who had attended as cadets the United States Military Academy at West Point, can be found on many a White House Presidential Staff with that of President Donald Trump's, being an example as to their use.

On July 2, 1975, my staff assignment in Europe ended for I had received orders to return back to the United States.

CHAPTER 11

The Frequency Hopping Radio

In the summer on July 7, 1975, I reported for duty at Fort Monmouth, New Jersey, then the home of the US Army Signal Corps Branch School and the headquarters of the US Army Communications-Electronics Command (CECOM). I was assigned to the Single Channel Ground and Airborne Radio System–VHF (SINCGARS–V) Program Management Office to the position of assistant program manager for Test, Evaluation, and Training for some four years. The program manager, Col. James E. Wyatt, was a respected Signal Corps officer with an established record.

I was surprised to receive this assignment because the focus was on the next generation of the Army and Marine Corps combat net radios used at the squad, platoon and company levels—a key radio in time of combat. The airborne version of the radio was even to be placed in Air Force Aircraft providing close air support to ground forces to facilitate communications between pilots, forward observers, and ground units in close enemy contact. The SINCGARS-V radio was to be much smaller, lighter, and able to receive and transmit digital data and incorporated frequency hopping to prevent enemy jamming of its signals. Compared to the then current VRC-12 VHF radio in 1975, it was a giant leap in solid state technology.

Such an assignment would be most appropriate for a Signal Corps officer, not that of an artilleryman. However, I had combat qualifications from Vietnam, was an electrical engineer (EE) from

170

Purdue University, and had taught EE at West Point. Moreover, I had served in the Office the Chief of Research and Development at the Pentagon and had experience in complex missile and radar test programs. Hence, I fitted the position, bringing experiences that were needed for this major Defense-wide program.

In particular, SINCGARS-V was to provide a replacement for the then present AN/PRC-77 and AN/VRC-12 series equipment then found in all Army and Marine combat and service units. Procurement of the SINCGARS-V was to include some one hundred sixty thousand new radios for the Army and twenty thousand for the Marine Corps.

The new capabilities of SINCGARS-V necessitated a review of employment doctrine for radios in the VHF-FM band both for amphibious operations and land operations. The new program with its frequency electronic counter-countermeasures and ability to transmit digital data caused the need to review doctrine and also the impact of SINCGARS-V on frequency spectrum management procedures.

The Monmouth County Community

However, the most pressing need upon our arrival from Frankfurt, Germany, to Fort Monmouth, was preparing for the pending birth of Christina, our second daughter. On post, family housing was not available. We were placed on the waiting list and living in the temporary visitor quarters, then all three of us plus my mother-in-law, Emorfia.

It was during that time that we were befriended by Georgia and Robert Burns. Georgia was a real estate agent and a long-time resident of Asbury Park. She helped us get adjusted to the Fort Monmouth area. We became members of Saint George Greek Orthodox Church located then in Asbury Park. She volunteered first to be Christina's godmother even before she was born. On August 29, 1975, some fifty-seven days after we had arrived back in the United States, Christina was born at Patterson Army Hospital at Fort Monmouth.

Soon thereafter, we moved to permanent Wherry Family Housing in a townhouse, among the putting greens of the Fort Monmouth Golf Course.

Antonia became involved with the Fort Monmouth Community Women's Club, plus the Saint George Daughters of Penelope and the Greek Orthodox Ladies of the Philoptochos Society, church women's organizations of Saint George Greek Orthodox Church, that supported various philanthropic programs in the county. She taught school on post in Fort Monmouth to the children of military families. This assignment later led to her permanent position in the Shrewsbury Borough School as the art and English teacher for kindergarten through eighth grades. She even attended Monmouth University in Long Branch, New Jersey, and earned her master of arts in teaching (MAT) degree. Her active style prompted Col. James Wyatt to whom I reported for duty to write in my first performance report on May 5, 1976, after our first year on assignment in his project office that

> "wife is equally dynamic, sets the example and provides great inspiration to other wives."

Action in a Defense Program Manager's Office

Working in a major program manager's office was a first for me. It brought me into close contact with American industry for the second time since my assignment on IHAWK and Raytheon in the Pentagon and while in the Office of the Chief Scientist of the Army. This time Rockwell Collins, ITT, Plessey, Harris, Thompson-CSF, Cincinnati Electronics, GEC Marconi, RCA and other defense communications firms would be interested players.

Although not a major weapon or fighter aircraft system, the Single Channel Ground and Airborne Radio System Very High Frequency (SINCGARS-V) was designated a major Defense program due to its impact on the military services. The new VHF radio was to replace thousands of radios throughout the Army, Marine

Corps, and even the Air Force, which needed to communicate with the ground forces.

There was excitement as General Thomas Reinzi, the Chief Signal Corp officer of the Army, Colonel James Wyatt, the program manager, and I were literally running through the basement corridors of the Pentagon. We were en route to our first Defense Systems Acquisition and Review Council's (DSARC) meeting to obtain DoD's approval to launch this multimillion-dollar Army program. Major General Reinzi had been one of my Tactical officers at West Point in 1955 when I was a yearling (college sophomore). He was known by the entire Corps of Cadets for parachuting or helicoptering into gathered cadet football rallies to lead the cheers to "On Brave Old Army Team." His entry and presence electrified and drove the entire Corp of Cadets to a frenzy.

Colonel Wyatt was a skilled program manager, also being a most highly qualified presenter. He was responsible for articulating the acquisition strategy (industry firms that could bid for the program and the criteria for selection, type of contract(s), development of the specification, and other requirements to achieve program objectives) for the new radio system, identifying the risks to the program, and presenting its special logistical aspects. The project office team had developed the budget for the new system and milestone schedule for the presentation to the council.

The project office staff was small, but a highly compatible and integrated team, supporting each other. In particular, I recall Cary Fishman, a civil service engineer, and Major Charles L. Fisher, a talented signal officer of the West Point class of 1962 with whom we worked closely. Charlie and his wife, Roseann, and two beloved children, Marith and Sean, became close friends with Antonia and our children. We would attend football games at West Point together. Colonel Wyatt was a solid leader and program manager. He allowed each of his key members of the team, to include me, to run with the "football." He expected us to perform our duties and did not micro-manage our daily actions in promoting the SINCGARS-V program.

We had prepared the Coordinated Test Plan (CTP) for the radio after months of working with a fifteen-member organization, the Test Integration Working Group (TIWG), which also included contractors. In addition, we had developed an upgraded reliability program that would be implemented by the winning contractor to design and build the new VHF radio.

For the first time, we had, in cooperation with several Army laboratories, developed an Electromagnetic Compatibility (EMC) Vulnerability Simulation, using frequency hopping, allowing us to assess the new radio's spread spectrum electromagnetic counter-countermeasures potential against enemy jammers. The hop rate and the dwell time at each changing frequency to be used for the new hopping radio were key adjustment parameters to defeating the jamming of an enemy's Electronic Warfare campaign. In today's terminology, we were involved in the forefront of a new technology to operate in a "cyber warfare" environment.

Needless to say, we were granted approval by the DSARC to proceed in a phased manner (engineering development, prototype development, test and evaluation, initial limited production, operational testing, and full-scale production) with periodic review points to develop and eventually manufacture for deployment the new radio. The first contract for the design and development of the SINCGARS-V was awarded to ITT, which was selected over Cincinnati Electronics and Rockwell Collins Corporations.

Still in 2018, the SINCGARS-V remains the Army's and Marine's VHF legacy radio system being fully deployed down to squad and platoon levels. It is compatible with mid-tier networking vehicular radios (MNVR) with its Capability Set (CS)17, which allows soldiers to rapidly exchange digital information with battalion and brigade levels.

Preparing for Future Assignments by Graduate Study

It was during this assignment that I decided that it was essential to prepare for the future. I had not been selected as yet for attendance at any of the senior service colleges such as the Army War College or the Industrial College of the Armed Forces. I was looking to the future to better refine my military and civilian value. Hence, I started attending evening classes at the Education Center at Fort Monmouth. A master in business administration program was offered on post in the evenings by the traveling faculty from Fairleigh Dickinson University (FDU). Permanent and adjunct professors came from the FDU Florham Campus in Morris County and the Metropolitan Campus in Teaneck, New Jersey.

After attending the MBA program for almost eighteen months, I decided to also attend night law school in downtown Newark at the private Seton Hall University School of Law evening program. Fairleigh Dickinson agreed that I could still receive my MBA with submittal of a research paper; hence, I did not lose any time in also earning my master in business administration.

My daily routine at the SINCGARS-V Program Office started at 6:30 a.m. and ended daily at 5:00 p.m. The two-story apartment-townhouse on the Fort Monmouth Golf Course was very near to our program offices. The backyard was adjacent to the ninth hole of the golf course where our young children—Stamie, Cosmas, and Christina—would often set up a card table and sell ice-cold punch to the golfers. As I stopped by our family quarters, Antonia would hand me my prepacked fully cooked supper on a tray. She was an angel. By five thirty o'clock in the afternoon, we were on the Garden State Parkway to the New Jersey Turnpike en route to downtown Newark for Seton Hall. One Marine Corps officer, who was also my next-door neighbor, one civilian newspaper reporter whose wife was a friend of Antonia, and one Army officer, me, comprised our rotating weekly car pool.

New Jersey has three law schools of which Seton Hall School of Law even to this date is rated the first, followed by the Rutgers University School of Law in Newark and the Rutgers State University of New Jersey School of Law in Camden. The dean of Seton Hall's School of Law was pleased to have as graduate students two active-duty veterans, an Army and a Marine Corps officer. We attended the evening school under the Vietnam GI Education Program which provided education benefits similar to those offered to veterans of WWII and the Korean War.

Vietnam veterans' education benefits at that time for school were subsidized by the federal government. Payments were issued directly to educational institutions on behalf of the veteran. They could be used for a variety of education and training programs, and separate subsistence payments were also provided directly to me, separately from my active duty regular military salary.

In my case, all our tuition fees were paid to attend law school at Seton Hall University and, concurrently, Business School at Fairleigh Dickinson University in Newark, New Jersey.

Hence, I was able to obtain both my JD law and master in business administration (MBA) degrees. Fairleigh Dickinson allowed me to conduct an independent research project in order to be able to receive my MBA.

We went to law school every day of the week either to class or to do research at the Peter W. Rodino Law Library. Class started at seven o'clock in the evening and ended by ten thirty o'clock in the evening. We were back at Fort Monmouth by midnight. The routine continued for three and a half years and included full-course loads each summer. On the weekends, we did our reading and written legal assignments. The instructors were members of the permanent law school faculty to include active judges still on the bench and experienced adjunct professors in specialty areas.

My evening classes were full with students commuting from New York City after work to Newark Penn Station and walking diagonally across Raymond Boulevard to the School of Law. My classmates were primarily working investment professionals and accountants from Wall Street with one doctor and several schoolteachers plus my car pool occupants.

Despite my busy travel schedule for the project office, I always made it back to Newark International Airport just in time to walk into law or business class by seven o'clock in the evening even traveling from Tucson. As a lieutenant colonel, I was known for scheduling short and to-the-point, no-nonsense, effective meetings. I had found that unclassified meetings could be held much more effectively at the airports that I landed. Most airports had conference rooms that were readily available for business travelers.

The Unexpected Visitor

Having commanded a nuclear rocket battalion in Europe in lieu of a howitzer battalion was not conducive to receiving an artillery promotion to colonel to command an artillery group. Artillery groups were comprised primarily of several howitzer-gun battalion units. Command of a howitzer battalion was key to group command. More importantly, commanding a rocket battalion with an absolescent missile being phased out of the army inventory with soldiers not interested in the Army, volunteers, and conscripts, many who had avoided going to fight in Vietnam, was a difficult task at best for achieving "stellar" command performance.

In addition, the proficiency and security of nuclear warheads for artillery missiles, engineer demolitions stockpiles was not a burden that a normal howitzer or infantry battalion commander was saddled. Little credit was given by promotion boards for such out-of-the-mainstream critical assignments.

As fate would have it, in early 1978, at his request, I met with a known but unexpected visitor on his official tour of Fort Monmouth. To his credit General Shy Myer, the then newly appointed chief of staff of the Army, sought me out while on his visit of research activities at Fort Monmouth. He unexpectedly deviated from his planned schedule. Privately, he wanted to freely discuss my status. The Army still had not selected me to attend any of the senior war colleges. I had been passed over for promotion several times. I was still a lieutenant colonel. I had made quite a few enemies in the Army loyally serving him on his staff and as executive officer, not to mention the command of an outdated nuclear missile battalion, which had been eliminated from the Army's inventory and tables of organization. We both talked frankly.

The meeting was a surprise and overwhelmed me. During the meeting, his senior escort officers who were standing by for some time were left wondering what was so important to the Army chief of staff to impact his schedule by having such an unscheduled, closed, extended meeting. One year later on February 12, 1979, I was promoted to the rank of colonel. No doubt the Army's new chief of staff had a hand in that promotion.

The New Commander of the Army Test Unit

In November 1979, now as a colonel, in lieu of an Artillery Group Command, I was assigned as commander of the Army Test Unit in support of the Joint Interoperability Tactical Command and Control System (JINTACCS) stationed at Fort Monmouth. Although I was prepared to defer the completion of law school for a troop command, this assignment was accepted. It did not involve a change in permanent station and disruption of the family or the completion of law school at Seton Hall. The combination of the promotion and assignment allowed us to move off the golf course to Colonel's Row in a separate standalone brick home on the Fort Monmouth Main Post. Now our backyard opened up to the Post Parade Field in lieu of a golf course.

The Army Test Unit was a new test organization created to participate in joint test programs. I became the director for tests demonstrating Joint Interoperability (between Navy, Air Force, Marines) of various tactical command and control computer systems. The effort involved coordination with multiple contractors and diverse Army commands. I reported directly to the commander of the Research and Development Command (RADCOM), then Major General Emmett Paige Jr.

We became deeply involved in communications, computer test instrumentation, software programming, budgeting, and multiple contract management. The buzzwords then were C3I, standing for Command, Control, Communications and Intelligence. Instead of combat troops, I led some twenty civil service employee engineers with grades GS11-15 and several Army officers and noncommissioned officers. Our efforts were the forerunner for simplified manual message preparation systems pending the availability of the Army's automatic data processing systems. My team of engineers pioneered the development of computer test software and test methodology for conducting joint interoperability tests.

I well recognized that no Army promotion board would consider this assignment a "choice key position" for promotion to brigadier general for a division artillery command much less attendance to a senior military school such as the War College. In lieu of an artillery command of soldiers, I was still basically for the second assignment involved in leading office bound professional civil servants in lieu of soldiers.

On the other hand, I had become skilled and seasoned in meeting and dealing with the rising industrial communications and computer industry catering to the needs of our military, managing major defense programs, and in the practice of awarding and administering federal contracts.

CHAPTER 12

Rookie Barrister

The Fort Monmouth Post band played our *Star Spangled Banner*, as I stood on the parade field and in front of the guest bleaches on that hot afternoon in July 29, 1981. I was a colonel in the Army after some twenty-three years of service. I had been offered as my next assignment to become the military attaché to the US ambassador in Greece. I felt this assignment was too late and certainly would not lead to general officer rank. Even more important, it did not excite me. Perhaps it would have, if it was offered to me earlier in my military service. It was time to move to another new career. I had served my country; now it was time to directly serve the general public as private counsel—despite the many overtures at the end to remain in service and the offer of future plum military assignments and even perhaps receiving a star as a brigadier general.

More importantly, I had decided that I was young enough, at forty-five years old, to start a civilian service-oriented career. This was the time to start or never. I finally was going to get involved in economics, business, and the social sciences as an attorney. I had loved and excelled in the social sciences and in military law as a student at West Point. As an adjutant, I had administered many a court martial.

In the bleaches were my wife, Antonia, and my three young children, Stamie, Cosmas, and Christina, and of course my beloved mother-in-law, Emorfia. Antonia was called up to stand next to me. She was recognized and presented with a bouquet of flowers.

The commanding general of Fort Monmouth conferred on me the Legion of Merit for my current services as Commander of the Army Test Unit as part of the Joint Interoperability Task Force (JINTACS). Such military medals are awarded for services previously rendered. However, one must never forget, whether in the military or civilian environments, promotions are for the "potential" of the performance of future service excellence, not because of prior accomplishments. Finally, the adjutant read the important Army's Retirement Order.

A week prior to my retirement ceremony, my family had all moved from government quarters to live temporarily in a one-story beach house at Bradley Beach just south of Asbury Park on the Jersey Shore. Although that winter was quite cold on the Jersey Shore to be living in a wooden beach house, after school and on the weekends, we all still had fun walking and playing on the beach. Aunt Georgia, Christina's godmother and now our realtor, had found the rental home for us.

Concurrently, we had also contracted for a new colonial brick-style two-story home to be built in Shrewsbury by Optimo Builders, a Long Branch, New Jersey, reliable builder. The lot was spacious and the backyard even had a flowing pond able to handle a canoe for the children. The home at 46 Winding Brook Way was within walking distance adjacent to the Avenue of the Commons office complex area where one day perhaps I could operate a law office. The west gate of Fort Monmouth was within a short walking distance. At the end of our block was a branch of the Monmouth County Library System, which housed a complete law library. Its children's wing was wonderful for all three of our children. Primary school was within walking distance and there was bus service to nearby Red Bank Catholic High School where Stamie attended school and also to Red Bank Regional High School later for Cosmas and Christina.

Our savings from our Germany military assignment made this construction possible. Antonia's appointment as the full-time art schoolteacher at Shrewsbury Borough School was also central to our decision. In the past twenty-three years, we had never owned a home before. On a temporary basis, the rented beach house served its purpose well, despite the cold, living on the Jersey Shore while construction was ongoing.

The Newly Admitted Attorney

On the day of my retirement, I had already been admitted into the practice of law in several jurisdictions. One year previously, on June 8, 1980, I had been at another ceremony in Newark, New Jersey, where I was awarded by the dean of Seton Hall University Law School the juris doctorate degree. With my degree in hand, in a period of less than several weeks, I had then flown to the Tampa Convention Center where some one thousand candidates and I sat to take concurrently the National Multistate Bar exam and the bar exam for the State of Florida.

Thereafter, within twenty-four hours, I flew back to Newark to take the New Jersey State Bar Exam. I was admitted to the Florida Bar on November 11, 1980, and New Jersey Bar on December 18, 1980. The District of Columbia Bar Exam followed thereafter with my admission occurring on August 11, 1981.

Although I was not a JAG officer, my commanding general recognized my law degree and had already assigned me a special confidential mission to investigate contract fraud allegations of several high-tech firms doing business with the Army's Communications Electronics Command. General Emmett Paige really respected me and my family. He knew I had completed law school and had passed the bar exams. His command had a problem with certain contracts involving possible fraudulent invoices from a number of contractors on the West Coast.

I was asked to lead the conduct of an investigation of these firms. So as an additional duty, I had worked out of the Judge Advocate General's (JAG) office to lead the investigation on a very close hold basis despite the fact that I was not a JAG officer. This assignment provided my first experience for my future law practice in federal contract administration.

During the one year between the receipt of my juris doctorate degree, preparing and taking the multiple bar exams in three-state court jurisdictions, and being accepted in the Federal Court System, I studied and took the US Patent and Trademark Office Patent Exam. My graduate degree in electrical engineering from Purdue and work in the Army plus teaching assignment at West Point made it easy to sit for the Patent Office exam. Hence, I had added prior to my retirement ceremony the ability to handle complex intellectual property matters as a patent attorney. This certification was an essential qualification that served many of my future clients starting up small businesses and high-tech firms.

Law school had re-energized me mentally and physically. I, in essence, had performed my duties in the Army during the day and in the evening as necessary. I had learned how to use each minute of the day and night to perform my Army duties as the commander of the Army Test Unit at Fort Monmouth, fulfill some minimum duties as the father of three children, and even attend law school. If it were not for my beloved wife, Antonia, and her mother, Emorfia, I would have never been able to complete my law studies even despite my Army salary and the GI Education Bill for all my tuition due to my combat service in Vietnam.

I distinctly recall hearing my oldest daughter, Stamie (nine years old) tiptoeing in the hallway outside my small study room and whispering to her younger brother, Cosmas, and sister, Christina, to keep quiet because "Daddy is studying!" This ritual went on for some four years. I only regret the sacrifices my family made to ensure I graduated Seton Hall Law School. I had sacrificed the times missed in not being available to play with my children and lead perhaps a normal life during that period. Such sacrifices, however, paid off as my three children thereafter attended and graduated from Smith College, MIT, and Tufts University and thereafter attended graduate schools in medicine, law, and education.

Stamie attended Smith College (1984–88) after graduation from Red Bank Catholic High School in 1984 in Red Bank, New Jersey. At Smith College, Stamie earned her bachelor of arts degree cum laude in economics. It was at Smith College that Stamie met and dated Aris Despo. The two were introduced during a Christmas Eve service at Saint George Greek Orthodox Church at the Jersey Shore during Stamie's winter break.

While practicing law in downtown Red Bank, I had lunch at the famous Molly Pitcher Inn in Red Bank to discuss some client patent work with another attorney, Bill Despo, Aris's brother. It was at that luncheon that Bill and I made the arrangement for Aris to meet Stamie at Sunday services at Saint George. That meeting eventually led to their marriage and my two grandchildren, Orion Chris and Alexander.

Later, Stamie attended Monmouth University (1989–1991) earning her master of arts in teaching (MAT). More recently, Stamie served as the director of Alumni Relations & External Constituents at the William States Lee College of Engineering, University of North Carolina-Charlotte, until July 2017. Stamie joined Susan G. Komen Charlotte in 2017 and is the Executive Director. The Susan G. Komen Charlotte mission is to save lives and end breast cancer forever by empowering people, ensuring quality care for all, and energizing science to find cures.

I recall the many fond times that Antonia and I had with Aris's dad and mom, Alex and Kiki Heleotis, in New Jersey. Whenever we visited each other at Loch Arbour, Long Branch, or Shrewsbury, Alex always brought a large platter of shrimp as our appetizer. Alex had attended school in Athens, Greece, graduated from Cornell University with a degree in hotel and restaurant management. He spent four and a half years as a forward observer for the artillery, having participated in four landings in the Pacific Theater during World War II. Later, he founded Despo Chemicals International Inc., which manufactured specialty chemicals for the food industry. Alexander Despo died in April 19, 2009, at age ninety-three. He was predeceased by his adoring wife, Kiki, in December 2008.

Aris, Alexander's son, grew Despo Chemicals into a regional chemical manufacturing business, which he managed for some twenty years, and negotiated the sale of its assets to a Fortune 500 competitor. Later as a senior executive of a publicly traded technology-licensing company, Aris led technology transfer and licensing negotiations on behalf of corporate and university clients. Later, he completed an assignment as interim CEO of a start-up operation providing a risk mitigation product and Intellectual Property (IP) advisory services to mid-market lenders by executing a five-year exclusive agreement with an A.M. Best "A" rated global carrier with their commitment to provide $20B of underwriting capacity to the program. Aris has an advisory firm that specializes in monetization of IP portfolios with life sciences, medical diagnostics and devices, therapeutics, applied sciences and renewable energy, knowledge-based products or services, and government-based research.

Cosmas, my son, attended Red Bank Regional High School where he played soccer and excelled in academics. Thereafter, he attended MIT, majoring in physics. Upon graduation, he attended the University of Medicine and Dentistry of New Jersey at Newark in 1998 for his medical degree. This was followed by a residency at Yale School of Medicine in New Haven, Connecticut.

He subsequently trained and joined the staff at the Massachusetts General Hospital (MGH) as a physician-scientist becoming an assistant professor at Harvard Medical School. After practicing and seeing patients for sixteen years full time and running a research lab, he joined Takeda Pharmaceuticals in their Cambridge, Massachusetts, office as a director for their Gastrointestinal (GI) Drug Unit, leading programs across a range of therapeutic areas in GI focusing on emerging and innovate approaches to treat human diseases.

Cosmas was married to Kathleen D. Kennedy on February 12, 2011, at the Ritz-Carlton Beach Club, in Sarasota, Florida. Cosmas lives in their home at Cambridge, Massachusetts, with Kathleen Kennedy, his beloved wife.

Kathleen is director of special projects at MIT, working as a lead organizer of the Engine, a venture fund and accelerator program for tough tech start-ups.

In addition, she is working with the MIT Center for Collective Intelligence, building a climate action program supporting climate policy planning and engagement.

In 2014, she cofounded HUBweek, a first-of-its-kind civic collaboration and weeklong festival that brings together the most creative and inventive minds making an impact in art, science, and technology. Hubweek is a partnership between the Boston Globe, Harvard University, MIT, and Massachusetts General Hospital; and Kathleen currently serves as vice chair on the executive board. In addition, she is an adviser for Good Growth Capital, a new venture fund.

She was president of MIT Technology Review, where she led the business, redefined the iconic magazine brand and expanded its global reach. She also served six years as president of the MIT Enterprise Forum, MIT's global entrepreneurial support organization.

She started her career in accounting at Deloitte and Touche, but quickly found her true calling and left the financial world to join a start-up, which specialized in media research for the film industry. She studied accounting at James Madison University and she was in the Rising Scholar program at the University of Virginia.

Kathleen is a frequent speaker at technology and entrepreneurship events around the world and is a skilled moderator on a wide variety of topics. She is very active in the community, serving as a judge for many competitions including the MacArthur Foundation, the Inclusive Innovation Competition, and the Lemelson-MIT prizes, also known as the Nobel Prize for Innovators.

She was awarded the Folio: 40, which recognizes the most innovative and influential people in the media industry and named by the Women of the Harvard Club as one of Boston's Most Influential Women of 2017.

After attending Tufts University, Christina, my youngest daughter, returned to Seton Hall University School of Law (following in my steps), but as a full-time law student, and earned her law degree. Her first assignment job was her selection as a Presidential Management Fellow (PMF) in Washington, DC, from 2000 to 2002.

At a rotation while Christina was a Presidential Management Fellow, she was sent to the US House of Representatives, Subcommittee on Immigration as Counsel to the Minority Staff in 2001. Christina advised and counseled ranking congresswoman Sheila Jackson Lee, of the Eighteenth District of Texas on restructuring INS, Section 245I, Democratic Statement of Principles on Immigration and the

PATRIOT Act. She also drafted floor statements, attended hearings, wrote memoranda for members, established and maintained effective working or collaborative relationships with immigration community stakeholders.

Christina currently (2018) works as Associate Counsel in the Adjudications Law Division in the Office of the Chief Counsel at US Citizenship and Immigration Services (USCIS). USCIS is one of the many agencies that is part of the Department of Homeland Security. Christina remains involved with all aspects of "Green Card" policy. A green card holder is also known as a lawful permanent resident who may reside and be employed in the United States.

It was at the PMF meetings of the various young professionals who had been admitted into the program in Washington, DC, that Christina met Aakash Thakkar, her husband, which led to their marriage and the birth of our two grandchildren Kira Antonia on March 9, 2010, and Kai Aris on November 20, 2012. Aakash, on his own, had visited Antonia in her hospital room when she was ongoing her last battle against ovarian cancer and received her blessing for his marriage to Christina.

On August 21, 2017, at approximately 2:42 p.m., Kai and Kira Antonia, then some four and one half and seven years old respectively, attended the Smithsonian's National Air and Space Museum, National Mall Building area in Washington, DC, along with Grandmother Irma Thakkar, Grandfather Rohit Thakkar, and Jaeska Pool, their au pair from Capetown in South Africa, to witness "The Great American Eclipse." A total solar eclipse was visible only in parts of the United States that Monday from Oregon to South Carolina and nowhere else in the world since the United States was founded in 1776. A solar eclipse occurs when the moon passes between the sun and Earth. The moon appears to completely cover the disk of the sun. By blocking the sun's light, the moon casts a shadow that turns into an eerie twilight here on Earth. The sun is some four hundred times wider than the moon, but is also four hundred times farther away, so they appear to be the same size in the sky. The next total eclipse will occur on April 8, 2024, in the United States.

Aakash is the son of Rohit and Irma Thakkar. Rohit was born in Bombay, India, in 1941 and arrived in the United States on January 29, 1969, with an Indian diploma in architecture and civil engineering at the age of twenty-nine on a student visa to attend computer school in New York City. Rohit became a licensed architect in Virginia and New Jersey.

Rohit met Irma Chatterjee, who was born in 1948 in the town of Lucknow, state of Uttar Pradesh of India in September 1969. She was in the United States on her own student visa. They were both married in 1970 in Newark, New Jersey, and thereafter gave birth to Aakash and his younger brother, Saagar.

As of 2017, Aakash served as a senior VP of Development and Partner at EYA (www.eya.com), one of the District of Columbia region's most reputable and active urban development real estate firms. Prior to that, he served in the federal government as a presidential management fellow, focusing on housing and development issues. Aakash completed a bachelor of science in accounting and political science from LaSalle University in Philadelphia, Pennsylvania, and a master in business administration and a master in city and regional studies from Rutgers University in New Jersey.

He remains active in community and civic affairs including membership on DC Mayor's Local, Small and Disadvantaged Business Council, the Obama for America Mid-Atlantic Finance Committee, the Urban Land Institute, and as a member on the Board of Trustees at the Maret School in the District of Columbia.

Green Card refers to an immigration process of United States lawful permanent residency, which is the immigration status of a person authorized to live and work in the United States of America permanently. The United States Alien Registration Card (USCIS Form I-551) is known as the *Green Card*. A valid Form I-551 verifies that a person is lawfully admitted to the United States for permanent residence. The instruction for application to register permanent residence or adjust status (USCIS Form I-485) to include its formats, written instructions, and processing procedures are required to be read and completed by each applicant to start the process.

The Green Card serves as proof that its holder, a lawful permanent resident (LPR), has been officially granted immigration benefits, including permission to reside and take employment in the United States. The holder must maintain permanent resident status and can be removed from the United States if certain conditions of this status are not met.

Within the Department of Homeland Security (DHS), the United States Citizenship and Immigration Services (USCIS) handles applications for immigration benefits. Two other DHS agencies oversee the functions of immigration enforcement: US Immigration and Customs Enforcement (ICE) and US Customs and Border Protection (CBP), respectively.

Christina's office in 2017 was impacted and will continue to be so because of the recent "tweets" and multiple executive orders issued on the subject of "Protecting the Nation from Foreign Terrorist Entry into the United States" (so-called Muslim ban from seven countries and subsequently revised to six) by the newly elected President Donald J. Trump, commencing on January 27, 2017, which have led to federal court rulings and public outcries, which continue to this very date. Christina's service to America is just one example of our country's professional senior civil service corps, essential to the smooth functioning of government from one administration to the next.

There are texts currently written toward those who want to start a new business and career. In my case, I started a new career without any student loans to payoff. However, the practice of law commencing at the age of forty plus presents significant challenges especially when one has no established client base to bring to the table or experience practicing law.

The ability to transition from one career to another requires patience and preparation—from acquiring additional education and new skills to conducting successful job searches. Even as of this writing, there are many unemployed men and women in the United States who need to be retrained and educated in information technology, data analysis, computer science, economics, statistics, artificial intelligence, et. al., to be able to be hired in the "new" business environment. Without such retraining, there will be little hope finding employment with reasonable salaries.

At the urging of newly elected president Donald Trump in 2017, many high-technology firm executives, to include manufacturing ones such as Apple, Boeing, Lockheed Martin, et. al, have promised to return or keep jobs in the United States. To assist such multinational corporate entities to meet their promises, the new executive administration has vowed ensuring fair export or import taxes, establishing border taxes, building a border wall between the United States and Mexico, corporate tax reform, and renegotiating one-sided trade agreements that do not favor the United States The new Trump administration has pledged to take the necessary actions to keep jobs in the United States, bringing manufacturing jobs back and repatriating corporate assets kept off-shore. Such promises will need time to materialize and will need a retrained national labor pool.

In my case, it was not necessary for my family to be relocated. I had traveled to the Tampa and West Palm Beach areas interviewing at various law firms. However, I concluded that I was being treated as just a new law school graduate without experience, which was true, and one that was too old at the age of forty-five. The salary offers reflected that view. Just as important was the need to consider fact that the New Jersey elementary and high schools were better than those in Florida not to mention our opinion that the Northeastern Ivy League colleges would provide more opportunities for our three children.

Moreover, I would not have had the potential Hellenic contractor base that existed in New Jersey from the Greek Orthodox Community, which surrounded the St. George Greek Orthodox Church of which my family was a member for over four years. Hence, the grass did not look rosier in Florida than right where we lived in New Jersey. My transition into the legal profession in New Jersey had the minimum impact on my family thus avoiding school disruption. Not to mention that Antonia would have had to apply for a new K-8 teaching position in art—a difficult specialty area to find a vacancy. Most primary and high school art teachers hold their tenured positions until they retire.

In essence, I was similar to the West Point second lieutenant who, for the first time, stood in front of a platoon at Fort Bragg, North Carolina, facing some forty soldiers. I was saved then by the experienced, senior Korean veteran platoon sergeant who understood the challenges I faced despite my recent schooling and training. I had no mentor for the practice of law except to turn to my experiences in the Army.

As I am writing this chapter, I cannot help but reflect on the anxiety of the USMA June graduating classes of 2017–18 and forward who would soon be second lieutenants. These new officers will be standing in front of platoons that may have career volunteer men and women, enlisted and officer, that wear services patches of the units that they served multiple tours of combat duty in Iraq, Afghanistan, and elsewhere.

With a different type of anxiety, I was interviewed by a number of New Jersey law firms despite my age. In many interviews, I noted myself to be older than the partners of the law firms that interviewed me. I had no client base. I had never been before a judge except in law school's moot court. Despite all the anxiety, one Red Bank firm (Evans, Koelzer, Osborne & Kreizman Law) hired me. The partners' hiring decision, I am sure, was based upon the fact that they projected that I would be able to grow the firm's client base from the then surrounding Fort Monmouth, Fort Dix, McGuire Air Force Base military communities. The fact that I was also a licensed Patent and Trademark Attorney with the US Patent and Trademark Office (USPTO) was very helpful. My base salary was set at below $20,000, but I was given 20 percent of all legal fees paid by my own "new" clients, if any. However, I had none to bring to the established practice.

My Initial Public Law Practice Experience

The New Jersey Hellenic Community was silently exuberant that I had become a lawyer. Many in that community at St. George Greek Orthodox Church in Asbury Park were first-generation Americans who had migrated from Greece and were employed in their own start-up small construction firms. Many teamed up with each other to perform construction work so that they could meet the insurance bonding requirements for major federal and state construction projects.

It was not too long before my small assigned office on the second floor of Evans, Koelzer, Osborne & Kreizman located near the Merrill Lynch offices in Red Bank, was providing legal services to numerous small Hellenic-owned businesses. They sought advice on federal construction projects from how to

- o   interpret the Federal Acquisition Regulation (FAR),
- o   prepare a construction estimate,
- o   bid on federal contracts,
- o   bid protest a wrongful award to the US General Accountability Office,
- o   prepare claims, conduct negotiations, and
- o   appear in the US Federal Claims Court in Washington, DC.

Some even had employee immigration issues, which I became quite skilled in handling at the then US Immigration and Naturalization Service offices at the federal building in Newark. In addition, I became involved in the legal aspects of the requirements for export licenses.

Early in my practice, I was retained by a corporate client that manufactured special air conditioning units adapted to serving as "radar dumps" on naval ships to obtain an export license. These units allowed the radars of naval ships to turn on the radiation power of their radars to test systems without radiating electromagnetic waves into the atmosphere. Such radiations could be picked up by an enemy ship or aircraft, then used to jam the radars or to effect the location of a ship.

My client sold these special air-conditioning units to the Navy. They were capable of handling the high heat generated by the contained radiation, thus allowing the various radars onboard a Navy vessel to be tested and exercised at a low-radar profile with minimally radiating signals into space, thus reducing enemy detection.

The client was interested in selling these units to foreign customers and hence was required to obtain export licenses to do so from the Department of Commerce. The item had an Export Control Classification Number (ECCN). The radar radiation capture system was a military item to be controlled; however, it did not warrant being placed also on the US Munitions List (USML).

A key in determining whether an export license is needed from the Department of Commerce is knowing whether the item you intend to export has a specific Export Control Classification Number (ECCN). The ECCN is an alphanumeric code that describes the item and indicates licensing requirements. All ECCNs are listed in the Commerce Control List (CCL) of the Export Administration Regulations (EAR), which controls military items that do not warrant export control under the US Munitions List administered by the US State Department.

In some cases, dual licensing would have been also required from the Department of State for the export of defense articles and services that provide the United States with a critical military or intelligence advantage governed by the Arms Export Control Act ("AECA") passed by Congress. The International Traffic in Arms Regulations (ITAR) implement the AECA.

Hence, I found myself taking the train from Red Bank, New Jersey, to Washington, DC, to visit the Commerce Department's Bureau of Industry and Security licensing office administering the Export Administration Regulation. My mission was to file the license application and obtain on the same day the authenticated license for my client. No cargo carrier, such as UPS or FEDEX, would pick up the air-conditioning units without the Commerce Department's export license.

I arrived early in the morning and went to the Commerce Department's Licensing office and filed the license application; then sat in its adjacent waiting room. Some four hours had past and no official or clerk called me. Finally, I calmly opened the door to the processing center and noted desk after desk of busy clerks all working in one extensive room—it was one large processing nucleus similar to a call center. Quite a few faces turned to see the lone person in a dark blue pinstriped suit and tie standing in the entrance way. In a firm, loud voice, I asked, "Is there a Greek in here!" I closed the door quickly and sat back down in the waiting room.

In less than five minutes, the door popped open and a staff officer came out. He was a first-generation "Helene." Within fifteen minutes thereafter, aside from the previous four-hour patient wait, I had the requisite license. The train ride from Union Station was peaceful. I even had supper in the dining car, a treat for me. I got back home by midnight in New Jersey. The next day, my client was amazed at how fast I had gotten the license, which would normally take at least several weeks. I learned that patience is a virtue even for new attorneys. The client was beholden to the law firm.

The law firm of Evans, Koelzer, Osborne, & Kreizman had served its purposes well. I learned how to do estate planning from one of the senior partners, did research for various partners in support of their court appearances or just for their clients, accompanied law partners to the Freehold County court house holding their papers and even their attorney luggage, learned how to use legal secretaries and paralegals, and above all, how to invoice clients. The use of the Internet, in-house computer systems, or cloud services for integrating law firm operations were not available. I had served Evans and Koelzer and its partners well not only as one of its oldest attorneys in age but its only "second lieutenant counsel."

The partners of the law firm became apprehensive, alarmed at my independence, rate of success, and captured use of law firm resources for my client work from secretaries to office space. Within six months, I had more clients than most partners. My monthly salary was on a rapid climb due to the 20 percent commission on new client billing. We mutually agreed on an amicable basis that it would be better off for me to resign.

I moved to my own rented offices several blocks away on Ninety Monmouth Street also in Red Bank. The space was excess to one of my new defense contractor clients. I took no client files with me. I was starting from scratch once again but this time under the umbrella of my own law firm, the "BILL COSMAS GIALLOURAKIS, A Professional Corporation, Attorney at Law."

CHAPTER 13

The Seasoned Counsel

Now that I was on my own in 1981, I needed capital to start my law firm and income to fund family college tuition costs. It was at this time that I concurrently turned to my engineering education as an electrical engineer from Purdue. Application was initiated for a small business innovated research program grant—the Phase I DoD Small Business Innovative Research (SBIR) program in 1983. Incidentally, the federal SBIR Program continues to this very day, involving federal executive agencies such as DoD, NASA, NIH, Agriculture, Education and others.

To my surprise, I was awarded a grant by the US Air Force to examine the technical feasibility of automating the use of the underlying learning curve (ULC) approach for use by contract administration organizations entitled "Small Business Innovative Research (SBIR) Phase I," program winner for Air Force (ASD/YZD). Abstract: Cost Analysis Software for Contract Administration (CASCA, 1983).

The Air Force was interested in analytic tools in estimating the cost of the manufacturing its aircraft jet engines at such plants as those of General Electric and Pratt Whitney located at Cincinnati, Ohio, and Hartford, Connecticut, respectively. I was thrilled to inspect the aircraft production plants in my research, where, surprisingly, I was welcomed to examine the plants' production lines, interview their managers and technicians, and receive requested technical production data.

So concurrently, while working on growing my embryonic law firm in the day time, in the evenings I was writing software in FORTRAN. Since I held a federal defense contract, I was assisted by the computer team at the National Institute of Standards and Technology (NIST), not to mention the written research support from the Defense Technical Information Institute. I had even attended a course in software coding using Fortran IV in preparation for being awarded the Air Force contract.

Within a span of a year, I earned the contract's fixed price of $42,782. I was honored by a request from Computer Science Corporation, reaching out to me to form a joint venture to proceed into a phase II of my research project in which the Air Force offered to provide some one hundred fifty thousand dollars to assist with further development and the commercialization of the software.

Winning a SBIR Phase I project had fulfilled my ego to prove myself able to win a grant and successfully complete a project. I must add that the SBIR program to this very day remains in place and is funded annually by many agencies of the federal government, from DoD to National Institute of Health (NIH) (https://www.sbir.gov/ sbirsearch/award/all). Going into the full-time business of software development and becoming a defense contractor was inconsistent as to why I went to law school.

Concurrently, the Hellenic construction clients followed me without any need to urge them. It was at this Red Bank office at Ninety Front Street close to the historic landmark, the Molly Pitcher Inn overlooking the Navesink River, where my law practice really took off. The office space was leased to me and was quite roomy that other lawyers came to start or continue their law practices. My office space attracted law firm "start-ups" similar to the open space provided for rent in current times at Palo Alto just outside the gates of Stanford University to high-tech incubators and their entrepreneurs.

In particular, one such lawyer was Gil D. Messina, a close friend and practicing professional lawyer even to this date. We each had our own clients and shared the rent; however, we served as sounding boards for each other on various legal issues. It was with Gil D. Messina that we bought jointly our first desktop computer system.

It was one of the first models, the IBM PC, model number 5150, which was purchased from the IBM backed ComputerLand store in Eatontown, New Jersey, in August 1981 along with its IBM monitor and keyboard for some five thousand dollars.

IBM had decided to move to the desktop computer in addition to being in the large main frame computer business. I must say that the use of this tool when added to the facsimile and Xerox machine changed the shape of our law office landscape. These tools eliminated the traditional role of the "paralegal" as we knew it then. As lawyers, we could now do our own typing and even research rather than dictating into a machine tape or waiting for a research assistant's memorandum.

Before long, I was involved with clients who competitively had won by sealed bid or negotiation on best-value basis federal construction contracts. Examples of such projects involved repainting the hallways of the Pentagon in Virginia, building a new federal court house, working on the nuclear submarine base facilities in Groton, Connecticut, to the two hundred plus Air Force family housing unit modernization of kitchens at Hanscom Air Force Base, Massachusetts. The success of my solo practitioner law firm was sealed.

Representation of Clients Before Agencies

Aside from my expertise in federal contracting, my clients respected my ethics. I often met with clients in the district offices of the Corps of Engineers at 26 Federal Plaza on Foley Square in Manhattan to discuss construction solicitations or issues related to ongoing projects for which the corps was responsible. We were known in the counsel offices of the US General Accountability Office (GAO) on 441 G. Street, NW., in Washington due to filed bid protests and subsequent hearings.

In other cases, I met with various procurement government agency offices with my clients to be present at public bid openings or to discuss contract issues. Government counsels were always present. We got to know each other professionally, and we respected each other's opinions. In many cases, these government offices ruled in our favor after hearing the matters. Clients could sense that their positions were always fairly represented and the word traveled.

On one such occasion, I was invited by a client to attend a public bid opening at the CECOM Bid Room at Fort Monmouth. The procurement was to be the award on a firm-fixed price contract to the lowest, responsible offeror. The specification in the solicitation was for the domestic manufacture of a large order of special non-commercial batteries to fulfill an Army requirement for their use in the United States. At that time, a wooden bid box with a lock was used similar to a secure voting box. My client was a Long Island, New York, manufacturing firm, which had brought its prepared written bid on the requisite Standard Form (SF) 1447, entitled Solicitation/Contract, with its necessary attachments. The client then placed the bid into the bid box as did a number of bids from other bidders prior to the time scheduled for the bid opening. We were timely. Today, most public bids are submitted electronically.

We were then seated with a number of other bidders when at the appointed bid closing time, the contracting officer appeared with his assistant, unlocked the bid box, and commenced to read aloud each submitted bid—the amount and the submitting firm. His assistant would record the information on the submitted bids using Standard Form (SF)1409, Abstract of Offers.

As it turned out, my client had submitted the second lowest bid. At that time, my client asked me to right then and there inspect the winning bid. After all, it was a public bid opening. After some confusion, several government counsel were called by the contracting officer and hurriedly appeared. After some discussion among us, the counsel concurred with the right of the public at such a bid opening to examine the submitted bid documents of the lowest bidder.

By examining the winning bid, my client stated to me that the person signing the bid was without authority to have signed such a large bid. He stated that he knew all the key persons able to commit that firm and the signature that appeared was not one of those key individuals with authority. He was confident that he knew his competition well. The signature was not that of a key corporate officer

198

whose signature had been submitted in advance and thus authorized to unequivocally bind his firm with the government.

Moreover, my client mentioned to me that the batteries to be manufactured and delivered in response to the solicitation were bid so low because the many cells that were to compose each battery were manufactured offshore and, when assembled in the US to form each battery, would cause violation of the Buy American Act. My client asserted that the manufactured batteries being offered were not a domestic end product. Even the cost of the domestic components in comparison to the foreign cell components would not exceed 50 percent of the cost of all the components.

My client was found to be correct on both counts and was soon thereafter awarded the Army's battery contract. Hence, the US government for its contracts already has in force Federal Procurement Laws (48 CFR 52.209-10) requiring use of American-made products and precluding doing federal business with "inverted" corporations. Corporate inversion is one of the many strategies companies employ to reduce their tax burden. One way that a company can re-incorporate abroad is by having a foreign company buy its current operations. With the inauguration of President Donald Trump in January 2017, more emphasis is expected to be placed in this area to the benefit of US workers and American companies.

At the US Federal District Court in Boston

Initially, I was tempted to form my own construction firm and ask several of the newly formed Greek firms to merge into my firm or team with my own firm in various joint venture projects, especially when the projects required the combined experience of the venture partners. Joint ventures reduced the project risk to the government. The federal government then, as today, was found to favor joint ventures (JV) on large projects. This idea was quickly discarded. I believed that it was important to focus on the legal side of procurement law rather than expand to ownership of my own construction firm, concurrently creating serious conflicts of interest in any further practice of law.

My clients respected my opinions and sought me out to be their counsel, since they recognized that I was not partnering with any construction firm to share in profits. I was paid on an hourly basis and received retainers in advance. They considered me expensive but valuable, worth it, confidential, and fair.

I was surprised to find out how comfortable I was appearing before distinguished judges in their chambers or before open court, especially when prepared as was the case. My perception, and as it actually turned out, was that a judge was no different than the numerous general officers I had always stood before to brief in the Pentagon or served as their executive officer in Heidelberg.

Early in my solo law practice, I was called upon to represent a construction firm that had a major construction renovation contract with the Air Force at Hanscom Air Force Base located near Medford and north of Boston. The contract specification was to basically remodel some two hundred kitchens of the family housing on post. The renovation project included replacing all the kitchen cabinets.

My client had subcontracted the construction and delivery of the cabinetry to a Texas cabinet manufacturer. The controversy arose after the kitchen cabinets had been installed. The finishes of the cabinetry were defective, basically the finish would peel off the wood. The Air Force wanted full replacement of the cabinets. The subcontractor of the cabinets refused to honor the AF detail specification provisions. Since we had several state jurisdictions involved, I filed the complaint to enforce the specification provisions in the district of Massachusetts, US Federal District Court in Boston.

That morning, one day before our first hearing, I was walking with two large briefcases heading for the John Joseph Moakley US Courthouse at 1 Courthouse Way, Suite 2300. I arrived early in the morning and found a seat to the rear of the court room of the judge that was assigned to my case. A preliminary hearing was about to start on an unrelated matter.

I sat in the rear of the court room all day taking notes and listening to the court activity. In essence, I was on a "scouting" mission to determine how the judge handled matters so that I could adjust my strategy. At about three o'clock in the afternoon, which was the end of the open-court period before the judge was to withdraw to his chambers, the judge stood up and asked me to stand and tell him who I was and what I was doing.

To say the least, I was startled. I recall standing up and informing the judge I had come up from New Jersey for the diversity case, which I was to present tomorrow before his court.

I basically said, "Your, Honor I had come to watch and learn from you."

He chuckled, smiled, and stated, "I will see you tomorrow."

He withdrew to his chambers. The next morning, I arrived at the judge's chambers and was waiting outside for my meeting with the judge and opposing counsels. Inside the chambers I could hear laughing, football chatter, and reflections by the occupants. I surmised by the chatting that the occupants, to include the judge, had been classmates in college or law school. The persons in the judge's chambers had graduated from major Boston law schools including Harvard.

Eventually, I was escorted to join the conference. The mood quickly changed to business. I explained to the judge and the three opposing attorneys in the office that our filed complaint was based on the legal theory applicable in federal contract law. That theory was that even though this was a contract between a prime and its subcontractor, the Air Force specification for the kitchen cabinets with its specified exterior wooden cabinet finishes, automatically flows down from the prime contractor to its subcontractor. In this case, the defendant subcontractor for the kitchen cabinets knew full well that the cabinets were to be built to military specifications and installed on a military reservation. The cabinet subcontractor had been given a copy of that specification.

I could tell by the comments made by the judge that he was not going to accept the implied flow down of the Air Force specification's provisions that had not been explicitly written into the subcontract contract between my client and the defendant subcontractor. The judge asked all the counsels to huddle to discuss the possibility of a settlement before the start of the trial.

The case was settled to no one's liking before trial. Neither party wanted to test the case law on the implied automatic flow down provisions of federal government specifications written into a prime contractor's contract to its subcontractors. Such provisions may automatically flow down from the prime to the subcontractor's contract without having to be explicitly scribed therein. I also did not want to test the partiality or conflict of interest of the judge due to barristers appearing before him with whom he had been classmates. I might add to this date, the law of implied federal flow-downs of various clauses from prime contractors into their subcontracts remains a difficult and controversial topic.

Lunch at the US Court of Federal Claims in DC Next to White House

On another occasion, I had the privilege of arguing a case before the US Court of Federal Claims located on Madison Place in the District of Columbia adjacent to the White House, involving an Immunization Case. This court, which has been in existence over one hundred forty years, has original jurisdiction to this very day primarily for money claims founded on the Constitution, federal statutes, executive regulations, or government contracts to include tax refund suits, Indian tribe claims, and those involving intellectual property. In 1982, it was given jurisdiction on bid protests and vaccination compensation cases.

Parents of children who take their series of mandated children's immunization shots and become ill with life-lasting maladies, such as learning disorders and even death, may proceed directly to this court for compensation. In such instances, the pharmaceutical firms are protected from the suits because the federal government by congressional statute passed the National Vaccine Injury Compensation Program ("Vaccine Program"), which protects the pharmaceutical industry to allow for the continued conduct of research, develop, and production of childhood vaccines.

This congressional vaccination program is similar to the anti-terrorism bill, known as the SAFETY Act, which protects firms who develop and field anti-terror detection systems in the event they fail when called upon. Otherwise, firms would not engage in such developments for the good of the overall public. The act's purpose is to ensure that the threat of potential liability suits does not limit or deter the development, manufacture, deployment, use or commercialization of products, technologies, procedures, software, system integration, advice, and services (known as QATT-Qualified Anti-Terroism Technology) that could prevent or mitigate a terrorist attack.

Likewise, the Vaccine Program is a no-fault compensation program whereby petitions for monetary compensation may be brought by or on behalf of persons allegedly suffering injury or death as a result of the administration of certain compulsory childhood vaccines. Congress intended that the Vaccine Program provide individuals a swift, flexible, and less adversarial alternative to the often costly and lengthy civil arena of traditional tort litigation.

I was nervous when I brought this first case from New Jersey in as much my experience was not in this area of the law. However, the family trusted me and were confident with my experience in federal contract law. I could have referred the case to a Washington law firm, but they insisted that I represent their child. They were not disappointed. Their child, after the vaccination was given, had suffered serious permanent disabilities, which were noted the very next day laying in her baby crib. The child required hospitalization whose ailments were the direct causation attributed to the received vaccine. My case before the court was accepted, and an appropriate monetary award was made. I might add that the best court lunches I have ever had were at the justices' cafeteria inside that very courthouse.

As I was writing this past experience, the issue of vaccinations has surfaced and risen for national debate with respect as to whether parents should be required by law to submit their children to early vaccinations in preparation of school attendance. Moreover, vaccination could have avoided the recent outbreaks of measles, a serious viral disease, in both young children and even adults that occurred after attending or working at theme parks. There are parents this very date that never undertook the measles vaccine. Some now also have children. The initial dose of the combined measles, mumps, and rubella (MMR) vaccine is recommended routinely for all children at age twelve through fifteen months, with a second dose at age four through six years.

The United States experienced a record number of measles cases during 2014, with 667 cases from twenty-seven states reported to CDC's National Center for Immunization and Respiratory Diseases (NCIRD). This is the greatest number of cases since 2000 when measles elimination was documented in the United States. In 2015, some 188 people from twenty-four states were reported to have measles. Most of these cases were part of a large, ongoing multistate outbreak linked to an amusement park in California. In 2016, 70 people from sixteen states were reported to have measles. Immunizations rightfully have become part of the national discussion and debate that will continue well into 2018 and beyond. Hence, parents be forewarned and become prepared.

My Paid Law Interns

After several years, I moved from Ninety Monmouth Street in Red Bank to my second rented office on the second floor at Forty South Street in Eatontown, New Jersey, which was also close to our home in Shrewsbury and Fort Monmouth. It was at this office that I had the opportunity to hire two interns over a period of two years who had graduated from Rutgers University. Both were English majors. It was an exciting time. I was especially busy with client work. Each year I would interview possible candidates for a paid internship after their graduation from undergraduate colleges in the New Jersey and New York areas. My main criteria were that the candidates had to be good writers and willing to attend law school at the end of the one-year internship. The term of each internship was not extendable.

In my interviews, I noted that the undergraduate engineers did not have good writing samples. However, the English majors were great in their writing samples. So over a two-year period, I hired two—one year apart. They received a reasonable compensation package, which included the agreement that they would apply and, if accepted, attend law school. As an incentive, I promised each intern that depending on their attitude and performance of duties with my law firm, I would personally intercede with the dean of Seton Hall University School of Law for their admission. No further employment would be offered by my law firm after the one year of internship. Everything was up front so that each intern could plan for the future.

The intern would accompany me in all my court appearances and would attend all client conferences. My clients were pleasantly surprised and impressed by these interns. In summary, both interns got once-in-a-lifetime legal experiences—they learned how to do legal research, write legal memoranda, prepare complaints for filing with county and federal courts, conduct discovery, and prepare invoices. They accompanied me in all client office conferences and attended trial court sitting in a chair at the counsel's table next to me. Incidentally, they joined me also carrying legal suitcases to court loaded with discovery documents too without a blink.

Most important, these interns learned and witnessed the key role of ethics in the actual practice of law. Subsequently, both attended New Jersey law schools and are now seasoned practicing New Jersey attorneys and live in New Jersey with their families. I must add that all my three children—Stamie, Cosmas, and Christina—also at one time or another served as part-time law clerks in my law firm in various capacities to include doing janitorial duties.

I cannot emphasize the importance of college students to "seek" internships each summer during their college years and/or right after college graduation at firms in and outside the United States in various disciplines, geographic areas engaged in the business or specialties such as nursing, pharmacy, laboratory, factories, investment banking, computers, cloud services, artificial intelligence, et. al., thus exploring their interests to test and research out where their interests match for future long-term employment.

To this day, I am thrilled that my oldest grandsons, Alexander and Orry (Aris and Stamie's children), undertook internships. Alexander, while in high school, went to school in Costa Rica as part of his Spanish language immersion program. Thereafter, Alexander Despo graduated from Wingate University in North Carolina where he had been awarded a four-year lacrosse scholarship. In 2011, Alex Despo played in fourteen games and was an integral part of the Bulldogs' face-off rotation winning some thirty-two face-offs on the season. Alexander, while at Wingate University, interned at Capitol Hill in Washington, DC, in the office of Sue Wilkins Myrick, the then US representative for North Carolina's Ninth Congressional District. Congresswoman Myrick served from 1995 to 2013. She was the first Republican woman to represent North Carolina in Congress. Upon graduation, Alexander served as an investment banking analyst with AGC partners in Boston, in the private equity venture at Paulsen Investment Company in New York City, and as a financial consul-tant with Laidlaw & Company UK Ltd in New York City. Currently, he is an associate in the oil investment banking firm of Johnson Rice & Company, LLC in New Orleans.

His brother, Orry Despo, a June 2017 college graduate of Stanford University with a bachelor of science degree in mathemat-ics and mathematical computations with university distinction had completed internships in big data and computer science during all his undergraduate summers with a variety of firms. He interned with Ubiqua, a B2B software development firm located just outside of Panama City, Panama. Ubiqua is focused on developing enterprise software in an effort to make products commercialization more efficient, thereby increasing sales and decreasing manual work by empowering workers with technology and real-time information.

Thereafter, he interned with Tableau Software in Seattle, Washington, and his junior year he interned with Facebook at Palo Alto, California. Upon graduation, he elected to intern with Point72 Asset Management, L.P. in New York City before returning in the fall of 2017 for his master's degree from Stanford University. Point72 invests in multiple asset classes and situations and innovates its investment style, products, and business model to deliver top risk-adjusted returns, relative to changes in markets and capital allocations. Orry graduated from Stanford University in March 2018 with his master's degree in statistics. Upon receipt of his master's degree, Orry was employed by BREX in San Francisco, California. The start-up BREX allows one to sign up for your corporate credit card instantly.

Immigration Services and the Russian Connection

From Forty South Street, I had the privilege of representing several foreign defense firms that had invested in the United States by purchasing existing US firms or started up new wholly owned subsidiary firms before the Immigration and Naturalization Service (INS). (The reader should note that INS was replaced and reorganized under the Homeland Security Act of 2002.) INS had offices in Newark at the Peter Rodino Federal Building at 970 Broad Street in Newark near Seton Hall University School of Law.

Peter W. Rodino Jr. had presided over the impeachment articles in House Judiciary Committee in 1974, which led to the resignation of President Richard Nixon. He was a well-known Democratic congressman with his roots in Newark and Orange, New Jersey; hence, his name often appears on or in various buildings in Newark. The Peter W. Rodino Library at Seton Hall University School of Law was my best study venue while in evening law school and, after graduation, served as my research center of choice for client work.

In March 1, 2003, the US Citizenship and Immigration Services (USCIS) officially assumed responsibility for the immigration service functions (preparing and filing forms for immigration benefits for clients) of the federal government under the Homeland Security Act of 2002. The other two remaining Immigration and Naturalization Service (INS) functions of border protection and enforcement were separated into two other components within the Department of Homeland Security (DHS) known as the Customs and Border

Protection (CBP) and US Immigration and Customs Enforcement (ICE).

The foreign firms I represented were from countries with which the United States maintained treaties of commerce and navigation, such as England. Although hiring many US workers, such foreign-owned parent firms eventually needed non-immigration visas for their key managers and technical and professional engineers to be sent to work in the United States for limited periods of time. Such individuals were non-immigrant workers. The L-1A Intracompany Transferee visa was for primarily key managers and executives that were sent to the United States to work temporarily for foreign-owned US subsidiaries on limited terms. The L-1B Intracompany Transferee visa was obtained for a transferee with special knowledge.

In other frequent instances, some established US defense firms had shortages in key engineering disciplines and would recruit foreign college and graduate students attending US colleges and universities upon their graduation. This latter category of foreign students who had had student visas, such as the F-1 (Academic Student) now required new visas to work in the US. I quickly studied and properly assisted such persons and firms with the Treaty Trader (E-1) visa whose citizens where from countries that the United States maintained treaties of commerce and navigation. The E-2 visa, a nonimmigrant classification, allowed a national of a treaty country to be admitted to the United States when investing a substantial amount of capital in a US business. Certain employees of such a person or of a qualifying organization would also be eligible for this classification. L-1, Intra-Company Transferee (for one year allows entry into United States for foreign executives, managers, or individuals with expertise).

I also handled the processing of the H1B Visa, Specialty Occupation, which allows US companies to petition for temporary employment by individuals in a specialty occupation (bachelor degree, engineer, law, et. al.) particularly essential in those occupations that American firms needed skilled high-technology employees in short supply or not available in the United States.

The H1B Visa category came under scrutiny in 2017 with the election of President Trump with various political groups arguing that such visas take away jobs from Americans. Other political groups support such visas because high-tech firms cannot find qualified American employees to work in their high-technology research, development, and production facilities. This immigration discussion will continue past 2017. It should be noted that H1B visa holders working in the United States concurrently after a year or so also apply for the Green Card leading to permanent residency.

I usually represented business firms or their employees, but on one occasion, I deviated from my stated policy. A Russian immigrant from the Russian community in the Toms River of South Jersey came to my office. The lady was in distress because her Russian husband, a US citizen, had just recently died and would not be able to accompany her to the scheduled marriage interview in Newark before an Immigration Officer for her "Green Card.". She had entered the United States on a current US visa from Argentina.

Her husband had been a former Soviet Union admiral in the Russian Navy and had escaped from Russia to Argentina. Thereafter, he had migrated to the United States and obtained his citizenship. At the time of his death, he was some eighty-five years old. He had filed the necessary petition and applications for his wife, the I-130, Petition for Alien Relative and the I-485, Application to Register Permanent Residence or Adjust Status.

As a one-time experience, I accompanied her to the Peter Rodino Federal Building in Newark. We waited together in the lobby and soon were called to the office of an immigration officer for the marriage interview. After some brief discussion, the immigration officer asked to speak with me in private. It was at that time that he informed me that my client was not "legally" married under New Jersey law, since under New Jersey marriage statutes, marriage between a women and her uncle were illegal. She was not eligible to be granted a Green Card for permanent residency. Needless to say, I was floored.

My client never had told me that she had married her elderly uncle. At that instant of time, I was reminded that clients often do not tell their attorneys their innermost secrets. At my request, the immigration officer, as a courtesy to us, suspended the interview until I had had time to research the marriage state statutes and to return in one week.

As it had turned out, my middle-aged female client had escaped as a refugee from Russia to Africa and then via Argentina came into the United States. She had been married to her uncle in Maryland in lieu of New Jersey. A Holiday Inn in Baltimore was where the wedding was held. She had a justice of the peace marriage license and photographs of family and friends in attendance to confirm the wedding and associated party.

The issue now was whether or not Maryland law allowed for weddings by a niece with her uncle. The weekend found me camped out at the Peter W. Rodino Seton Hall School of Law Library in Newark in its state statute archives. That weekend, I confirmed that New Jersey statutorily precluded marriages of a niece with an uncle although not using those exact words. The state law was not repealed or amended.

Based upon my research then, Maryland's marriage statutory law was found not to specifically preclude marriages by a niece to a distant uncle. It was my legal opinion based upon my research that my client had been legally married in Maryland, and due to reciprocity, the marriage was valid even if she lived in New Jersey. The matter in a New Jersey court of law could have gone the other way depending on interpretations of the statutes.

On August 31, 2014, the New York Court of Appeals allowed an uncle and niece to marry. The case had been brought by a Vietnamese woman who appealed an unfavorable ruling for permanent residency by an immigration judge.

The immigration officer was gracious and accepted my research report and legal opinion Although I was prepared, he did not want to test my legal opinion before an immigration judge. He granted approval to my client's Green Card application, allowing her to become and remain a permanent resident with the opportunity to obtain employment in the United States.

Several weeks thereafter, upon coming to work early one morning at my Forty South Street, Eatontown law office, I noted a line of women at my front office door. They had come from the Toms River of New Jersey area. The word had traveled fast. I handed off all these Russian prospective clients to a counsel who specialized in family and immigration law.

Mining the Prior Art of Intellectual Property (IP)

Little did I realize when I started the practice of law the extent that my registration with the US Patent and Trademark Office (USPTO) and electrical engineering background would allow me to have exciting times reading and registering new technology created by industry and government engineers. I was given the opportunity to examine and protect for clients their intellectual property (IP)— their trade secret (technical data), copyrights, patents, and trademarks. I prepared numerous reports on the patentability of their future devices and innovative solutions from cyber warfare defense software systems to teaching dolls for elementary schools. Later, I prepared numerous patent applications in a form ready for clients to file directly with the USPTO.

Clients realized that a registered US patent gave the inventor(s) and the firm to whom it may have been assigned, a legal monopoly for twenty years to use, manufacture, and sell the described invention with its claims. A patent is enforceable in US courts against infringers and in those countries that have treaties with the United States agreeing to recognize the US patent. The enforceability may be geographically extended by filing an international patent under the Patent Cooperation Treaty (PCT) of 1978 reached in Washington, DC. As of my writing of this section of the memoir, some 152 countries have agreed to abide by its terms. In 2017, Jordan and, in 2016, Kuwait, Cambodia, and the Republic of Djibouti located in the Horn of Africa became the most recent countries to be bound by the PCT.

Through 1998 and after 2004, one could find me periodically in the library stacks of the Public Search Room in Arlington within eyesight of Reagan National Airport. I would be shuffling through "shoe" boxes that served as the "paper depository" of issued patents in a particular classification under the filing system of the US Patent and Trademark Office. The US Patent Classification System provides the identity of the subject matter for the storage and retrieval of every patent document that a patent examiner needs to review when examining patent applications. Next to me would often be standing patent agents, patent counsels, and hired search agents likewise conducting their searches of the contents of similar boxes. It was not unique to chat with searchers from Japan, other Asian countries, or Europe.

Clients had found out primarily by written word or mouth that I was a registered patent attorney. Some were individuals while others were corporate clients for whom I had provided business legal services such as incorporations, litigation of their federal claims, or had been previously counseled on federal procurement regulations. Some had even attended my classes on "Contracting with Uncle Sam."

Over the years, especially before the Internet facilitated distant searches to be conducted and before the US Patent and Trademark Office (USPTO) had digitized its issued and pending patents and trademarks, I spent quite a bit of time in Arlington, Virginia. I would fly early in the morning from Newark Airport to Reagan National Airport and return back late in the evening. The USPTO still to this day maintains the Scientific and Technical Information Center with its Public Search Room in the building at Crystal Plaza 3, 2C01 at 2021 Jefferson Davis Highway in Arlington, Virginia.

New Jersey clients came to my office and brought their business trade secrets (such as engineering and production drawings, testing procedures, and drawings of their test fixtures and test instruments); rough apparatus or semi-working models; and even software coding for various processes involving manufacturing controls, business management, or financing operations. They came seeking to file design or utility patents for computer software programs, electronic systems, various processes, and much more.

Others came for the registration of trademarks and service marks related to their business names and products; still others came wanting just to obtain advice as to how to protect their conceptions, literary works, and business practices (e.g. then trade secrets), which they were reluctant to share with anyone. Most wanted an opinion as to whether their invention was "patentable," meeting the criteria of *usefulness, novelty, and non-obviousness* to one skilled in the art.

In some cases, we prepared and filed a provisional patent with the USPTO to protect their invention for twelve months, thus allowing the inventor time to diligently complete the technical aspects of the invention's conception from its reduction to practice in some form of a model to filing the actual patent application with its associated distinguished prior art, specification, drawings, claims, and oath. This period also provided us time to conduct a search of the prior art before being required to file the complete formal patent application and deliver our patentability report. We had used the simpler Document Disclosure Program up until 2007 when it was discontinued in lieu of filing a provisional patent.

With few reliable data bases to verify that a conceived invention was useful, novel, and non-obvious, I would advise the client to travel to DC or travel to the nearest public library that contained a Patent Resource Center to conduct a search of the prior art under the appropriate classification depending if the alleged invention was for a chemical composition, biological idea, aeronautical conception, computer, medical devise, or one of the other classes. The classification guide could be consulted and the appropriate section of the Patent and Trademark Resource Center's (PTRC) holdings could be searched for copies of prior registered patents. If a patent was found that had incorporated the client's conception, then it surely would not pass the test of novelty and would be rejected by the patent examiner.

A similar process would be followed for trademarks and service marks that had already been registered. The Trademark Electronic Search System (TESS) is available in all Patent and Trademark Resource Centers. Also, these libraries now have CD-ROMS containing the database of registered and pending marks; however, the CD-ROMS do not contain images of the design marks.

If the idea involved concurrently copyrightable matter, then the search would be extended to the US Library of Congress, which was responsible for registering copyrighted material.

The best person to conduct such searches, I advised then and even now, is the inventor or author that had developed the conception of the device or system, had read all the trade journals in the specific field of the invention, and could assess the novelty of the prospective invention. If they needed assistance, one could retain a patent search firm that could be found in the Washington area (for example: search@national patent services.com) whose researchers conduct searches in the mechanical, electrical, chemical, computer, business methods, communications, optics, biotechnological, and medical arts.

Multiple search firms are listed in the yellow page section of telephone directories under the heading "Trademark Search Services" or "Patent and Trademark Search Services." A detail search report on the findings of a search firm could be provided at a reasonable price. There is no sense in filing a patent application on an alleged new invention or a significant improvement to the existing art, until a search was done to assess the elements of patentability.

In today's improved web search environment, I first encourage inventors to personally as a minimum search the USPTO's patent database to see if a patent has already been filed or granted that is similar to their conceived innovation. The USPTO Patent Full-Text and Image Database is a good start. The US Patent and Trademark Office (PTO) offers world-wide web (web) access to bibliographic and full-text *patent* databases (http://patft.uspto.gov/). This USPTO database houses full text for patents issued from 1976 to the present and Portable Document Format (PDF) images for all patents from 1790 to the present. PDF is an Adobe file extension and is a fairly standard file extension for exchanging documents due to the fact that the program that reads these files is free. The Patent and Trademark Resource Centers Program(PTRCP) administers a nationwide network of eighty public, state, academic, and special libraries in some forty-six states designated as Patent and Trademark Resource Centers authorized by 35 USC 12 to disseminate patent and trademark information and support diverse intellectual property needs of the general public at no cost.

These PTRCs have shifted from the paper depository ("shoe" box) concept to an expansion of access to electronic information since 2011. These PTRC's employ USPTO-trained librarians to provide customer assistance on the use of the agency's patent and trademark databases and public seminars on intellectual property topics for all users. For a list of current PTRC libraries and their locations, one may visit www.uspto.gov/ptrc. In addition, the World Intellectual Property Organization (WIPO) maintains a database known as PATENTSCOPE, which allows a user to access millions of patent documents including some two and one-half million patent applications filed under the Patent Cooperation Treat previously discussed.

The intellectual property (IP) of any business is key to its success and particularly its financial well-being, regardless whether such property comprises its trade secrets or its registered patents, trademarks, and copyrights. In fact, firms often have their IP appraised and insured. Some firms actually sale their multiple patents associated in a particular technical area to which they are no longer interested in conducting business. Others even use their IP as collateral to receive loans from financial institutions. Hence, firms must, in every manner possible, protect and defend their intellectual property, by registering their inventions, proceeding to the courts to stop infringers, and maintaining sound cyber security systems for all their trade secrets that have not been registered.

Today the Patent Cooperation Treaty system and other treaties, such as the Paris Convention for the Protection of Industrial Property signed as far back as 1884, work for member nations that have agreed to abide by treaty to respect the patent rights of the other signatories to promote business and world innovation. However, at the same time, there are countries and organizations that have not signed such treaties and are engaged in business espionage to obtain the business secrets of successful firms. Concurrently, there are other countries, organizations, and individuals that are intent to creating disruptions and harm by using cyberspace to appropriate the Intellectual

Property business secrets of other entities. These threats will continue more intensely as we head into the future.

Over a period of some ten years, my solo-practitioner law firm, Bill C. Giallourakis, P.C., was fortunate to support the IP department of the US Army Armament Research, Development, and Engineering Center, which, to this day, is located at Picatinny Arsenal in New Jersey, known as the Joint Center of Excellence for Guns and Ammunition. Large numbers of new advanced weapons, munitions, and auxiliary equipment are produced and fielded by the engineers and scientists of Picatinny, providing US forces increased effectiveness on the battlefield. As one example is the engineers' work to provide the ability to manufacture essential parts using 3-D printing at the "point of need," applying a system called Rapid Fabrication via Additive Manufacturing on the Battlefield.

My law firm became one of its selected support contractors. Over the ten-year period, I would receive the confidential invention disclosures from its engineers. My firm would convert the disclosures into complete patent applications ready for filing with the USPTO. I had retained a subcontractor who prepared the accompanying unclassified fine drawings of the invention consistent with the rules of the USPTO. In essence, my law firm operated a separate miniature branch to just handle my federal contract work that later expanded from IP to teaching federal contract law to Army, Navy, Marine, and Air Force procurement professionals at various military installations. Most large US corporations have divisions that cater to federal government work providing a support base for the entire firm during periods when their commercial business slows. My miniature IP branch served the same purpose.

By 2015, this part of my work was completely transferred by Picatinny Arsenal to another firm that was awarded a multiyear Indefinite Delivery Indefinite Quantity (IDIQ) contract. The award was based upon a solicitation on a Lowest Price Technical Acceptance (LPTA) basis. Under the IDIQ type of contact, a one fixed small guaranteed amount is ordered using a written task order. Thereafter multiple task orders are issued as a Federal Agency's need arises and funds are available.

Teaching Face-to-Face from the Platform

While practicing law in New Jersey and to this very day in Florida, I had the privilege of teaching for the Armed Forces Communications Electronics Association (AFCEA) located in Fairfax, Virginia. AFCEA International, established in 1946, is a non-profit organization serving its members, both in the military and industry, by providing a forum for the ethical exchange of information and dedicated to increasing knowledge through the exploration of issues relevant to its members in information technology, communications, and electronics for the defense, homeland security, and intelligence communities.

It has been my privilege to have taught numerous combined classes of industry and government professionals the Federal Acquisition Regulation (FAR) and such terms as Reverse Auctioning associated with sealed bids, best-value contracting by negotiation, what is a commercial item, when do cost and pricing data have to be provided and certified, cost analysis, contract administration techniques, how to write a performance-based work statement, procurement data bases such as the key System for Award Management (SAM), which incorporates the former proliferated data bases such as the Central Contractor Registration (CCR), Excluded Party List(EPLS), Online Certifications and Representations(ORCA).

Important topics that are still with us today even more so in 2018 that impact contractors that reorganize as inverted domestic corporations or become a subsidiary of an inverted domestic corporation, for such entities may not be paid for activities performed after the date when they become an inverted domestic corporation or subsidiary, nor are they eligible for new federal government contracts.

Moreover, the push by the Trump Administration is on the repatriation of such entities by new tax reform legislation, to bring the large sums of money kept overseas in tax friendly foreign countries such as Ireland and bring back their jobs to the United States. In particular, the Tax Cuts and Jobs Act, which amends the Internal Revenue Code of 1986, passed through both chambers of Congress on December 20, 2017, and was signed subsequently by President

Donald Trump on December 22. While the bill lowers taxes for many Americans, it also provides benefits to America's biggest companies. The measure slashes the federal corporate tax rate from 35 percent to 21 percent and allows a one-time repatriation of overseas cash. Goldman Sachs estimated S&P 500 companies hold $920 billion of untaxed cash overseas. US companies as a whole have $2.5 trillion stashed overseas, according to Citigroup.

The classes were professionally exciting for me and found informative by the professional students, both civilian and uniformed, as evidenced by their end of course written critiques. Life was breathed into what would be a "dry" course on the Federal Acquisition Regulation. It was made exciting with short student required problem-solving exercises and use of recent actual service and product agency procurement solicitations, federal contracts, claims, bid protest decisions from the General Accountability Office (GAO), and Armed Services Board of Contract Appeals (ASBCA) and Federal court decisions. Tales from my consulting experiences were especially popular.

My teaching technique unknown to these students was forged and molded in 1964–1967 by my experiences teaching "juice" (electrical engineering) to junior college students (known as cows) at West Point. Then and now while teaching "Contracting with Uncle Sam" no professional student falls asleep or gets bored because there are always ongoing classroom student hands-on practical exercises leading to lots of team groups and discussions.

This continuing education teaching effort for AFCEA and the feedback from students led to the writing of my first text, *Contracting with Uncle Sam*. It was published by the United States Naval Institute Press in 2008. The text would not have been written without the encouragement of my beloved wife, Antonia, and Fred Rainbow at AFCEA. Fred had previously, before his appointment to AFCEA, been the editor-in-chief of the Naval Institute *Proceedings* magazine among other duties at the Naval Institute Press in Annapolis. The outline of the text and many of the chapters were written over a period of five years while Antonia, my beloved wife, was an inpatient in her fight against cancer at Memorial Sloan Kettering Cancer Center in

New York City, the Kessler Rehabilitation Center, in Union, New Jersey, and other medical facilities.

Never Give Up the Ship (NGUTS)

In 2012, I was asked by Fred Rainbow, the then vice president for Education at AFCEA and the executive director of the AFCEA Education Foundation located in Fair Lakes, Virginia, to come up with an interesting topic to present a one-hour lecture for the attendees at the TechNet Land Forces-South on July 12, 2012, at the Convention Center in Tampa, Florida. The presentation was to have no stipend associated with it or any instructor fee.

The purpose of the conference was to provide a forum for the Army and Marine Corps, as well as the Navy, Air Force, and Coast Guard security forces, to discuss issues and share ideas for solutions. Representatives from US Southern Command out of Miami and Central Command from MacDill Air Force Base, Tampa, were to attend the conference in addition to invited speakers and numerous industry representatives plus exhibitors. We agreed that I would present the Report by the Congressional Appointed Commission on Wartime Contracting in Iraq and Afghanistan, dated August 31, 2011. My presentation was titled in the handouts as "Wartime Contracting—Lessons Learned."

I had studied for about two weeks and prepared a power point presentation to be show cased 1200-1250 in the afternoon at Session IV in Engagement Theater Four on the last day of the convention. At about eleven o'clock in the morning, I arrived early at the Engagement Theater at room 4 in the convention center lower level and sat in on the ongoing Class Session III. There were some fifty attendees for the class entitled: "Army Enterprise Email Migration to DISA" (Defense Information Systems Agency) a combat support agency of the Department of Defense (DoD).

DISA is composed of some seven and one-half thousand civilian employees and active duty military personnel from the Army, Air Force, Navy, and Marine Corps; and approximately an equal number of defense contractors. DISA provides, operates, and assures command and control and information-sharing capabilities and a globally accessible enterprise information infrastructure in direct support to joint warfighters, national level leaders, and other mission and coalition partners across the full spectrum of military operations. The session speakers were providing an overview of the Army's progress in moving to Enterprise Email in lieu of the e-mail services provided by each separate DoD armed service department or agency.

The presenters were discussing the requirements, processes, and responsibilities for successful transition from the current decentralized multiforest Exchange (e-mail) environments to the DISA as the e-mail service provider based on Windows Server 2008R, Exchange 2010. Current and planned activities were identified and were discussed to provide overall project status and identify project progress towards bringing functional organizations to the common standard. My class session was to follow this well-attended class, which was to end at 11:50 a.m.

When the prior class was dismissed, I moved to the podium and the information technology folks set me up with my computer with Power Point slides—lapel microphone, amplifier-projector, large screen, podium, electronic pointer. Soon, I was ready to present by noon. I was so excited to give the class since the Commission's report had been an eye opener on the waste and abuse of the service civilian contracting in Iraq and Afghanistan with warnings of significant more waste and abuse to take place as these two wars were to close down.

By twelve fifteen that afternoon, the entire previous class had cleared and I was behind the podium ready to start my presentation. The only problem was that, although my class was advertised on the main convention floor and identified by a tripod outside the classroom door, no attendees came into the room, nor were there any seated conferees from the previous class staying to hear my class.

Needless to say, I was starting to worry that the class had no interest despite the importance of the topic and the significance of the published report. Perhaps it was because my class was planned to be over the lunch period. It was at that very time that I decided that the class had to be presented. I needed to find some attendees—even if I just had several janitors come in and listen to the class. After all, it was, in my opinion, an important topic of national interest and would take only less than thirty minutes to give the presentation summarizing the findings of the commission.

I ventured just outside the classroom and noted that there was one well-dressed gentleman standing and chatting with two others in the hallway. I walked up to that gentleman and asked him if he would be so kind to come listen to my presentation despite the fact that I would have ruined his lunchtime. The gentlemen agreed, knowing the topic I was to present. After an hour and half later, we were finished. During this period, a second convention attendee representing a woman-owned small business (WOSB) had come and sat in the rear in the midst of our presentation and participated in our discussions. We had in a lively manner covered the commission's report in detail. We had exchanged numerous questions and answers.

As the gentleman stood up to leave, he thanked me and shook my hand. In a firm shake, he slipped into my palm what felt like a coin and told me to call him any time. As he left the classroom, I opened my palm. In it was a coin. To my amazement it was the gold coin of "Excellence" presented by the Defense Information Systems Agency. The gentleman who attended was Col. Aubrey L. Wood, commander of DISA Central Field Command located at MacDill Air Force Base. He was responsible for the expenditure of some $10 billion dollars in Information Technology and Telecommunications Federal Contracts to US firms and other multinational firms in support of combat and administrative operations in Iraq and Afghanistan.

I have repeated this experience to close friends and, especially, to my grandchildren with the intent for them to understand the importance of always being well prepared and never to give up the ship (NGUTS) on a worthwhile project. As I am writing this chapter, we have removed all major forces, leaving some five thousand US forces in Iraq, and have removed major U.S forces out of Afghanistan, leaving less than some nine thousand or less primarily to serve as trainers, advising the Afghanistan forces and supporting counterterrorist operations.

We are also seeing the return of havoc in Iraq, Syria, and even Afghanistan with the resurgence of various competing ethnic groups such as the Taliban, Islamic State of Iraq and the Levant (ISIL), and Kurds and the loss of order bringing tumult, displaced refugees, human suffering, and destruction to that Middle East region.

This turn of events required the US in 2017 to continue to provide material and close air support along with other coalition allies to the government of Iraq and Syria. The war lessons from the wars of Vietnam, Iraq, and Afghanistan remain critical for our military and civilian leaders as America's role in world order continues.

In the late fall of 2017, the leaders of Iraq and Syria both declared the terrorist group ISIS defeated militarily in Iraq and Syria. Iraqis and Syrians, with assistance from the United States and other regional militias, took their countries back from the terror group that had declared them its sovereign territory in 2014. However, ISIS still has territory in countries around the world despite the fact that ISIS has been brutally disrupted by a US-backed bombing campaign and advancing ground forces. In addition, the world will continue to see isolated significant ISIS terrorist activities of destruction and death reaped on the West and other nations, since its worldwide organization remains intact!

On May 17, 2014, as I walked up to my grandson Alexander, when he was returning from the stand accepting his college diploma from the Honorable Pat McCrory, the governor of North Carolina, at Wingate University, I shook his hand and hugged him. He had majored in finance and accounting. I firmly concurrently slipped into his palm the gold coin of excellence from Defense Information Systems Agency that I had received some two years earlier.

In essence, with the coin, I was passing the baton to Alexander for his college academic achievements and as an advance token to carry on his life's journey as a Wall Street investment banker and analyst and more. Work hard, always be prepared, focus, be honest, be benevolent, pray, and strive to do your best. *Never give up the ship (NGUTS)!* With such attributes, one increases his or her probability for achieving excellence in whatever one undertakes.

CHAPTER 14

When Love Calls

I started writing this chapter of the Memoir in Palo Alto at the Cecil H. Green Library, the largest Stanford University library, containing collections in the humanities, social sciences, area studies, and interdisciplinary areas from notes that I had jotted en route to San Francisco. We sat among a flock of students that February 15, 2014, Saturday morning before Monday's annual Presidents' National Holiday. Across the specially built large desk with multiple power strips for laptop connections sat my grandson Orry, then a freshman studying computer science.

I had flown up from San Diego early that Friday after teaching the day before my course entitled *Contracting with Uncle Sam,* to three students from industry and one Marine Corps officer. After arriving at San Francisco International Airport, I was taken to Palo Alto by Supershuttle service to the Stanford Inn. The Stanford Inn caters to family members of students matriculated at Stanford. Being driven for the first time through Palo Alto, the small town known as the Birthplace of the Silicon Valley, was exciting to me. The town includes portions of Stanford University and its headquarters to a number of high-technology companies, including Hewlett-Packard (HP), VMware, Tesla Motors, Skype, and Palantir Technologies to name but a few. It has also served as an incubator to several other high-technology companies such as Google, Facebook, Logitech, Intuit, and PayPal.

That same afternoon that I arrived at one o'clock at Stanford, I sat with Orry in a computer software coding class with some eighty other students in a lecture hall similar to the amphitheater style that I had taught cadets at West Point transistor solid state circuits some fifty years earlier. Once the coding lecture was completed by the Stanford professor, the students retired to individual small group classrooms for further instruction using assigned practical software coding exercises. With the assistance of a teaching graduate assistant, the concepts taught in the lecture hall were reinforced and questions answered. Later the student teams each took to the blackboards to present their respective coding solutions to the remainder of the class.

I must add that Orry graduated from Stanford University on June 18, 2017, whereat he earned his bachelor of science degree in mathematical and computational science with distinction. Our whole family was in the Stanford U. Football Stadium, cheering some 1,700 graduates and Orry. I could not help but allow my mind to wonder, thinking of the absence of my beloved wife, Antonia. It has been some thirteen years since her loss due to cancer. My option A was lost. Option B was now in the stadium—Antonia's three children, Stamie, Cosmas, Christina and their families—my grandchildren. The grief, denial, and anger had been replaced.

However, on that February 15, 2014, en route to San Francisco's International Airport, on United Airlines Flight 1272 from San Diego, I could not help but reflect on the first and only time my beloved wife, Antonia, had joined me in my annual trek to the West Coast to teach for the Professional Development Center of the Armed Forces Communications Electronics Center (AFCEA), a non-profit activity. AFCEA works to have industry and government officials meet in a legal, unofficial manner to discuss defense matters and solutions for the various Departments of Defense.

The San Diego Convention Center serves as the annual site for the West Coast defense industry meeting sponsored by both AFCEA and US Naval Institute in late January or early February of each year. Defense industry representatives and active uniformed military service personnel view displays of the latest communications systems, electronics technology, and big data computing applications for defense artificial intelligence enterprise solutions; attend various presentations by distinguished civil servants, industry leaders, and military leaders; and even attend lectures, professional development classes, cocktail parties and banquets.

It was that winter, mid-January of 1998 in San Diego, that after my three-day course was completed, Antonia had joined me from our home in New Jersey that Friday for the weekend. Early that Saturday morning, we had gone whale watching on a cruise ship—a tourist must-do when one is in San Diego—and later that afternoon, we had visited the famous San Diego Zoo.

It all began later that evening when we retired to our hotel room at the historic Sofia Hotel on downtown San Diego Market and Front Street. Antonia did not feel well. Something was wrong. Her lower body torso, especially lower back and right groin were experiencing severe pain.

We returned home to Shrewsbury, New Jersey, and Antonia promptly visited her orthopedic doctor, Dr. Cary Glastein, in Tinton Falls, New Jersey. Magnetic Resonance Imaging (MRI) was undertaken on February 7, 1998, and a Computed Tomography (CT) scan of February 10, 1998, of her spine due to her prior history of herniated disks (prior L3-4 disk lumbar discectomy). It was those scans that indicated a mass in the right adnexa, the appendages of the uterus, namely the ovaries, the fallopian tubes, and the ligaments that hold the uterus in place; and another mass in her left groin. The possibility of cancer led us to seek Antonia's internist on February 11, whom Antonia annually consulted for her physical exams.

On February 12, Dr. Marianne Roosels, her internist, met Antonia at the Review Medical Hospital Emergency Room and conducted a physical exam. Dr. Roosels felt the hard left mass on the exterior and the softer mass on the right internally. She prescribed for Antonia to have the CA-125 and CEA blood tests performed. The CA-125 blood test measures the level of a protein called CA-125 in the blood. High amounts of CA-125 may indicate ovarian cancer, as well as less serious conditions, such as endometriosis or inflammation in the abdomen. The Carcinoembryonic antigen (CEA) blood test is used as a tumor marker. An elevated or rising CEA level indicates cancer progression or recurrence.

For Antonia, the CA-125 Test eventually came back showing elevated levels of CA-125 (137 from 37) for ovarian cancer. The CA-125 Test was performed multiple times during Antonia's battle with cancer as a tool used by her doctors to monitor the presence of cancer cells in her blood associated with ovarian cancer and its metastases. Recommendations were provided to us by Dr. Roosels for appointments to two local doctors, an obstetrician-gynecologist and a gynecology-oncologist located in separate offices within two counties. The recommended oncologist was not available for a week or more. Hence, Antonia and I decided that we would go out of state promptly to a major full-service cancer treatment center, Memorial Sloan Cancer Center (MSKCC) in New York City.

Within twenty-four hours, Antonia was accepted at Memorial Sloan Kettering Cancer Center. Her assigned doctor was to be Dr. Carol L. Brown. Further tests as described were performed. Ultrasonography (US), Computerized Tomography (CT), and Magnetic Resonance Imaging (MRI) are generally used to evaluate ovarian tumors. Ultrasound is the first-line imaging investigation for suspected adnexal masses. Color Doppler ultrasound helps the diagnosis identifying vascularized components within the mass. Computerized Tomography (CT) is commonly performed in pre-operative evaluation of a suspected ovarian malignancy, but it exposes patients to radiation. When ultrasound findings are non-diagnostic or equivocal, Magnetic Resonance Imaging (MRI) can be a valuable problem solving tool, useful to give also surgical planning information. MRI is well known to provide accurate information about hemorrhage, fat, and collagen. It is able to identify different types of tissue contained in pelvic masses, distinguishing benign from malignant ovarian tumors. The knowledge of clinical syndromes and MRI features of these conditions were crucial in establishing an accurate diagnosis and determining appropriate treatment.

On February 13, 1998, we were both sitting in the gynecologic oncologist-surgeon's office of Dr. Carol L. Brown at Memorial Sloan Kettering Cancer Center on the east side of Manhattan, discussing the scheduling for the immediate removal of her ovaries. Dr. Brown had performed an internal and external exam plus had a transvaginal sonogram performed in her presence and that of another colleague. The transvaginal ultrasound test is used to look at a woman's reproductive organs, including the uterus, ovaries, and cervix. Dr. Brown confirmed that Antonia had cancer. She ordered additional testing to include colonoscopy, needle biopsy, among others in the preparations for surgery.

Ten days later, on February 23, 1998, a complete abdominal hysterectomy was performed by Dr. Brown. Upon the biopsy analysis of the removed ovaries on that day, Antonia was found to have pathology "stage III C," ovarian carcinoma (metastatic cancer)—multiloculated right adnexal mass adenopath, swollen lymph nodes, to her left groin and retroperitoneal. The retroperitoneal is the space in her abdomen behind the abdominal lining that houses her major organs, including kidneys, bladder, abdominal aorta, and adrenal glands.

The treatment of ovarian cancer is based on the stage of the disease, which is a reflection of the extent or spread of the cancer to other parts of the body. Staging is performed by the surgeon (gynecologic-oncologist) when the ovaries are removed. During the surgical procedure, the surgeon will obtain small pieces of tissue (biopsies) from various sites in the abdominal cavity. During this procedure, depending on the stage (extent) of the disease, the surgeon will either remove just the ovary and fallopian tubes or will remove both ovaries, Fallopian tubes, and uterus. In addition, the surgeon will attempt to remove as much of the cancer as possible.

Ovarian cancer is staged I–IV. Stage I cancer is confined to one or both ovaries. The cancer is stage II if either one or both of the ovaries is involved and has spread to the uterus and/or the fallopian tubes or other sites in the pelvis. The cancer is stage III cancer if one or both of the ovaries is involved and has spread to lymph nodes or other sites outside of the pelvis but is still within the abdominal cavity, such as the surface of the intestine or liver. The cancer is stage IV cancer if one or both ovaries is involved and has spread outside the abdomen or has spread to the inside of the liver.

Being classified as stage IIIC made the cancer for Antonia onerous, indicating that the cancerous cells had progressed so much not
only in the ovaries but that they had spread to other organs of the
human body. No wonder that ovarian cancer, similar to pancreatic
cancer, have been labelled silent killers.

The word carcinoma, or cancer, is a dreaded word to the ears of
a human. It was as though this malady had crept up on us so silently
passing through multiple stages with little warning despite Antonia's
annual female gynecological exams. There was no family history of
ovarian cancer or any other cancer to cause concern of inherited gene
mutations to undergo the BRCA1 and BRCA2 gene tests. These
human genes produce tumor suppressor proteins. These proteins
help repair damaged DNA and, therefore, play a role in ensuring the
stability of the cell's genetic material. When either of these genes is
mutated, or altered, such that its protein product is not made or does
not function correctly, DNA damage may not be repaired properly.
As a result, cells are more likely to develop additional genetic alter-
ations that can lead to cancer.

Based upon Antonia's experience, the BRCA1 and BRCA2 gene
tests should be seriously considered to be taken by female readers of
this memoir, even if no ovarian cancer, or even breast cancer, hered-
itary history resides in a family. Many insurance plans do cover such
genetic testing with certain conditions, and if not, consideration
should be given to privately paying to have the tests conducted for
peace of mind. However, the CA-125 and CEA blood tests should be
considered to be standard by family practitioners for inclusion in any
women's annual physical exam just as cholesterol, protein, salt, and
sugar levels are measured.

Antonia was released after ten days from MSKCC, on March 3,
1998, to return home following the surgery with a prescription for
home health care and a March 16 appointment back at MSKCC for
the beginning of chemotherapy discussions and scheduling.

I did not realize that all our actions that were to be undertaken
were really a delaying action to the inevitable continuing spread of
the cancerous cells to many of the key organs of Antonia's body overwhelming the healthy cells. The counterattack was started by Antonia

first with the surgical removal of her ovaries, followed by whole body chemotherapy to see how many of the dreaded cells we could "kill" that had spread throughout the body.

Antonia was given chemotherapy at various periods, as appropriate, intravenously (by vein) and intraperitoneally (through a catheter placed in her abdomen). Some of the chemotherapy drugs she was given were Cisplatinum, Paclitaxel, and Carboplatin. The common denominator of these three medications was the prevention of the cancer cells from growing by interfering with DNA (deoxyribonucleic acid), the genetic material in cells. Deoxyribonucleic acid, more commonly known as DNA, is a complex molecule that contains all the information necessary to build and maintain an organism. All living things have DNA within their cells.

The risk Antonia accepted was that to kill the bad cells, we would invariably be killing many healthy ones; thus defeating the primary purpose of causing remission and further weakening the human body leading to death. I remember Dr. David Spriggs, Antonia's medical oncologist at Memorial Sloan Kettering, telling us that whatever we do, we would not be able to kill every bad cell with chemotherapy.

Dr. Spriggs' principal responsibilities were to manage gynecologic malignancies (predominantly ovarian cancers) and to lead Memorial Sloan Kettering's program in early drug development. Dr. Spriggs coordinated the surgery, radiation oncology treatments, and chemotherapy to include all integrative medicine to help Antonia preserve her quality of life during treatment, finding the management approach that worked best for her.

Since we heard the diagnosis in 1998—ovarian cancer, stage IIIC, we both transformed ourselves. Antonia prepared for the fight for her life. I transformed myself from a practicing lawyer to a caregiver coordinator. My law clients were transferred to other counsels for face-to-face services, my rented law office on Forty South Street in Eatontown was closed and legal staff released, and my professional office was moved to our home. I had become a full-time caregiver and coordinator as a starter. Our entire family—Stamie, Cosmas, and Christina— suited up for the long haul. Antonia and I had become a team with even a greater bond. There was no thought of giving up or cutting and running. A major battle of life itself was unfolding, dropping right at our doorsteps in mental, physical, and spiritual terms. Antonia needed all the support.

There was no turning back. General Douglas MacArthur is remembered by the Corp of Cadets at West Point for his statement on May 12, 1992, in his acceptance of the Sylvanus Thayer Award and his farewell address to the Corps, which is engraved in his monument on the plain that reads, *"In war there is no substitute for victory."* Antonia and I had drawn the battle lines against cancer.

As the primary caregiver, the table 14-1 below depicts the tasks that we undertook.

Table 14-1. Functions by the Family Cancer Caregiver

- Maintained schedules for doctors' appointments.
- Maintained the schedules for surgeries, chemotherapy, x-ray therapy, speech therapy, physical rehabilitation therapy.
- Coordinated private and public transportation schedules to and from hospitals, doctors' offices, rehabilitation centers.
- Attended all doctors' appointments and cancer treatment sessions.
- Remained at bedside for all hospital admissions for the entire stays—day and evening.
- Kept written notebooks of all cancer treatments, doctor's meetings, and medications or prescriptions. This journaling of medical events was very helpful for me for it also gave me also the opportunity of putting feelings into words.
- Ensured Antonia had some fun (music therapy, art therapy, horse carriage riding in Central Park, "EVRA Estatorio" [Greek restaurant] between Third and Lexington Avenue in Manhattan, depending how she felt after her outpatient therapy).
- Hired and coordinated twenty-four–hour live-in home health aides and their schedules to ensure her personal care,

hygiene, and nutrition—home functions not performed by hospice.

We spent quite a bit of time at Memorial Sloan Kettering Cancer Center where Antonia was an inpatient or an outpatient in order to undergo procedures or to receive various therapies. For the various chemotherapy cycles, which lasted often three days, we often stayed several nights in hotels (Bentley Hotel, 500E Sixty-Second Street or Affinia Gardens, 215E Sixty-Fourth Street) near the hospital within walking distance rather than commuting daily from Shrewsbury, New Jersey.

We would often find ourselves in Central Park South, which was nearby and just sit and relax. Antonia enjoyed the horse-drawn carriage rides through the park. We both found the park experience just sitting on a park bench or riding in a horse-drawn carriage to be a wonderful way to experience the beauty and serenity of Central Park. It provided palliative care at its finest along with the art and music therapies that the hospital provided when Antonia was an inpatient at Memorial Sloan Cancer Center in her very own patient room. We would visit nearby restaurants to eat.

If practical, depending on how Antonia felt, on any Sunday, we would attend Greek Orthodox services at the Holy Trinity Cathedral on Seventy-Fourth Street. Believing in God, Christ, and the Holy Ghost gave us hope and resilience. Often an Orthodox priest or other denominational cleric would visit Antonia while a hospital inpatient. We both knew that those times of being inseparable were so precious, reminding us of our very mortality.

In May 3, 1998, Antonia's mom, Emorfia, eighty-two, who had been living in Tarpon Springs since 1980, fell and suffered a cerebral hemorrhage while gardening outside her one-story family home at 121 Bay Street on the Whitcomb Bayou. While at Helen Ellis Hospital in Tarpon Springs, she suffered cardiac arrest. We had never told Emorfia that Antonia was being treated for cancer even before these events occurred. While visiting with Emorfia in the hospital, sitting at the foot of her bed while she was still partially cognizant, Antonia still did not want her mom to know that her daughter was undergoing chemotherapy in the fight of her life. Hence, Emorfia never knew that her daughter had cancer.

We later traveled with Antonia to Grand Island, Nebraska, Antonia's birthplace and family home and where Emorfia had wanted to be laid to rest. Antonia's aunt, Zeta Caredis, had joined us from Raccine, Wisconsin. Aunt Zeta loved Antonia as her own daughter and treated our children as her own grandchildren. On May 13, 1998, funeral services were held at the Holy Trinity Greek Orthodox Church. Thereafter, Emorfia was interred at the West Lawn Memorial Park Cemetery next to her beloved husband, John, and son, Chris. We have never returned again to Grand Island. The trip to Grand Island for Antonia was very exhausting but she had insisted.

Antonia and I always marveled that despite all Emorfia had gone through, from being a Greek Christian orphan child in Turkey, surviving for many years in International Red Cross camps in Turkey and then Athens, becoming adopted in Greece by her stepmother, migrating with a US visa as a Turkish citizen at seventeen years old to America under sponsorship of a stepbrother, the loss of her beloved West Point son, Chris, a lieutenant in the US Air Force, and finally, even the loss of her husband, John, whom she had cared for many years due to a severe stroke; she was not bitter. A sacred guardian protected and strengthened Amorfia. She had learned to survive and cope with adversity. She was fiercely proud to be independent. She was kind, frugal, honest and very proud of all her family. To this day she continues to provide an example and an eternal memory to her family and to all whom she touched.

During one of our summers together in 1998, we had gone for a weekend at Ship Bottom on Long Beach Island, New Jersey, and rented a condominium on the beach. Antonia loved Long Beach Island (LBI) and wanted to live in her own beach house. That weekend, we had found a newly built beach house, 323 Tidal Drive in Loveladies of Beach Haven, facing a lagoon with a swimming pool and even a dock. It was located within walking distance of the beach. We had to make the purchase decision within an hour.

The newly constructed home was being shown in an open house to multiple buyers standing in line with their realtors to view the new home. Stamie and Aris were asked to quickly go to nearby Barnegat Light to see another home and to report back which of the two homes they liked. They reported that 323 Tidal Drive was far superior as a beach house. I have never bought a home so quickly, thanks to the builder, who was escorting us. He dismissed the other prospective buyers accompanied by their disgruntled realtors. The builder made the sale himself due to the happiness he noted in Antonia's eyes.

From 1998 to 2003, as it turned out, Antonia enjoyed our short one-hour drives from Shrewsbury to the beach house on the weekends on the Garden State Parkway to rest, especially after her sessions with radiation and chemotherapy. The sacrifice was worth it to see how happy Antonia was at the beach house on those special weekends over some five years until she could no longer travel. As for myself, the tradeoff was executed without hesitation. To finance the purchase of the beach house, we sold the commercial lot located at Avenue of the Commons in Shrewsbury onto which we had planned to build our law office complex. Once we signed the purchase papers for the beach house within twenty-four hours, I had sold the law office property back to the construction firm from which I had purchased the vacant prime commercial property. Antonia's happiness was more important than my professional ego of owning and operating an office building occupied by attorneys.

My focus was to be on supporting Antonia in her fight from coordinating her medical insurance, being with her during all her appointments, hiring home health aides, remaining with her while in hospitals, and meeting with physicians. We were fortunate that, by that time, all our three children—Stamie, Cosmas, and Christina—had completed high school and college and even graduate schools. My most important function was providing Antonia mental support and emotional strength. Stamie, my oldest daughter, was married and lived with her family in Wayside, New Jersey, a short distance by car to our home in Shrewsbury. Stamie and her husband, Aris, would often visit Mom. Their two children, Alexander and Orry, our first two grandchildren, brought great happiness and joy to Antonia as she struggled to win her fight against cancer.

Antonia was no longer able to be the art teacher at Shrewsbury Borough School where on, any given day, she taught art to an average of over one hundred students per day. Different kindergarten through eighth grade classes would enter her classroom every forty-five minutes, thus creating a need for different lesson plans and preparations for each grade level as well as frequent changes of art supplies and materials. Antonia had attended George Washington University to earn her master in fine arts in June 6, 1971. Thereafter, she attended Monmouth University in West Long Branch, New Jersey, for her master in science in education in May 1995. She was recognized by Governor Jim Florio, of New Jersey, in May 9, 1991, for her excellence in teaching as part of the Governor's Teacher Recognition Program at the Shrewsbury Borough School. The recognition was for having made exceptional contributions in the use of effective instructional techniques and methods, the establishment of productive classroom climate and rapport with students, and the development of feelings of self-worth and love of learning in students.

In 1993, Antonia was the co-author with Claire B. Gallagher of the text calling for discovery through architecture, entitled *Eyes on Insects*, an interdisciplinary teacher's guide. The guide developed a special art curriculum for grades 3–6 that was inter-disciplinary, setting a standard for others to follow. The guide provided teacher and student reference information on specific insects, lesson plans and teacher templates. Its goal was to inspire students to "develop new eyes" to "see" their natural environment as a means of inspiration. Students were to focus on the insect world as a means for designing and building models for humans.

As an artist, Antonia enjoyed watercolors and egg tempera, a fifteenth century Russian, Byzantine technique. She had ventured into iconography more than thirty years earlier while studying for her master of fine arts. In 1996, Antonia studied periodically under the recognized master Russian iconographer Vadislav Andrejev, who had emigrated from Russia and founded the Prosopon School of Iconography in the Byzantine Russian Tradition at Whitney Point, New York. She attended a number of weekly classes at Whitney Point. Her icons are today found in private collections. Antonia had also donated icons for philanthropic purposes and to Saint George Greek Orthodox Church now located in Ocean Township, New Jersey.

Antonia had used up all her sick leaves and subsequently filed for unpaid leave and ordinary disability retirement on July 14, 1998, from her school and the state of New Jersey as a teacher. Her world had drastically changed overnight. Antonia felt it would be unfair to the children of Shrewsbury to teach, if she could not provide the day-in, day-out proper vitality needed for teaching. Antonia was "disability retired" in 1998 after more than twenty years of teaching preschool through eighth grade in the United States (New Jersey, Nebraska) and Germany (DoD Dependent Schools) with a pension and medical benefits with Horizon Blue Cross Blue Shield of New Jersey.

Even before halfway through her chemotherapy treatment protocols, Antonia had the side effects described at table 14-2 below. No one was able to assess whether or not she will have suffered lasting effects from her treatments, which would continue to prevent her from fulfilling her teaching responsibility much less any household duties. Little did we both comprehend until several years later, the significance of the transformation that was taking place.

Table 14-2. Antonia's Experienced Side Effects —Chemotherapy

- Nauseousness, vomiting, and anorexic from Cisplatin (Zofran and Decadron medications given to offset effects)
- Swelling of face and body
- Constant and severe fatigue—loss of energy level
- Sore throat and mouth sores
- Hands and feet turning purple—neuropathy
- Difficulty in walking—feet and leg joint pain, cramping
- Loss of hair
- Restless sleeping, heavy breathing, heat flashes, and sweats
- Weakened immune system—risk of contagious disease

Some two years had passed since her first major surgery in 1998, when on March 3, 2001, Magnetic Resonance Imaging was performed at Monmouth Medical Center in Long Branch, New Jersey, of her brain and the carotid arteries providing blood flow to the brain. Lesions were found to be present in her brain and the possibility of carcinoma.

Hence, on March 4, 2001, Antonia was transferred to Memorial Sloan Cancer Center (MSKCC). A tumor growth was pinpointed about one and one-half centimeters in her left occipital lobe, indicating brain metastasis caused by the ovarian cancer, quite small but deep down in her brain. The tumor was impacting her visual association cortex, which interprets what one sees. Due to the size of the tumor and its location, Antonia was a candidate for stereotactic radiosurgery. Stereotactic radiosurgery, or SRS, is a method for delivering radiation to brain tumors, which may be given in place of surgery. It is used to treat tumors that start in the brain as well as brain metastases (cancer that has spread to the brain from other parts of the body). The technique uses advanced imaging technologies combined with sophisticated computer guidance to deliver a highly targeted and intense dose of photon radiation. The radiation conforms to the three-dimensional shape and size of a tumor, resulting in minimal exposure to the rest of the brain and fewer side effects than conventional radiation techniques.

On March 13, 2001, Dr. Josh Yamada, radiologists oncologist, and Dr. Blasberg, neurologist, performed Stereotactic Radiosurgery–Cyber Knife at MSKCC. Stereotactic radiosurgery (SRS) is a form of radiation therapy that focuses high-power energy on a small area of the body. Despite its name, radiosurgery is a treatment, not a surgical procedure. Incisions are not made. SRS targets and treats an abnormal area without damaging nearby healthy tissue, especially those in the brain. Cyber Knife slows the growth of small, deep brain tumors that are hard to remove during surgery that involves incisions.

Antonia was discharged from MSKCC on March 14, 2001. Within three days thereafter, Antonia was experiencing seizures affecting her eyesight, experienced memory loss, and had difficulty walking, being very unsteady. She also had severe dizziness and had visual white light flashes and rotating flashing lights with severe headaches. By May, she was also having in her vision multiple rotating black triangles. These seizures, although lasting a few minutes, continued for over one year up to May 2002.

On May 17, 2002, Magnetic Resonance Imaging showed significant brain swelling and an increased necrosis area in comparison to the original area. A brain positron emission tomography (PET) imaging scan was also performed, which allowed her doctors to see how the brain was functioning. The scan captures images of the activity of the brain after radioactive "tracers" have been absorbed into the bloodstream. These tracers are "attached" to compounds like glucose (sugar). Glucose is the principal fuel of the brain. Active areas of the brain will be using glucose at a higher rate than inactive areas. When highlighted under a PET scanner, it allows doctors to see how the brain is working and helps them detect any abnormalities.

Due to the increased size of the brain metastasis, in lieu of another round of radiosurgery, the decision for brain surgery with the acceptance of the risk to eyesight and other possible neurological functions was made. This led on August 5, 2002, to surgery (craniotomy) to remove the brain tumor from the left occipital lobe by Dr. Philip H. Gutin, chief of the Neurological Service in Oncology at MSKCC.

This brain medical intervention led to substantial loss of sight and her field of vision concurrently became restricted from both her eyes. On August 12, 2002, Antonia was released from Sloan Kettering and was transferred by Emergency Transfer Service (EMS) to Kessler Institute for Rehabilitation, Acute Care at East Orange in New Jersey. It was at Kessler that Antonia threw herself to recovering. She took special eye classes to strengthen her vision in addition to the physical therapy classes to allow her to walk and brain training therapy. Her champion was Christopher Reeve who, in 1995, had spent several months at Kessler rehabilitating from permanent injuries suffered after an equestrian event fall in which he sustained complex fractures to the first and second cervical vertebrae that resulted in an injury to the spinal cord. He became a paraplegic, wheelchair bound, and required the use of a respirator to assist him in his breathing. Reeve had acted the role of *Superman* in the movie and related sequels before his accident.

On November 1, 2002, Antonia wrote a letter to Mr. Christopher Reeve and family stating,

> I want you to know that I, along with millions of others, appreciate you and your family's supportive role model of love and fighting spirit ... You continuously give the gift of hope to families around the world. You give this gift to all those who are quiet, "unsung heroes." These unsung heroes are struggling and facing their life-changing challenges, just like you and your family. "Thank you. Thank you. Thank you" seems inadequate.
>
> Keep fighting and so will I.
>
> Sincerely,
Antonia J. Giallourakis

While my energy, focus, and all available resources became redirected in support of Antonia's efforts to beat the cancer, Antonia insisted that her three children's focus was to remain on their own families and careers. No mother could ask for more care, support, and love from Cosmas, Stamie, and Christina and her two young grandchildren, Orry and Alexander. Cosmas remained a physician at Massachusetts General Hospital in Boston; Stamie's family lived within a few minutes' drive to our home in Shrewsbury. Stamie and Aris frequently visited Antonia to provide her encouragement. On those occasions, she loved to play with her first two grandchildren, Orry and Alexander, and Christina, as a second-year law student at Seton Hall University Law School, remained living in Hoboken, New Jersey.

For Antonia, when she was not undergoing outpatient treatments, or in the hospital, she focused on starting up of a non-profit foundation for art therapy for children with cancer and other serious diseases. Her close friend Margaret Scandalios would assist her and drive her to visit children's hospitals and public schools in New Jersey. She was no stranger to Massachusetts General Hospital for Children with Cancer, Pediatric Hematology-Oncology Center in Boston; Memorial Sloan Kettering Cancer Center, Children's Day Center, Pediatric Center in New York; Robert Wood University's Bristol-Myers Squibb Children's Hospital in East Brunswick, New Jersey; Levine Children's Hospital in Charlotte; Morgan Stanley Children's Hospital of New York Presbyterian Hospital; Red Bank Regional High School, Little Silver Elementary School, Shrewsbury Borough School, and many other pediatric hematology-oncology centers and public schools. On those days that she felt well, she delivered art therapy classes using specially prepared lesson plans to children, their teachers, and child life specialists on the art of giving art therapy and its importance as a therapeutic integrative medical modality.

Her passion lead to the activation of Children's Art for Children's Cancer Foundation (CACCF) Inc., a New Jersey non-profit organization, that promoted art therapy for children with cancer in which children in schools (the Art Pals) created art for sick children (the Unsung Heroes) in hospitals—"children helping children." The foundation provided monetary grants to the art departments of numerous schools, which in turn during their art school classes, had students create art works appropriate for children with cancer to complete while inpatients or outpatients or just provide uplifting feelings while undergoing various cancer treatments.

By September 2001, Antonia authored, tested, and refined the "Hero Approach Lesson Plan," a service learning approach, using drawing. Teacher heroes motivate student *art pal* heroes to create original stickers, posters, or bandannas with positive slogans. In these ways, drawing was used for service learning. This process helped children understand that each of them could make a difference in the life of a sick child.

Antonia's motivation for founding Children's Art for Children's Cancer Foundation came after she realized that having cancer is a gift of time. She decided to use her passion for working with children and the visual arts to help others. The foundation had fundraisers whose donated receipts were used to provide monetary grants to numerous schools to have children create art works for inpatient children in cancer centers. This effort kept Antonia's mind busy and provided a needed refuge from the overhanging specter of serious ongoing organ body damage by the cancer cells.

Some of the items created by the "Art Pal" heroes in their schools and thereafter delivered and completed by pediatric hospital patients were designer bandannas, designer caps, posters and slogans, designer canvas tote bags, personal journals, and loveable Lumpy Sea Creatures on canvas. In addition, the foundation shipped to numerous pediatric cancer centers over several thousand printed ABCs coloring books for young pediatric patients. Activity books with pencils and crayons, whose uncolored drawings and SUDOKU puzzles therein were created by Art Pal heroes. These were used for coloring by older students undergoing cancer treatments.

Antonia served as a stellar example to numerous Art Pal heroes, to the art teachers of New Jersey, and to her community as well as family. Her legacy continues in an endowed fund. On December 3, 2012, CACCF was assimilated for perpetuity into the Antonia J. Giallourakis Endowed Fund in Art Therapy for Children with Cancer at the Massachusetts General Hospital *for* Children (MGH*f*C) Cancer Center in Boston.

In that regard, Alan Salisbury, whose family supported Antonia's art therapy program, was instrumental as the author in developing and marketing the children's Christmas package known as "The Legend of Ranger: The Reindeer Who Couldn't Fly" with book, music CD, and toy. Ranger's net profits are today directed primarily to the Antonia J. Giallourakis Endowed Fund for Children with Cancer.

In 2003, our next medical trauma was that new body scans had located cancer growths that had appeared in Antonia's spine. Once again, at MSKCC, surgery was conducted to remove the cancerous tumors from her spine followed by chemotherapy and radiation, plus further rehabilitation. At table 14-3 that follows is a summary of the medical procedures and treatments that Antonia underwent in her campaign to defeat cancer.

Table 14-3. Summary Oncology Procedures, Treatments Antonia Underwent.

The Metastisis Ovarian Cancer Trail, Stage IIIC

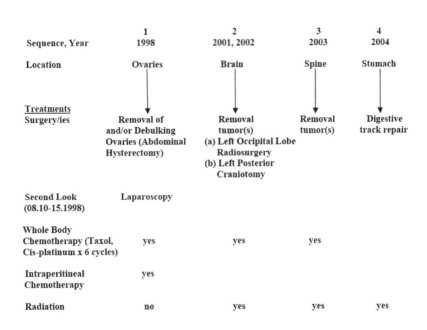

Sequence, Year	1 1998	2 2001, 2002	3 2003	4 2004
Location	Ovaries	Brain	Spine	Stomach
	↓	↓	↓	↓
Treatments Surgery/ies	Removal of and/or Debulking Ovaries (Abdominal Hysterectomy)	Removal tumor(s) (a) Left Occipital Lobe Radiosurgery (b) Left Posterior Craniotomy	Removal tumor(s)	Digestive track repair
Second Look (08.10-15.1998)	Laparoscopy			
Whole Body Chemotherapy (Taxol, Cis-platinum x 6 cycles)	yes	yes	yes	
Intraperitineal Chemotherapy	yes			
Radiation	no	yes	yes	yes

It was a cold winter day in January 2004 and the ambulance drive to First Avenue and Sixty-Seventh Street in NYC was uneventful. Antonia was sleeping in the ambulance's bed with me sitting in a stool beside her as we passed the car and truck traffic on the New Jersey Turnpike and entered the Holland Tunnel, then crossing the avenues and streets onto York Avenue.

The emergency room at Memorial Sloan Kettering Cancer Center in New York City was quite busy. We had arrived by ambulance from Monmouth Medical Center, in Long Branch, New Jersey. Antonia was quite ill. Earlier in the month, she had received several directed doses on an outpatient basis of radiation at MSKCC to stem the metastasized cancer in her spine. We were in our fifth year of fighting the ravages of ovarian cancer, stage IIIC.

The Monmouth Medical Center Emergency Room (ER) CT scans revealed that the spinal radiation had collaterally damaged Antonia's intestine in several locations. Her bowel had become obstructed. It had to be repaired by immediate surgery. That day would, indeed, be a long one. The issue was whether or not Antonia wanted to live or die. Since she was now alert, Dr. Carol Brown, her surgeon, wanted her approval for any further surgery. Antonia asked that Dr. Brown call Cosmas, my son, a newly minted doctor, who had completed his residency at Yale-New Haven Hospital and was practicing at Massachusetts General Hospital in Boston. Dr. Brown reached out to Cosmas and explained the options related for the surgery and obtained his thoughts. Antonia wanted the family involved in the decision of her life. Antonia made her mind up to have the surgery immediately. She wanted to live so that she could be "with all of us."

The surgery was undertaken to remove the damaged intestines and to repair the digestive track. Within a week, we were released to return home to Shrewsbury with no further appointments issued by Antonia's medical team at Sloan Kettering—a sign that we were coming to the end. We returned back to Shrewsbury whereat I personally took care of Antonia with the aid of Hospice for the first time supplemented with our private nurse aides.

Hospice care is end-of-life care usually for a patient that is expected to live six months or less. The care can be given at home, at a hospice center, in a hospital, or in a skilled nursing facility. A team of health care professionals and volunteers provide it. They give medical, psychological, and spiritual support. The goal of the care is to help people who are dying have peace, comfort, and dignity. The caregivers try to control pain and other symptoms so a person can remain as alert and comfortable as possible. Hospice programs also provide services to support a patient's family.

I found that hospice at home does not provide twenty-four-hour on-duty services, nor does that organization cook meals, feed patients, clean the patients' bedroom, change sheets, bath patients, or do laundry. The family members are responsible for those functions. I supplemented hospice with private caregivers to cook, feed, and bathe Antonia.

A number of years earlier in my private law practice, I had accepted a court case from a military officer and friend of mine, to sue a nursing home in Neptune, New Jersey, for the premature death of his elderly mother. The staff of the nursing home had failed to periodically turn my client's bedridden mother on her sides during each twenty-four–hour period, allowing the creation of bed sores in her back and buttock that eventually became highly infected. This negligence led to fever, open wounds, severe pain, and death. Despite the monetary award to my client's family, the loss was avoidable.

That case made a lasting impression on me to such an extent that I vowed never to allow such an event to occur to any member of my family. Hence, I took special interest in the hiring of my own nurses and home health aides and to properly overwatch their activities while at home with Antonia. It is not a question of just qualification, certifications, competence, and compensation but also of an aide that cares for her patient and sincere interest in the health profession. The same caution I exercised when Antonia was hospitalized, hence the reason I spent all my days in the hospital room at the hospital when Antonia was admitted. I literally moved my one-man office with laptop to be within sight of Antonia and the care she was receiving. My clients did not care from where I was working their legal matters.

After five years, the battle was lost despite the heroic stand Antonia made. We fought a good fight. I was by her side as she slept, and as the hours went by, I could feel her body temperature dissipate to the chilling level. On April 12, 2004, the spirit of Antonia passed into heaven in the early morning hours while she was in her bed in our bedroom at home in Shrewsbury. She had preceded her earthly champion, Christopher Reeve, by six months who passed on October 10, 2004. I waited until sunrise came up to awaken my children that had been sleeping in the other upstairs bedrooms, then called hospice to come to our home. Hospice came and pronounced Antonia had died officially; hence, we had no need to transport her to the emergency room of Monmouth Medical Center in Long Branch.

Concurrently, I had notified our priest, Father Andrew Eugenis, from our Asbury Park parish of Saint George, who came promptly to comfort the family and to commence the Orthodox last rites. Once Father Andrew had finished, only then did we call for the funeral director from the Braun Funeral home in Eatontown to come to our Shrewsbury home.

The Trisagion Orthodox Service and wake were held on Monday, April 19, 2004, at the Braun Funeral Home. Funeral services were held at the St. George Greek Orthodox Church at 700 Grand Avenue, Asbury Park, New Jersey, the next day starting at 9:30 a.m. on Tuesday, April 20, 2004.

The solemn funeral procession of the hearse and family sedans proceeded from St. George Greek Orthodox Church in Asbury Park turning onto the Garden State Parkway north onto the Palisades Parkway. Thereafter, it then followed the winding route along the Hudson River to Bear Mountain and onto Highland Falls and West Point, New York. Two leased academy Buses of parishioners, who dearly loved Antonia, accompanied us to West Point.

Antonia had returned to be laid to rest on the hallowed grounds of the West Point Cemetery where her monument now overlooks the Hudson River. As the hearse and accompanying vehicles entered the cemetery and passed the Old Cadet Chapel, one could not help but note the gravesites of recent returning West Point graduates from Iraq or be far from such gravesites as those of Generals George Custer, Westmoreland, and "Stormin'" Norman Schwarzkopf, not to forget even Coach Earl "Red" Blaik, the revered West Point football coach.

Without any equivocation, Antonia had loved living in Grey Ghost Housing as a newlywed Army bride to a recently minted captain. In the years that followed, she had taught art and pottery classes to the West Point cadets, academic faculty, and their families on post. She had been the teacher in art and English to American students in Germany, Nebraska, and New Jersey public schools. She had given birth to her first beloved daughter, Stamie, at the West

Point Hospital; Cosmas at Fort Belvoir, Virginia; and Christina at Monmouth Medical Center, New Jersey.

She was the perfect Army wife—educated, family-oriented, understanding, who as a teacher of K-8 children was not only competent, respected, but loved by her students and their parents. Her students over the years and we shall always remember Teacher/Mom/Grandmom Antonia's birthday (March 17, 1944, during WWII) and how she was so excited when Saint Patrick's Day came around each year. Antonia would dress up and paint herself "green" and bring the whole Shrewsbury K-8 School into a day of special celebration anticipated each year. May her memory always be eternal. Mom would want us to celebrate always on March 17 in some way.

She had raised her family under the true spirit of Greek Orthodox Christianity. She served all the parishes in their choirs, philanthropic organizations such as Philoptochos and the Daughters of Penelope, and their schools. She had touched the lives of children undergoing cancer treatments through art therapy in multiple pediatric hematology-oncology centers. Her friendship was sought by all whom she met. The world is better for the years that Antonia lived.

I lost my partner in this world and have accepted coming to terms with the title "widower." Now, I cannot look back for I need to make every day count, having gained strength because of Antonia's loss.

In the private notebook of our daughter Stamie, one discovers the following scribed, unedited notes about her beloved mom, Antonia, which speaks for all of us:

> *She loved beauty*
> *butterflies & dragonflies*
> *good & generous soul, honesty*
> *always strived to do her best in everything*
> *proud of you*
> *Alexander—1ˢᵗ grandson*
> *play with you for hours*
> *on the floor with blocks*
> *mythology and Egypt*

Orry—loved to hold you
paint next to her for hours
create beautiful pictures together
play the piano ...
LBI
She loved to come to soccer games,
piano recitals, karate tournaments,
geography, bees, enrichment
fairs. Play games for
candy
She will travel with all of us in our
hearts as we continue our journey.
Mom was my best friend
biggest supporter
taught me what a good education
means—light up a child
holidays—Easter egg hunts, X-mas, birthdays
nurtured the artistic side
encouraged me to reach for the
high bar in all aspects of life.

A private burial immediately followed at her gravesite, surrounded by her close family and friends. West Point was her selected resting place where also she knew her partner and husband, Bill, would one day lay too. West Point was from where her brother, Chris, had graduated.

Below the reader will find an essay that Antonia, by her personal hand, wrote, summarizing her life and feelings.

WATER JOURNEY

I believe that validating children's power to under-stand and uplift sick children is monumental. If children are guided and nourished, they become empowered to become contributing citizens. All children are gifted and have the potential to be empowered to use their individual gifts to make a difference to others. As parents, teachers, neighbors and friends we need to engage, guide and convince our youth of their emotional power to make a positive difference. Children around the world need to know that others care. We can express this care through images that heal and uplift.

I am now a five-year survivor of ovarian cancer and four metastasis—two brain and one in the spinal fluid. Even as I write, it seems surreal. During this time, I have taken the most remark-able, meaningful, comforting and jolting journey. There have been multiple full circles. I have jour-neyed through a winding, calm, sometimes stormy weather and back to free flowing. In a short span of time, there have been many miracles that I want to share in hopes it will help others.

My life is not extraordinary in the sense of headlines but I have been blessed since childbirth. As a child, I arrived cocooned and surrounded by embryonic fluid filled with love. The gifts of my family's river have had their own cadence and emo-tions—some gloomy, some indigo, and mostly ceru-lean blue moments.

The joys of family, marriage, raising children, teaching, working with children, and friendships are like bubbles (full circles), bobbing gently, burst-ing, reforming, and revitalizing the river of life. I have traveled on my personal river of life, some-

247

times clashed against opposing forces but mostly surrounded by a river—AGAPE love.

Symbolically, I would represent myself as a
dragonfly, transcient, in today's world, but reaching
and searching for something everlasting. My dream
is to touch children's spirits, even for a second, and
transform or role model positive, healing, comfort—
as my mother, husband, children, grandchildren
have role modeled for me. I have always felt that
on the very second I was born, my embryonic family
river released me, a microcosm, which was graced
from generation to generation.

As a child (bubble) I was cocooned and floated,
protected by family. At eight the bubble surfaced
and sprang unsolicited unwanted bobbling franti-
cally. My father had a severe stroke.

Like "The Pianist" I am a survivor but not
from the holocaust proportions. Like the Pianists,
music and art have touched my spirit, but delicately
balancing logic and intelligence to provide equilib-
rium. Unlike the Pianist, I have continually (as far
back as I can remember) traveled via visual images
accompanied by color, form, and sound.

The first 13 years of my life, I had no reason to
feel anything but love and comfort. Days were filled
with happy times and happy thought. My days were
filled with childhood exploration, making pretend
food such as mud pies, trailing my older brother,
painting, and creating a front yard snow animal
sculpture garden. I was inquisitive. As a first generation child, I was instilled with the idea of education
being a means of a better life and as an instrument
to help others. I constantly wanted to know about
the beauty of the natural world. I dreamed of traveling and working at the United Nations—a far cry
from my physical surroundings of flat land, the daily

multiple visits to the corner grocery store for my five cents ice cream or elephant pastry, and small town living in Grand Island, Nebraska. Starting at the edges of town were rows of corn stretching as far as you could see.

I am now 58 years young and filled with many gifts. Looking back at childhood, I now realize that, in actuality, we were poor materialistically. We had no car and were the last to get a TV in our neighborhood. My dad would walk to the grocery store miles away two to three times a day. My Mom's friends would see my artwork and ask her where I got my love and appreciation of nature and man-made beauty and, yes, even drawing. Mom would answer and I would have a quiet, inner silent laugh.

At the time she answered in this way, she had been making cards for the children and us. Every card was a stick figure chicken—no matter the occasion or special event. Yet when I look back now—I do realize that she was extremely aesthetic, snow animals, mud pies, playful, collected and loved crystal.

On June 11, 1959, I was jolted and knocked out by the sudden death of my older brother, Chris. He had graduated from the United States Military Academy at West Point, New York, and had been commissioned in the US Air Force as a second lieutenant pilot. On a routine, return flight, lightning struck the plane. At that very moment, I was sitting down under a tree, sat on my glasses, and felt a shattering emotion within me. Within hours, a priest came to our front door, and my mother and father collapsed from shock and grief.

On Friday, February 13, 1998, my doctor announced, "You have ovarian stage IIIC cancer." The cacophony of the shocking words were like symbols clashing, making all reasoning vanish, panic, fright, and confusion taking over. In my era, cancer equated with sure, hideous death. If you were lucky fast; if you were not, it equaled a vision of hell.

My river of life changed profoundly.

I have been greatly enriched, am filled with peace, joy, and the melding of logic and soul. Cancer is not always an immediate a killer. It will probably eventually kill me, but it will not kill my spirit or soul. For me, cancer is not a "killer" rather a gift of time.

—By the Personal Hand of
Antonia J. Giallourakis

CHAPTER 15

A Centenarian Calls

Becoming a Centenarian

The biggest celebrated family event, when Mom and I were in Tarpon Springs together on the Whitcomb Bayou at 121 Bay Street, was St. Anthony's name day on January 17 of each year. St. Anthony is considered the Father of Orthodox Monasticism. His kind of monasticism, that of "living alone with God as his only companion," remained the most cherished monastic ideal for the monks of the Christian Orthodox Church throughout the ages.

Since Mom was born on St. Anthony's name day in 1911, starting in 2009, we had a birthday party here on the Whitcomb Bayou on the weekend of St. Anthony's celebration in January. When Mom hit a hundred years old in 2011, she even received a signed letter from our forty-fourth president, Barack Obama, and his wife, Michelle Obama.

Being born in 1911 on the Island of Kalymnos, which was under Turkish rule until May 1912, Mom was less than two years old when, as a result of the Turkish-Italian War, Italy took over rule of Kalymnos and the other eleven islands that comprise the Dodecanese Islands with Rhodes being the most famous of the group. Italian rule over the Dodecanese was firm and efficient but never popular. Italian became the official language, and in 1925, the Dodecanesians were obliged to take Italian citizenship. The generation of islanders that remained under that regime were forced to become bilingual. In reading my mom's USA Certificate of Naturalization issued on January 18, 1944, by the US District Court for the Southern District of Florida, it had filled the space for "former nationality" with "Italian."

Earlier in 1927, as a schoolteacher on the Island of Symi, one of the twelve Dodecanese islands, Mom lived through the occupation of the Italians. She recalled to us how she quickly self-taught herself Italian so that she could speak to the Italian inspectors who would come to her classes. On those occasions, she would speak Italian to her class and even had the children memorize selected words in Italian to repeat. However, as soon as the inspectors would leave, she would revert back to speaking Greek in her classroom.

After World War II in 1945, the Dodecanese temporarily came under British occupation, with Greek participation. Until finally with the conference of foreign ministers in Paris, it was agreed in 1946 that the islands should pass to Greece, and they were formally ceded in 1947.

Archbishop Iakovos, of the Greek Orthodox Archdiocese of North and South America, in June 23, 1961, recognized my mom, Stamatia, as a leader in early Greek parish education. This recognition was mirrored and justified not only by her education but by her peers, students, and parents. Stamatia lived and breathed the importance of education, teaching it to several generations of children and stressing the importance of their Greek heritage, physical exercise, the Orthodox religion and love of family.

Mom provided exceptional and meritorious service to Saint Nicholas Greek Orthodox Cathedral for some forty-one years. She was a 1927 graduate of Kallithea Teaching School in Athens. She became a respected pioneer teacher and principal of the afternoon Greek Primary School and Nursery of Saint Nicholas Greek Orthodox Cathedral in Tarpon Springs, Florida, during the period 1935–1976.

By her eightieth birthday, Mom had been living alone in our large home at 170 Spring Boulevard where I grew up. She continued to use the home to provide private Greek school classes to preschool children and for married couples who wanted to learn to speak Greek. After some urging, she finally agreed to sell 170 Spring Boulevard, our original family home, and downsize. So she purchased a villa (two-bedroom townhouse) at Green Dolphin Park in Tarpon Springs where she lived for several years.

She was able to walk from the villa to the nearby Winn-Dixie for groceries using her cart and even some eight blocks more each Sunday to attend services at Saint Nicholas Cathedral. The center of town was not far away, so she enjoyed walking to window shop at the numerous antique stores in downtown Tarpon Springs.

Eventually, she found that the villa was too big and in fact lonely, especially, when the "snow birds" (retired seniors) who migrated to Florida primarily from the Midwest, Northeast, and Canada left their villas and condominiums at Green Dolphin Park prior to Easter each year and returned after Thanksgiving for the winter in Florida. Moreover, the first story unit had no view and was located adjacent to a noisy main traveled road to the Howard Park Beach.

Hence, she moved from the villa to a second-story, two-bedroom end unit condominium, which she bought in Green Dolphin Park. She had by this step downsized further to a smaller two-bedroom corner unit. From her unit location, with multiple "golf-proof" windows and a screened-in porch, she had a panoramic view of the Tarpon Springs Golf Course with easy access to her unit by elevator.

Eventually, Mom was not able to walk the many blocks to Saint Nicholas on Sundays or to Winn-Dixie for groceries, so she purchased and moved to a first-floor condominium at Villa Plumosa within view of the Whitcomb Bayou. She was so happy to be across the street and able to walk along the periphery of the bayou. This condominium also allowed Mom to walk easily one block to church and two blocks to downtown Tarpon Springs. Moreover, she was in the daily travel path for their work and homes of several relatives, Mercury and Duchess, who often dropped in to see her before or after work. She often visited Duchess's home to be with her children, Irene and Damian. She was no longer out of the way, thus had more company just coming to see her. She was just closer to her past students too, such as Mercury, Damian, Duchess, and Russell, and other family relatives and friends. This was to be my mom's last experience in "independent living."

My widowed mother, Stamatia, had joined us in New Jersey from Tarpon Spring, Florida, in 1998 at the age of 87. We had constructed a one-story modern addition to our home by adding a large bedroom with a built-in full bathroom and separate sitting room for health aides to our Shrewsbury home. Stamatia would have her privacy and be able to have space for a live-in caregiver. It was easier for me to keep my eyes on both my wife, Antonia, in the main house in her battle against cancer and my elderly mom under an adjacent roof.

My brother, Mike, had passed away due to heart complications in 1996. I certainly have become an advocate for a family to have more than two children just to increase the probability that at least one child will be around to perhaps at least manage the geriatric care of a parent. I had drawn the only lot for this duty. I never left a wounded soldier of mine behind when I was in Vietnam with the First Infantry Division. So I was not going to leave my mom in a nursing home or abandon her to live by herself. For others, this level of care may not be feasible for financial or other reasons. Each family team should address the most practical manner to care for an elderly parent or seriously ill and handicapped family loved one.

However, I reflected a number of times whether or not Mom should have just been left in Tarpon Springs rather moved to New Jersey for ease in management. The reason is because I often think I should blame myself for the two hip repairs that she had to undergo while in New Jersey in my home while even under the close care by me and a twenty-four hours, seven-day-a-week live-in home health aide.

The first fall occurred in 2007 and the second fall occurred in 2008. The first fall cracked the right hip and the second fall the left—both were intertrochanteric fractures. Mom was just standing in her living room area next to her sofa when she just dropped to the floor. Due to her age, hip repair was the order of the day rather than hip replacement. Such a fracture occurs between the neck of the femur (thigh bone) and a lower bony prominence called the lesser trochanter. The lesser trochanter is an attachment point for one of the major muscles of the hip. Intertrochanteric fractures generally cross in the area between the lesser trochanter and the greater trochanter. The greater trochanter is the bump you can feel under the skin on the outside of the hip. It acts as another muscle attachment point.

Intertrochanteric fractures are usually repaired with a metal plate and screws. The patient is given a general or spinal anesthesia in the operating room. They are then positioned in a manner to realign the fractured bone. Once the fracture is well positioned and confirmed to be in a good position using x-ray, an incision is made on the outside of the thigh. The femur (thigh bone) is exposed, and a metal platinum plate is placed along the outside of the thigh bone using several small screws. A large platinum screw is inserted across the fracture and into the femoral head. This large screw is held to the plate. Together, this plate and screw implant hold the broken bones in place to allow for healing.

I recall succinctly the orthopedic surgeon coming out of the operating room to the hospital's waiting room and informing me after Mom's first hip repair surgery that "elderly patients normally pass in twelve months." One-year mortality rates of 12–36 percent have been reported. We had a repeat of such a repair on the left hip when she fell almost a year afterward.

The predominant mechanism of hip fracture in the elderly population is a fall from a standing position. Mom had osteoporosis. Due to her advanced age, Mom, with her slower gait, had less forward momentum. Thus, without warning, when such an elderly falls, they tend to buckle and fall to the side, making a fracture more likely. The decrease in bone mass in the elderly is caused by a number of factors, including reduced biosynthetic and replicative potential of osteoblasts, increased osteoclast activity, reduced physical activity (a stimulus for bone remodeling), genetic predisposition, decreased calcium intake, and hormonal influences. The net result is that bone resorption outpaces bone building. Hence, as one becomes elderly, such falls occur without any notice and not from any slip and fall incident causing intertrochanteric fracture of the hip.

After each surgery, Mom was sent to a rehabilitation center where on the first hip repair she regained the use of her legs with the use of a walker. After the second fall and hip repair, Mom no longer wanted to stand and refused to stand or walk. She was prematurely

BILL GIALLOURAKIS

released from the rehabilitation center under Medicare rules since Mom showed no improvement in her rehabilitation plan.

My self-blame wore off in as much as I decided that these falls would have occurred even sooner and would have been more traumatic had she not been with me under the same roof in New Jersey. On both occasions, the on-duty health aide felt guilty in not being able to prevent Mom from falling. However, I quickly moved to dispel those thoughts, assuring each of them that we had all done our best for Mom. It would have been intolerable to keep Mom strapped in her bed or a wheelchair for fear of what happened.

Bringing Mom Back Home and the Maze of Geriatric Care Options

Now, some five years later after Antonia had succumbed in her battle with cancer, I arrived at Newark International Airport, New Jersey, at curbside by sedan with my beloved Mom. We were to board a US Airways flight to Tampa. We were returning back to our three-bedroom family home at 121 Bay Street on the Whitcomb Bayou in Tarpon Springs. One twenty-one Bay Street had been owned by my beloved mother-in-law, Emorfia. Upon her death, the home was devised in her last will and testament to Antonia and me. It faced the Whitcomb Bayou with a magnificent view of the blue Gulf of Mexico tidal waters, which flow first into the Anclote River and then into the bayou. Directly in front of it was a miniature city park with two benches, several trees, and planters. It enhanced the view and appearance of the home.

Mom was now ninety-eight years old. She was more frail than when we had left Tarpon Springs some ten years earlier. The car driver helped me lift my mom from the front passenger seat of the airport shuttle onto her wheelchair once we had removed the leather side arm rests. Thereafter, we re-attached the previously removed extended footrests and arm rests. Incidentally, having a wheelchair whose arms can be removed is essential in sliding a disabled person into and out of a vehicle not to mention in and out of bed. Adjustable, removable

256

leg rests are also essential, allowing a disabled person to be seated at a supper table to eat with her family or just traversing an airport to get to a waiting gate area. It is essential that legs should be partially raised when one is in a wheelchair to assist in the flow of blood and its circulation throughout the feet. Otherwise, one will find a patient's legs and feet swollen after sitting in the wheelchair with legs touching the floor for hours in the day. In addition, a chair sitting "air mat" is essential to be placed on the top of the wheelchair seat to prevent sores to one's buttock from extended sitting.

I had alerted US Airways in advance to have assistance, especially in getting my mom from the long walkway ramp to the air plane's entrance doorway and then to her seat. I was restless since I was not sure how we were going to get Mom from the aircraft's entrance with her wide, standard wheelchair then down the narrow aisle to her seat. To my surprise, the airline stewardess provided a special narrow rolling wheelchair without any arm or leg rests onto which we lifted my mom from her foldable wide wheelchair. The stewardess then rolled her down the narrow aisle in the narrow wheelchair to her sitting row. We then both lifted and slid her into her passenger aisle seat. We were going home back where it all started for Mom when she had arrived as a young bride in 1933 and from where I left to attend GMA in 1950 and West Point and the Army in 1954.

Once we were back at 121 Bay Street in Tarpon Springs, Florida, Mom initially had the care of several home health aides from the agency called Visiting Angels Home Health Care. Other health care agencies located in the Tampa Bay area that could have provided home care aides where Ascentia Home Healthcare, Right at Home, and Accurate Home Care. These agencies, through their subsidiaries, provide services in multiple states throughout the United States.

For a beginning family that needs a caregiver, I wish to offer some insights because of my experience of the live-in and hourly caregiver options available to one that is elderly or approaching the twilight years. The health aides from Visiting Angels were a mix of independent contractors while others were actual employees of Visiting Angels. These health aides were known as Certified Nursing Aides (CNA) who had taken and passed the state of Florida CNA examination and were qualified, registered, and vetted as certified nursing health aides with several home health providers. This allowed them to be able to receive work depending on which local agency had hourly assignments for them.

Table 15.1 below depicts the standard transition of the elderly in retirement living and care, which is explained in more detail in the text that follows. Specialized Care Centers are also shown, such as bariatric care, which consists of pre- and postoperative care and education for people who undergo bariatric surgery such as gastric bypass or lap band surgery. One may want to initially consult a web site, such as http://www.APlaceforMom.com, to determine what geriatric facilities with transition centers are available near where an elderly person would like to live and to chat with a counselor linked to that website.

Table 15.1. Transition Stages of Retirement Living and Geriatric Care

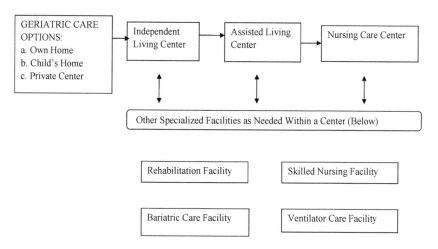

Mom was not able physically to move back into a facility such as Villa Plumosa from where she had last left for independent living. She did not have a husband or other special full-time person to live with her and to coordinate her care. She was wheelchair bound.

She also was not interested or physically able to socialize with other persons such as attend swimming classes, golf, attend movies, go out to dinner in a bus or van with a group to a local restaurant or local operas much less attend a traveling Broadway musical at Ruth Eckerd Hall located in nearby Clearwater as one could in a full-service independent living center.

Another alternate for Mom was an "assisted living" center, which generally offers a housing alternative for older adults who may need help with dressing, bathing, eating, and toileting, but do not require the intensive medical and nursing care provided in nursing homes. The choice of moving into an assisted living facility also was not feasible because she required extensive personal attention at all time.

"Nursing home" residents have physical or cognitive (short-term or long-term) impairments and require twenty-four–hour care during their stay. Nursing centers provide hospital-type bedrooms, private or shared with roommate, with prepared meals, and twenty-four–hour care by nurses, certified nurse health aides, and onsite visiting doctors. Generally, one will find nurses and nursing aides are assigned specific tasks to perform for numerous residents on a specific ward. The primary care giver in a certified nursing home is a certified nursing aide (CNA)—not a skilled professional such as a nurse or doctor. In other words, most of the resident care in various nursing facilities is provided by a combination of licensed certified nursing assistants and non-licensed individuals supervised by generally one nurse for a group of patients.

The cost of staying in a nursing home can cost more than several thousand per month or more. Some people deplete their resources due to the often high cost of nursing home care. If eligible, Medicaid will cover continued stays in nursing home for these individuals for life. However, they require that the patient be "spent down" to a low-asset level first by either depleting their life savings or asset-protecting them, often using an elder law attorney. Moreover, the federal and state budgets for Medicaid are under continuous reviews and recently under more scrutiny and controversy, especially since the

2016 election of President Donald Trump and 2018 budget, which cuts the budget in Medicaid for the elderly and disabled.

Medicare covers nursing home services for twenty to one hundred days for beneficiaries who require skilled nursing care or rehabilitation services following a hospitalization of at least three consecutive days. Medicare does not cover nursing care if only custodial care is needed —for example, when a person needs assistance with bathing, eating, walking, or transferring from a bed to a chair. To be eligible for Medicare-covered skilled nursing facility (SNF) care, a physician must certify that the beneficiary needs daily skilled nursing care or other skilled rehabilitation services that are related to the hospitalization and that these services, as a practical matter, can be provided only on an inpatient basis. For example, a beneficiary released from the hospital after a stroke and in need of physical therapy, or a beneficiary in need of skilled nursing care for wound treatment following a surgical procedure, might be eligible for Medicare-covered SNF care at a special facility located within a nursing home.

Moving Mom into a nearby nursing home where she would be provided twenty-four–hour assistance, seven days a week was considered and discarded based upon my experience. Nursing homes, in most cases, are just one profit center of a larger facility that transitions the elderly from independent care to assisted living to skilled nursing and rehabilitation therapy to even perhaps bariatric and ventilator care. Such multiple centers market skilled nursing care, rehabilitative services, respite care, long-term care, and palliative care with select centers offering specialized programming for dementia and Alzheimer's disease care.

They are owned generally by large for profit corporations. For example, Opis Management Resources, Tampa-based, has about eleven centers in Florida; Brookdale Senior Living, headquartered in Tennessee, operates well over five senior living facilities in the United States to include Florida. Although such facilities are professionally staffed to meet federal and state licensing requirements, generally, their skilled nurses and assistant health aides are assigned too many patients to monitor and care, much less have the time to feed, bathe, cloth, and prevent bed sores. Due to staffing shortages, medical funding cuts, and an array of issues, patients tend not to be turned in bed in the daytime and at night, cleaned and fed as often as the ideal standard of nursing care would dictate.

Such lack of care of the elderly inevitably leads to the development of decubitus ulcers (skin open wounds), reflecting some form of neglect (nutrition, hydration, positioning, infection control, etc.). Such wounds are preventable injuries and are not excusable. In addition, in most cases, the nurses and their aides have little professional empathy or interest for the care of any particular patient.

The geriatric care centers depicted at table 15-1, starting with independent living (e.g., condominiums or apartments) above generally charge an admission fee and monthly rental or service fees depending on the size of one's selected living unit and level of care. For example, a studio for single occupancy in independent living could have an admission fee of $60,000 with a monthly service fee of $1,395 in comparison to a one-bedroom apartment located in the same retirement community such as St. Mark Village in Palm Harbor, Florida, (http://www.stmarkvillage.org) for two occupants in independent living would have had an admission fee of $92,000 with a monthly service fee of some $2,460. In contrast, a one-bedroom apartment for a single person occupancy in assisted living level of care would have a monthly service fee of $3,800. For a semi-private apartment in skilled nursing or nursing home, the per diem rate would have been $250 or $7,500 per month. Annual cost of living adjustments should be expected to be applied as appropriate.

Hence, one needs to have saved sufficient funds to meet the admission and monthly service fees. Such additional payments for hospitalization, ambulance, physician, therapists, dentists, opticians, podiatrists, private duty nurses or aides, companions, medications, treatments, laundry, housekeepers, and other services and supplies are not ordinarily included in residential or nursing care. They are paid separately and directly by the residents or by their insurance carriers such as Medicare or private insurers.

Overall, the best option in my mom's case was to come under the "homecare" of her son in his home. I elected the family homecare option with certified nursing aides (CNA or home health aides

[HHA]) being my mom's employees rather than temporary, variable assigned employees associated with an agency such as Visiting Angels or Girling Health Care. It was time to form our own caregiver team. This option is today being selected by more and more American families as the US population ages and economics play a major role where the principal caregiver is a family member assisted by private certified nurse assistants or home health aides on an hourly basis or as live-ins over a twenty-four–hour period.

We initially, for several months, enlisted a home health care agency (Visiting Angels) to provide certified health aides to care for my mom. The agency would send a screening nurse out to our home at 121 Bay Street in advance to meet with my mom and me. This meeting is essential for the nurse conducts a survey of the needs to match the elderly's need with their available health aides. Thereafter at our request, the firm would send their prospective choice of employees or independent contractors who were to service my mom for my interview. The agency would bill the family the health aides as either employees of the agency or independent contractors and then in turn compensate them.

Within this option, one could elect to advertise in the local area papers and take on the responsibility to interview prospective employees, have them vetted through the county police and criminal court records to assess their trustworthiness, verify training and licensing requirements with the state, and then only hire on your very own payroll the certified health aides or home health aide.

My experience proved that the best health aide or caregiver providers were former immigrants rather than born American women. In particular, after trying both categories of aides and caregivers over a number of years, I found that the best ones had emigrated from the Philippines, Greece, Jamaica, Russia and its independent republics, such as Ukraine. However, their immigration status was critical to avoid hiring someone illegally here in the United States. They all had the immigration status for permanent residency, thus allowing them to live and legally work permanently in the United States (Green Card, USCIS Form 551). The aides that were hired were found to have empathy and cared about the personal care they delivered. Some were US citizens or had made their applications for citizenship before or while they were employed with my mom.

For these employees selected to be on our payroll, we paid on a weekly basis each home nurse aide after deducting from their gross income the withholdings for (1) federal income tax, (2) Social Security tax, and (3) Medicare tax. The latter two taxes were matched by the undersigned and all withholdings quarterly reported as required to include state unemployment taxes. At the end of each tax year, we paid all employment taxes collected plus unemployment taxes federal and state. Weekly and other periodic home skilled nurse visits prescribed by Mom's primary care doctor or by her doctors when released from hospital stays would be paid by Medicare and her secondary medical insurance carrier, USAA.

Let there be no doubt that there were weekly, quarterly, and annual payroll employee paperwork involved, which I personally handled. The burden could have been outsourced to an accounting firm or specialized payroll company handling such matters for a monthly fee such as INTUIT Full Service Payroll or PAYCHEK Customer Payroll Service.

Caregiving by Mom's Dedicated Health Aides

For some four years here in our home in Tarpon Springs, Mom had the care of two health care live-in professionals. For her last three years, Maria was the weekday health aide and Lidiya was the weekend aide. Both health providers were married and had grandchildren. Both were extremely strong and able to lift my mom as necessary.

For safety reasons, both had been qualified to lift Mom, with a "Hoya" hydraulic manual lift with full-body patient slings, in and out of her bed. Both were excellent cooks and housekeepers too, ensuring Mom was properly fed, the house was cleaned, and all medications were taken as prescribed. Maria spoke Greek and Lidiya spoke Ukrainian. Both spoke and wrote English. Most important of all, both were professionally competent, were dedicated in their work, and had empathy and concern for my mom's well-being.

During their employment with my mom, each applied for their US citizenship (USCIS Form N-400) and soon thereafter took their Naturalization Oath as citizens at a ceremony in the Tampa Field Office of the US Citizenship and Immigration Services (USCIS). Mom had encouraged and supported her immigrant health aides to become US citizens. Just as Mom had received her Certificate of Naturalization on January 18, 1944, some fifty-nine years earlier. Before the end of 2003, both Maria and Lidiya turned in their Green Cards and had received their US citizenship papers certificates (USCIS N-600). Mom's goal of US citizenship for her health aides was fulfilled before the end of their employment with her.

A special health aide notebook, "HEALTH AIDE AND HOUSEKEEPING INSTRUCTIONS" for Stamatia C. Giallourakis, had been prepared, which included instructions for the care of my mom by each health aide such as preventing decubitus ulcers by changing Mom's bed position every two to four hours or more frequently as needed; specific menus for each day of the week; and necessary housekeeping. A decubitus ulcer, also called a pressure sore or bed sore, is an open wound on your skin, which, if untreated, will lead to tissue destruction and infections. Such ulcers are common for the elderly lying in beds or sitting in wheelchairs for extended periods of time without repositioning.

More importantly, each health aide was instructed personally on the Do Not Resuscitate Order (DNRO) patient identification papers signed by Dr. Nicholas Pavouris, Mom's personal physician, which were to be provided to any emergency personnel. The DNRO identified Mom as one who does not wish to be resuscitated in the event of respiratory or cardiac arrest.

The schedule in the notebook (table 15-2 below) was to be followed unless special circumstances arose in which case I would be called at my office or the St. Petersburg College Library at the Tarpon Springs Campus where I worked daily, writing and studying for contract classes, which I was to teach for AFCEA. Each evening I would review with the duty health aide the schedule and menu for the next day.

Table 15-2. Daily Schedule for Stamatia Giallourakis

Activity	Approximate Time
• Wake up, wash, and dress (in bed)	8:00 a.m.
• Breakfast (in bed, sitting room, or dining room)	9:00–9:30 a.m.
• Physical therapy (in bed, foot bicycle)	9:45–10:30 a.m.
• Wheelchair Promenade around bayou	10:00–11:00 a.m.

(Depends on weather. In summer go earlier.)

• Lunch 12:00–12.45 p.m.	
• Nap time in bed	1:30–4:00 p.m.
• Physical exercise in bed	4:00–4:15 p.m.
• Mental therapy and related activities	4:30–6:00 p.m.
• Supper 6:00–6:45 p.m.	

Then open time (TV, activities)	7:00–8:00 p.m.
In living room	

• Bed time	8:00 p.m.
• Lights out	9:00 p.m.

The above times were flexible, keeping in mind Stamatia's hip fractures, her then age of 102, her thin skin, and stamina. Mental activities included, but were not limited to, photo albums for memory training, coloring book, scribbling with pencil or pen on pad of lined paper, dominoes, cards, puzzles, and the *National Herald* Greek newspaper.

The availability of the "instructions" notebook was one key to the success of the care for my mom. It provided clear instructions as to the health aide's duties—what was to be cooked each day of the week; health aide dress code; and necessary guidance in the event of emergencies and contacts. The Notebook was a must-read document and was kept updated and handy.

Physical exercise was high in the daily schedule for my mom. Range of motion exercises using rubber stretching slings and a small foot stationary bicycle were followed by tossing tennis balls or a basketball between Mom and the health aide and then by Mom into a basket net held at ground level.

This exercise was followed by the daily morning promenade to the nearby Craig Park and around Whitcomb Bayou with its tidal Gulf of Mexico waters from the Anclote River. This wheelchair ride lasted for about an hour. During the promenade, Mom would be stopped to be cheered by a neighbor, former student, or a friend who recognized the elderly passenger with her snowy white fine hair in the wheelchair. This was part of Mom's socialization program.

Due to Mom's dementia associated with her decline in memory or other thinking skills, she often would just smile to the well-wisher, providing the impression that the person was recognized. She always tried. Often the caregiver and Mom would stop frequently and watch the antics of baby dolphin and manatee that had ventured into Whitcomb Bayou from Anclote River via Gulf of Mexico.

Sundays were very special. We took Mom to St. Nicholas Greek Orthodox Cathedral every Sunday unless the weather was too cold or it was heavily raining. Lidiya or Maria, whomever was on duty, would dress Mom with her Sunday dress to include a lady's hat. Thirty minutes before church services were to commence, a wheelchair accessible van would arrive at our home. The van and its driver would be provided by the Pinellas Suncoast Transit Authority (PSTA) through its Demand Response Transportation Services (DART) for a nominal fee.

Had it not been for the DART transportation services, we would not have been able to transport Mom to St. Nicholas Cathedral. The Pinellas Suncoast Transit Authority (PSTA) provides demand response transportation services for people who, because of their disability, are unable to independently use the regular, accessible PSTA buses. Such similar essential public services for the disabled are provided by other communities in Florida and other states.

The congregation was accustomed to seeing Mom arrive with her health aide and her son, Bill, through the ramped side entrance to the Saint Nicholas Cathedral and later seeing her proceed to the inside front of the cathedral to receive holy communion. I always pushed the wheelchair toward the altar for communion. We were all kept in suspense to the very end, wondering whether or not she would open her mouth to receive the holy sacrament. She seldom disappointed Father Michael or me. This act of opening her mouth at the right time reassured us that at some level Mom's brain was still working.

With Mom's monthly Greek schoolteacher's pension received from the Greek Government, and Social Security payments, plus invested savings, we were fortunate to be able to afford the twenty-four hours, seven days each week services her two caregivers provided over a span of fourteen years—four years in Tarpon Spring and New Jersey for some ten years earlier. Medicare and her supplementary insurance from USAA fully covered her hospital and doctor-prescribed medical services to include skilled nurses who came to our home.

Maria and Lidiya treated my mom with empathy and great care. Their performance enhanced Mom's quality of life and extended her life. I lived in our home where I assisted, especially for the full-body bath showers that were done twice a week. To prevent flooding of the bathroom, I operated the wet and dry vacuum cleaner to remove the water from the shower that dropped outside into the bathroom hallway floor on a plastic mat. The shower stall was too small to fit the special wheeled shower chair.

Sitting with my mom and health aide at the family dinner table for supper each evening was the highlight of the day. No one likes to eat alone. After dinner, I always daily sat with my mom in the living room while the health aide cleaned up the supper table and completed related housekeeping in preparation for the next day.

It was during that time that I also received reassurance each evening after watching the early evening Tampa Bay news on TV or playing dominoes with my mom that her brain and memory were functioning. I would lower my head and voluntarily be given a kiss before she was wheeled to her bedroom by her health aide. She knew it was me! I then retreated to my closed-in porch where I had set up a small law office from which I often worked into the late evenings.

The most difficult time for me was to watch Mom slowly degrade in being able to perform her daily living activities of walking, eating, talking, laughing, standing, and dressing. The loss of mobility could be understood with the two hip repairs. As the years from 1998 grew to 2013, more of her daily living abilities slowly were degraded or all together lost. This "outward" noticed degradation was similar to my beloved wife's, Antonia's, degraded mental, eye, and overall physical abilities that were directly attributed to cancer as the disease metastasized and the aftereffects of her chemotherapy and radiation treatments associated with her care became evident.

However, for my mom, the cause, although never formally identified as Alzheimer's disease, had all the indicia of that disease plus very old age. Alzheimer's disease is a condition in which nerve cells (neurons) in the brain die, making it difficult for the brain's signals to be transmitted properly. Alzheimer's symptoms may be hard to distinguish early. A person with Alzheimer's disease has problems with memory, judgment, and thinking, which makes it hard for the person to work or take part in day-to-day life. The death of the nerve cells usually occurs gradually over a period of years.

In Mom's case, she eventually was not able to speak often. This phenomenon was followed by not being able to assist in getting out of bed whatsoever. Before she was able to sit up in bed with her feet hanging at the edge so that a health aide could transfer her into her wheelchair easier. She now did not cooperate whatsoever in being moved in and out of bed. At times, she was highly belligerent. She was exceptionally strong and provided a challenge to the health aide in just dressing Mom each morning.

In 2013, Mom stopped holding a fork and spoon and would not eat on her own. She could not find her mouth with a fork for her brain was not fully functioning. Hence, we shifted to spoon-feeding Mom. It was a slow process that required patience to get enough food and water into her. The health aides really got good at spoon-feeding, using "smoothies" plus all kinds of tricks to entice her.

In the interim, Mom was found to have blood clots in both her legs and was placed on the blood thinner, Coumadin. She had her fingers pricked periodically by a skilled nurse to measure blood thickness and report her findings to Dr. Nicholas Pavouris, Mom's family practitioner. This was painful for me to watch. Eventually, within nine months, the clots had disappeared.

Once off the Coumadin, which had thinned her blood, Mom was found after a biopsy to have skin cancer on her nose—Squamous Cell Carcinoma. By September 2013, we could address removing the skin cancer. We were amazed that she hardly flinched when her dermatologist, Dr. Roger W. Altman, numbed her nose with a local anesthetic and skillfully, progressively removed and examined layers of cancer-containing skin under a microscope until only cancer-free tissue remained.

The goal of the Mohs micrographic surgery was to remove as much of the skin cancer as possible while doing minimal damage to surrounding healthy tissue. Mom was brave while in Dr. Altman's office. In late October 2013, further skin cancer was discovered on the nose. It was at that time we decided that Mom had had enough of the skin cancer removal due to the minimum health risk that postponing such further care could cause.

However, it was a not until Mom was hospitalized initially on December 02–07, 2013, and then later December 13–16 that same year, initially first for low nutritional magnesium levels, and then matters became life-threatening for she was diagnosed with pneumonia. We had taken Mom to just have her blood drawn for examination as recommended by her physician, Dr. Nicholas Pavouris. Her magnesium level was found to be seriously low. She was hospitalized to relieve the imbalance using intravenous feeding. Nutritional magnesium is deeply involved in energy production, oxygen uptake, central nervous system function, electrolyte balance, glucose metabolism, and muscle activity, including that all-important muscle—the heart.

Magnesium plays an essential role in many of the functions of energy production itself. It is an integral part of the energy (ATP) and protein (enzymes—as co-factor and as a structural component of the muscle protein, myosin) molecules—without which the energy to contract and relax the heart does not occur properly. Magnesium is also an essential element in the construction of the cell membrane and vitally important to the electrolyte balance of cells. When magnesium levels begin to get too low, the body tries very hard to adapt, but these basic functions of energy production and cell structure can be affected, and when they are, symptoms of heart or cardiovascular disease can begin to manifest.

Enough Is Enough

Since Mom was found to have pneumonia, she was placed on penicillin-based antibiotics intravenously while in the hospital and later at home. Walgreen's Infusion Services were used to provide the antibiotics (piperacil-tazobact, 3.375gm VL) and the visiting home skilled nurses trained Lidiya and Maria to conduct the infusions. While at Helen Ellis Hospital (now Florida Hospital), we noticed that Mom would not eat except sporadically despite all the urging by both Maria and Lidiya.

The pneumonia was caused by food particles that had gotten lodged in her lungs and decayed creating bacteria. Mom's brain was not functioning, and when she was being spoon fed, the food was, instead of being swallowed down her throat, going into her lungs. Mom would also quench her chin and keep her mouth tightly shut. The doctors wanted to feed Mom intravenously. Since Mom was having serious trouble swallowing and could not get enough food or liquids by mouth, a feeding tube was recommended to be put directly into her stomach through the abdominal skin. This procedure is called a percutaneous endoscopic gastrostomy (PEG). The tube allows feeding directly into the gastrointestinal tract to occur bypassing the mouth and esophagus (the "food tube" leading to the stomach). It was at this point that I made the decision that Mom had had enough, and so I informed her doctors we were going home to 121 Bay Street on the Whitcomb Bayou.

In 2006, Mom had executed a Durable Power of Attorney containing Health Care Surrogate Provisions, appointing me as her Health Care Surrogate, giving me final authority to act for her and make health care decisions during her incapacity. More important, earlier in July 6, 2000, Mom had executed a Declaration stating clearly,

> I desire that nutrition and hydration be withheld or withdrawn when such procedures would serve only to prolong the process of dying …
>
> I specifically refuse my consent to the treatments below, but it is not my intention to limit my refusal of treatment to these measures:
>
> 2. Artificial sustenance or nutrition by gastric tube feeding, nasogastric tube feeding, intravenous feeding, or any other type of artificial means if I am paralyzed or otherwise unable to take nourishment by swallowing.

We may have been able to lengthen Mom's life but certainly not its quality. In the early afternoon of December 17, we arrived home. Mom was placed in her very own bedroom and was resting comfortably. Her health aides and companions, Maria or Lidiya, were with her at all times. Carter Nursing sent skilled nurses, which were ordered by Mom's doctors to the house to check her vitals plus administer the requisite antibiotics for several days. For some six days, Mom would not eat or drink anything substantive. She was comfortable and close relatives came to visit.

A Miracle Followed as the Journey Ended

Five days later on December 22, 2013, Father James Rousakis, our priest from Saint Nicholas Cathedral, came to bless Mom. He asked me to let us try to offer her the Holy Eucharist. We went together into Mom's bedroom. Father James wore his priest's robe and prepared to give her Holy Communion. Mom had been sleeping. Without any attempt yet to wake her, Mom suddenly "popped" her eyes open and opened her mouth to receive the Holy Eucharist. It is as though she had a premonition that she must wake up for this was to be the last Holy Communion she would receive on this earth. Having taken the Holy Eucharist, she closed her eyes and fell asleep. Father James and I were truly astonished. Surely, a miracle had occurred before our eyes.

Early next morning, December 23, two days before Christmas, I was sitting next to her bed holding her hand for several hours. Both Maria and Lidiya were present. Her body temperature was slowly dropping. Her hand was soon "freezing." I noticed her body temperature had drastically dropped just by placing my chin next to hers. Mom's spirit had gone to heaven. She was pronounced officially dead as of 10:38 a.m. I was at the bedside of my mom when she passed away in her bed, in her own room—a promise to her that I was allowed to keep.

As the tower bells of St. Nicholas Cathedral tolled exactly at eleven o'clock in the morning on January 4, 2014, outside the cathedral, the six pallbearers had assembled comprised of my cousins, Mom's nephews, and one great-grandchild. The evening before at the wake, His Eminence Metropolitan Bishop Nikitas (Lulias) of Dardanella, a former resident of Tarpon Springs and Greek School student of Mom's, appeared unannounced to participate with two other priests in the prayers and speak to the assembly. Mom had been his very special former Greek schoolteacher when he was a student in Tarpon Springs.

When he periodically would return to Tarpon Springs to visit his then-surviving beloved mom, Kaliope Lulias, and choir director, brother, John, His Eminence Nikita would stop the Sunday liturgy to recognize his Greek schoolteacher in the wheelchair at the rear of the church aisles. The entire congregation would turn to see the teacher in the white hair. His Eminence Nikita is the director of the Patriarch Athenagoras Orthodox Institute in Berkeley, California.

Kaliope Lulias, the mother of His Eminence Nikita and brother, John, joined their father in heaven, on July 11, 2017.

At my mom's funeral services, the cathedral choir had assembled and sang the special hymns for her funeral service, indeed a very special assembly. Many of the choir members had either been students of Mom or their children had attended Mom's classes. The United States' Stars and Stripes and Greece's national flag flanked the casket. Mom was making her last visit to Saint Nicholas Cathedral, the church that she so loved and served. After the funeral church service, Mom was laid to rest in the family plot at Cycadia Cemetery in Tarpon Springs next to her beloved husband, Cosmas, on one side and on the other her first son, Michael. Nearby laid her sister, Katina.

My mom had stood by my dad throughout all his sponge business endeavors. She was responsible for sending Mike and me to Georgia Military Academy, which gave us strong high school academic and athletic backgrounds. She then ensured I received a senatorial appointment to West Point, which led to my Army career. Mike went on to become a college professor. Mom took responsibility for her own mother and remaining sister who lived in Greece in the Panagias Argos Cloister as nuns while bringing her two other sisters, Katina and Ypapanti, to the United States. She provided a new start in the United States, in Tarpon Springs, to several members of her Kalymnian childhood neighborhood, which emigrated to the United States from Kalymnos.

She had served as the Greek schoolteacher for the Saint Nicholas Greek community with foresight, dedication, and distinction. Today, the Stamatia C. Giallourakis Saint Nicholas Cathedral Greek School Scholarship Fund exists, awarding scholarships to defray the cost of needy and gifted church member children to attend afternoon Greek school during the academic year. She was ahead of her times. I miss the presence of my mom.

Tips on Selecting a Retirement Community

Providing care to a loved one is at times strenuous on family caregivers, mentally and financially. By taking enough time and attention to finding the right place and level of care, which will eventually have to be adjusted for your aging loved one's specific needs, you can avoid overpaying for senior living.

Understanding the proper level of care your loved one needs is critical. Instead of assisted living, it might be less expensive to live in an independent retirement community and hire a home health aide to help with day-to-day needs for several hours each day. If a senior is seeking assisted living, ask for a written assessment done by the nurse of each community you are looking at and request that they put together a specific price plan for the requisite level of care.

Compare costs from different communities. Check to determine what is included in the monthly price for each one. The amenities will vary with each one, so understand what you receive for that monthly rate. Some may include meals, weekly housekeeping, and laundry services while other facilities charge extra for such services. Ask about the base rate and what it includes, and the costs associated for different levels of service.

Think about the size of apartment you really need. If you can downsize to a studio or one-bedroom apartment, the savings could be significant on a monthly basis. Plan to use the common areas available in the community in lieu of a larger apartment.

Many communities charge a deposit, an entrance fee, or a community fee. Generally, this is a one-time fee that varies according to the market and is usually nonrefundable. Read the small print and understand what these fees collected upfront are and whether or not they are refundable and under what conditions.

Check if there are incentives or specials that are not advertised by marketing managers of the geriatric center to cover moving costs or to waive selected fees. Also, some assisted living communities have a limited number of Medicaid apartments available for residents who may outlast their funds. Ask if the community will provide a guarantee for "continuing care" once your money runs out.

Compare facilities. If available, get on waiting lists whose fees are refundable if you do not select the particular community upon the availability of a unit. Ensure one reads the Waiting List Agreement carefully that is provided for you to execute. Read online reviews and talk to as many residents as possible during a trial stay in a retirement community. Conversing with residents and their staff during the visit is a must. Lastly, stay overnight several days to see how you like it.

EPILOGUE

Although I lost my father when I was nineteen years old, by that age, I had learned as a small boy sitting on a stool next to him and handing him sponges, the importance of the work ethic. I learned about love of family from Dad for he supported his parents, brothers and sisters financially and was their pillar of strength, which I have tried to emulate. I owe my math acumen to my dad from those early-year arithmetic problems that we solved together while I was stretched out on the living room carpet near his feet as he sat in his rocking chair near our fireplace.

From my mom, I learned about the importance of physical fitness, education, and Christian Orthodoxy, which she instilled in my brother and me. I still run into my mom's former students who relate to me that she was definitely ahead of her time. They never had a teacher who would teach them so much in a classroom while concurrently exercising mounted on a stationary bike.

At Georgia Military Academy, I learned what responsibility meant in taking care of fourth through seventh grade boarding students as their "house brother." While a West Point cadet, I gained a high sense of duty to others, even foolishly ignoring an ongoing Asiatic flu pandemic to visit my sick brother, Mike, at Fort Ord, California. In the peacetime Army, I sensed the need to fully train and prepare each soldier for actual combat under my command.

I have been asked periodically by family and friends as to whether I had any regrets in attending West Point and entering the Army in lieu of going on to John Hopkins University and becoming a doctor. My reply is an unqualified no.

For had it not been for West Point, I would not have never met Christ Poulos of the class of 1957 and, through him his sister, Antonia, whom I married. Nor would I have been alive to write this memoir for I would have died at an early age (sixty years) from heart disease as have the male members in my family—my dad and brother Mike, to include my some seven uncles and several male cousins. It was the physical workout ethic that started on Whitcomb Bayou and continued at West Point from gymnastics to those daily airborne runs at Fort Bragg and Okinawa to the current daily workouts walking around the Whitcomb Bayou or working out at the "Total Fitness" gym and pool every morning in Tarpon Springs.

That ethic has made the difference coupled with my open heart surgery in 2004, which have sustained me past the eighty-one–year marker. I survived quadruple heart by-pass surgery and even a bicycle fall in 2012, despite wearing a helmet, which required a craniotomy to relieve the pressure from several hematomas between my brain and skull.

The active Army allowed me to have experiences that would have been impossible to experience in a normal civilian career. To this day, I can still smell the projectile powder of howitzers firing, wake up feeling the sweat of launching nuclear capable tipped Honest John rockets during annual proficiency tests, marvel in my mind at the vista of Seoul while parachuting onto the Han River in Korea, wipe the tears down my face at family and friend funerals similar as those in the field morgue after identifying fallen artillery forward observers with the infantry companies in the Big Red One in Vietnam, experience periodic flashbacks of the unseen enemy below as our gun projectiles pounded the Viet Cong jungle trail and tunnels directed from my overhead flirting "Loach" helicopter, experience the excitement before a federal judge as when briefing the Army chief of staff on laser weaponry, and sense the tension at White Sands Missile Range of each IHAWK missile firing, whose drone intercept "kill" determined the effectiveness of an improved US air defense system and Raytheon's Defense business future and overseas foreign military sales.

I would be delinquent in closing this book without pleading with our political leaders— Congress and our commander-in-chief, the president of the United States. The plea has to do with the sacred use of our military. America has achieved its freedom and stability over several centuries in large part because our military services, starting with the leaders from our service academies, which respond to the defense of the United States when and wherever they are committed.

During the Civil War, history records that West Point cadets and graduates from the northern states fought for the Union. Likewise, cadets and graduates from the southern states fought for the Confederacy. That was the only time in American history where active political sides were taken by our military. In more recent times, the relief of General of the Army, Douglas MacArthur, under contentious circumstances by President Harry S. Truman, provided the only famous civil-military spat while the Korean War raged.

It is incumbent upon the executive and congressional branches of the government to prepare, maintain, and deploy our armed forces carefully and not to misuse the Armed Services. Aside from WWII, we have deployed American fighting forces in large numbers to various protracted wars in foreign lands from Korea to Vietnam to Iraq and Afghanistan and other places. In addition, especially in Iraq and Afghanistan, we have provided civilian support services by awarding billions of dollars of federal contracts in which the civilian contractors in many instances outnumbered our boots on the ground. In many cases, these contracted firms employed former veterans who had served in Iraq and Afghanistan, luring them back into harm's way, primarily by exceptionally high salaries plus bonus incentives to serve as security guards, truck drivers, logisticians, information technologists, operators, and project managers.

In Vietnam, each soldier knew that he would serve one year and would not be obligated to return for a repeated tour. We had a volunteer and lottery-type conscription in which newly drafted eligible men would be sent for their share of duty and life-threatening risks into the Armed Services. In Germany, we had other volunteers and conscripts, which wanted no part of Vietnam and were lucky enough not to be assigned to the Pacific Theater. They were just waiting their time in a safe assignment in Europe for their rotation date to come and the end of their conscription period.

With the current volunteer Armed Services and National Guard, we have sent our warriors individually or by rotating entire units on repeated assignments to war zones, basically placing the burden of fighting on those that have volunteered to serve rather than based on conscription or some form of lottery so that able-bodied persons (men and women) of the wider population and their families share the burden.

Today, as I am writing, we have soldiers assigned to containing the Ebola epidemic in Africa; some 8,400 soldiers after some sixteen years still remain in Afghanistan to train its army and to conduct counterterrorism operations against the Taliban; and more as advisers to Iraq in the defense against the Islamic State of Iraq and Levant (ISIL) terrorists. Our Air Force in concert with our Coalition military forces are flying bombers, fighters, and remotely piloted aircraft to conduct air strikes in Iraq and Syria against the ISIS threat. One need not be naïve, yes, the challenges are many and they will continue well into the future. I am sounding the warning to those who care to read that dependency on only a few to repeatedly carry America's burdens is fraught with the danger of exhausting our volunteer services (boots on the ground) even with contracted civilians providing service support.

The recent policy decision of August 2017 by President Donald Trump to increase the current 8,400 US presence in Afghanistan, in a conflict once called futile, by some 4,000 additional soldiers to train Afghan forces and conduct counter-terrorism operations is fraught with risks, even if it includes efforts to seek the cooperation of Pakistan and even the Taliban.

Encouraging are the efforts by the United States, to include President Donald Trump, to solidify a combined coalition of nations in the fight against ISIL known as the Combined-Joint Task Force Operation Inherent Resolve, providing air support to eliminate the terrorist group and the threat they pose to Iraq, Syria, and the wider international community. Coalition nations conducting airstrikes, during this writing, in Iraq include the United States, Australia,

Belgium, Canada, Denmark, France, Netherlands, Jordan, and the United Kingdom. Those conducting airstrikes in Syria include the United States, Canada, Australia, France, Netherlands, United Kingdom, Turkey, Bahrain, Jordan, Saudi Arabia, and the United Arab Emirates; and recently, air strikes were conducted in Libya by Egypt. As of August 9, 2017, the Coalition has conducted 13,331 strikes in Iraq, and 11,235 strikes in Syria, for a total of 24,566 strikes total in support of Operation Inherent Resolve.

In addition, the efforts in 2017 by President Donald Trump to rein in the belligerent nuclear threats of North Korea and his efforts to enlist the Chinese government to exercise its power to reign in its neighbor North Korea and, in particular, its nuclear missile threat provoking President Kim Jong-un, are important actions to the stability of the Korean Peninsula, Japan, and to overall world peace. Moreover, the strong positions of the United States and United Nations against the use of nuclear, chemical, and biological weapons by any nation to include North Korea is a clear warning that the use of such weapons is not to be tolerated.

Currently, the United States is overhauling its nuclear arsenal. The modernization of the US nuclear arsenal program was started in 2010 by President Obama's Democratic Administration with its ratification by the Republicans and is known as the "New Start Nuclear Arms Reduction Program with Russia," which is expected to continue well past 2020. Some 1,400 US nuclear warheads are deployed on missiles, submarines, and bombers. The modernization will replace all three legs of what is known as the nuclear triad—bombers in the air, submarines at sea, and Intercontinental Ballistic Missiles on alert in ground silos. In the future, a new launch cruise missile is projected to be developed and deployed

The repeated service of a "few" in constant rotations in the past sixteen years of the same US soldiers in what appears to be "endless wars" bodes serious consequences to those deployed all-volunteer service members and thus to the readiness of US forces. Such repeated counterinsurgency assignments have led to spikes in soldiers with post-traumatic stress disorders (PTSD), traumatic permanent bodily injuries from enemy improvised explosive devices (IED), suicides, and stress in military households. I am sounding the horn for those that may listen. The attention to the promises to the improvement of the defense forces and their fighting equipment by President Trump is encouraging; however, it remains for history to record the will by the Executive and Legislative branches of our government on a long-term basis to budget and appropriate funds to take actions to enhance US defense forces and weapon systems.

The Vietnam War Memorial teaches us to not only honor the some fifty-eight thousand who sacrificed but also to be honest and to question the policies that send Americans to war. The focus on Vietnam caused serious morale, racial, leadership, and readiness issues to our Army in its deterrent mission in Europe that had been neglected. These issues permeated also the Army's tactical nuclear enterprise at that time and, in particular, the nuclear tactical missile battalion that I was assigned to command. My experience as an Honest John Rocket Battalion Commander recorded in this memoir describes the personnel, readiness, and morale issues that occur when nuclear weapons systems and their security are not properly staffed, budgeted, and led.

The challenges are amplified when nuclear systems become obsolete and remain deployed too long. The Army tactical nuclear weapons inventory has been removed from Europe. Both the Honest John Rocket and Lance Missile Systems by 1973 and 1992 respectively, to include their nuclear warheads, have been eliminated. These eliminations were performed under the terms of the Intermediate Range Nuclear Forces (INF) Treaty of 1987 with the Soviet Union.

However, as of this writing, DoD nuclear enterprise strategic missile systems exist in the United States that since 1970 have been neglected due to our focus on Iraq and Afghanistan. History has been known to repeat itself. Evidence of the similar problems that I experienced in Germany after Vietnam are now appearing in Navy and AF strategic nuclear systems as evidenced by the US twenty-fourth Secretary of Defense Chuck Hagel's publicly announced comprehensive action plan in 2014 to reform the overall DoD nuclear enterprise.

The plan called for additional critical investments in sustainment as well as measures to address longstanding cultural issues that have hurt the morale of the nuclear force. The plan arose because leadership incidents in 2014 resulted in reviews that concluded that while US nuclear forces are meeting the demands of the mission, significant changes are required to address "systemic" problems that could undermine the safety, security, and effectiveness of the force in the future.

My life with Antonia was as close as one could come to paradise. The span was short, some thirty-nine years. It was a wonderful period of our lives filled with romance, three children, grandchildren, schools, fun, sweat, tears, happiness, prayers, argument, and teamwork.

Attending night law school, while also working full-time, would not have been possible had it not been for Antonia, my wife, friend, confident, and cheerleader. Emorfia, Antonia's mother, was our key supporter. I am a firm believer that one cannot really achieve success without a dedicated teammate. I respected Antonia's dreams and time too. She completed graduate schools at George Washington University with receiving her master of fine arts and later attended to Monmouth University for her master in education. We alternated, in and out of graduate schools, while working and raising our family. Self-improvement and growth were important to both of us.

Antonia's fight against cancer was epic. I have written her battle in this memoir in substantial detail in hopes that others will learn from her experiences. Antonia is not alone for there are many other women daily entering the battle against cancer. She joined the line as one truly unsung hero.

Not staying in the Army past twenty-three years was a major milestone in my walk through professional life. One must move on and not hang around hoping for a promotion whether in the military or civilian professions. One needs to create his or her own destiny. Having finished law school almost a year before the date I retired from the Army gave me the opportunity to make my career change as smooth as possible on the entire family. For me, the practice of law was exciting and fulfilling to this very day.

Periodically, I reflect on why I did not proceed to medical school after leaving the Army, especially after Vietnam. In that case, my Vietnam GI education benefits would have paid for most of my schooling as it had done for law school. Antonia would have supported us as a tenured teacher. However, that was not my calling. I do have a consolation though in as much as my son, Cosmas, went to New Jersey Medical School and is a practicing physician at Massachusetts General Hospital in Boston.

Caring for an ailing, elderly parent was a life-changing event. Beyond the sadness and suffering, the experience can teach us much about toughness, perseverance, and, especially, love. One must not judge those who do not opt for home hospice. To be sure, we had the room and financial means to care for my mom, Stamatia. As one's age progresses, the human body slowly loses physical and mental abilities in various stages. At some point as age progresses, life starts to end. Special measures to prolong life of the elderly are no longer warranted and should not be pursued. Perhaps the chronology and experiences of my mom with me, as her caregiver, described herein of my mom's progression from mother, widow, teacher, elderly, and end of life will be helpful to others in their walk through life.

As a teacher in the classroom and the field, one must think about the proper use of technology to promote learning but not allow it to replace the human's ability to assess and reason. In particular, it is just important to show how one got the answer than merely showing the right answer to a problem. Digital integration in all aspects of our lives from the classroom, home, business, offices, manufacturing plants, automobiles, hospitals to the battlefield, Army war rooms or Navy ship combat information centers (CIC) is a reality now and increasing. We must, however, let it not take away our capacities for critical thinking and problem solving. We need to be able to estimate the correct answer or the remedy to an issue and project the solution's consequences.

On April 25, 2014, some sixteen years later from its purchase, I sold the family beach house on Long Beach Island to a young family with two small children from Philadelphia. Their children were about the same age as my children when we had first purchased the beach house in 1998. The home was expensive to maintain and, more importantly, was not convenient to frequent use from my children's homes in Boston, DC, and Charlotte. However, in keeping with Antonia's last wishes, the "family" now gathers annually in the summer in a rented beach house convenient to all for a week. The gathering has become a "family" (the Giallourakis, Kennedy, Despo, Thakkar) tradition. Again in 2016, we had all assembled at the rented beach house in Isle of Palms, South Carolina, just northeast of Charleston. In June 16–18, 2017, as an exception, we gathered in Palo Alto, California, to celebrate the baccalaureate graduation of Orion Despo, my grandson, from Stanford University with the degree bachelor of science in mathematical and computational science with university distinction. We are scheduled to return to Charleston in August 2018 once again.

Such annual family gatherings at a family member's graduation, at a home for Thanksgiving, a rented beach house, on a cruise ship, or resort hotel are central to family members strengthening their ties to each other, relaxing, and rejuvenating its members for the new year ahead. Swimming with all my grandchildren is a gift. It is an event not to be missed. Stamie, my eldest daughter, has picked up Antonia's baton and coordinates the annual summer meeting of our family. We are fulfilling Antonia's wish.

In Vietnam, it was my duty to bring each soldier back home. Once deployed in Vietnam or in Germany, my concern was with the given mission and being the guardian of my assigned troops, meaning, ensuring they were kept trained, in good health, morale, and performed their missions—eventually bringing them back home safe. Soldiers can sense if their commander cares. In Germany during the Cold War, I was challenged but led reluctant missile-armed soldiers and guarded America's special "nuclear" weapons.

I never imagined how it would be when one's parents, my only brother, my wife, and my in-laws had predeceased me. I had been so busy being the guardian of someone close to me until now so as not to realize the vacuum that their absence created.

Having a nurse aide with my mom at all times was taken for granted. I always had looked forward to a daily great supper meal eating with my mom and her health aide in our home overlooking the blue Gulf of Mexico water of the Whitcomb Bayou. My main consolation now are the few friends I have in Tarpon Springs and DC but mostly my children, grandchildren, and their families—an irreplaceable, treasured legacy that was initiated and left to me by my beloved Antonia.

How do I fill the vacuum? Do I search for a romance? Do I move from the bayou in Tarpon Springs to live nearby, at least part time, with each of my children's families—in their homes in Charlotte, DC, or Boston or in a nearby rented apartment? Do I continue to bury myself in work—legal, accounting, technical, writing, and teaching? I have found putting feelings into words allows one to make sense of the past and rebuilds oneself providing confidence and resilience to navigate the present and future. Do I move to a full-service independent living facility with the built-in ability to transition to assisted living and other stages for geriatric care as inevitably one's health declines?

I recognize that I am not the only "elderly" or "senior" citizen facing such decisions, that are not so far distant as one would like, with the most important one that must eventually be faced—the end-of-life discussion. Having survived Beast Barracks, the rockets of the Vietcong, the tension of guarding a nuclear special ammunition weapons storage site, attending more than a handful of funerals for soldiers, West Point classmates and family, and the gavel of judges, I am up to the challenges ahead as we walk into the future. I am reminded that one is often at his or her best when life is at its worst. How well I make this transition, the reader will have to wait to read in my next published writing—novel or mystery.

My beloved Antonia came home to finally rest. Later, I also brought my dearest mom to rest at our home. I have been blessed by my God for being given the strength and capacity to have fulfilled my heritage as the **Spartan Guardian** of all I touched—those of my family, in the Army and as an attorney. I look forward to the future.

I am forever indebted to America for my many opportunities. One day, I will return to rest near Antonia at West Point—the place where all the action started that day in June when I stood at Trophy Point to be sworn in as a cadet in the class of 1958. What a ride!

SOURCE NOTES

Preface

[1]   http://www.businessinsider.com/largest-ethnic-groups-in-america-2013-8(2015)

Chapter 1. The Spartan in Me

[1]   http://www.secondworldwarhistory.com/1941-ww2-events-timeline.asp(2014).

[2]   http://www.the spongeexchange.com(2014).

[3]   http://www.harvardartmuseums-org/art/136670, Father Theophilos Karaphillis standing on the sponge docks (2014).

[4]   https://www.princeton.edu/~achaney/tmve/wiki100k/docs/Tarpon_Springs,_Florida.html (2014).

[5]   https://www.google.com/#q=picture+of+sponge+docks+tarpon+springs (2014).

[6]   Michael F. Giallourakis, *The Giallourakis Story* (January 26, 1992).

[7]   *United States v. The Tarpon Springs Sponge Exchange*, 142 F.2d 125, 127-28(Fifth Circuit, 1944).

[8]   Duchess Giallourakis Arfaras, untitled paper (January 26, 1992).

[9]   Michael G. Cantonis, *My Ancestors & My Life* (Staraphics, Seminole, FL, 2008).

[10]   http://www.seasponges.com.au/information/sea-sponge-facts(2014).

[11]   http://www.iaszoology.com/skeleton-in-sponges/(2014).

[12]   http://www.tcm.com/tcmdb/title/68458/Beneath-the-12-Mile-Reef/ (2014).

13 U.S Fish and Wildlife Service, American Alligator (February, 2008).

14 http://www.fws.gov/endangered/ (2014).

15 http://www.madehow.com/Volume-5/Sponge.html#ixzz3G2Y3vSmY (2014).

16 http://sp.uconn.edu/~wwwcoh/TIMELINE.HTM#1931(2014)

17 Torrance R. Parker, *20,000 Jobs Under the Sea, A history of Diving and Underwater Engineering* (Publishers Press, Quality Books, 1997)141-150.

18 http://www.youtube.com/watchv=rR6FApI1VlU(2014).

19 Semazzi.Dorothy@epa.gov

Chapter 2. Waiter to House Mother's Assistant

1 https://www.chegg.com/generalpolicies (2015)

2 http://www.woodward.edu/about/history/index.aspx (2014)

Chapter 3. Plebe to Lieutenant

1 https://www.enotrans.org/; Eno Center for Transportation and Florida East Coast Industries (2014)

2 http://tarponspringsareahistoricalsociety.org/About-Us/about-us.html (2014)

3 http://www.westpointcadet.blogspot.com/2013/02/beastbarracks/html. (2014)

4 http://www.usma.edu/chaplain/cadetchapel.aspx.(2014)

5 http://www.ehow.com/facts_7374720_history-hudson-river-reserve-fleet.html (2014)

6 http:/foundationsofamerica.com/index.php?option=com_content&view =article&id=420: the-battle-monument-at-west-point&catid=54:monuments-a-parks&Itemid=68 (2014).

7 http://engineering.dartmouth.edu/magazine/who-was-sylvanus-thayer (2015).

8 http://www.west-point.org/class/usma/ (2014).

9 *"50 Years of Service, USMA Class of 1958"* (Yearbook,1958)

10 Kevin Cahillane, *The Women of West Point (New York Magazine*, The Education Issue, September 7, 2014).

11 Robert Timbering, *The Nightingale's Song* (Blackstone Audio Inc., 2008).

[12] Midshipmen Second Class Thomas Q. Wester, *Technology Brings a Paradox of Power*, (US Navy, Proceedings USNI, September 2014), 10.

[13] Donald J. Palladino, *The Howitzer 1958* (Comet Press Inc. 1958).

[14] http://www.usghof.org/files/bio/t_maloney/t_maloney.html (2014).

[15] http://www.historyofvaccines.org/content/articles/influenza-pandemics (2014).

[16] http://www.jhsph.edu/.../19... Johns Hopkins Bloomberg School of Public Health (2014).

[17] http://www.sfgate.com/realestate/article/City-to-get-Treasure-Island-for-105-million-3206898.php (2015).

[18] http://www.loc.gov/pictures/item/md0916/(Bancroft Hall) 2015.

[19] articles.baltimoresun.com › Collections(Articles about Bancroft Hall–Baltimore Sun) 2015.

[20] http://www.navysite.de/ships/lha1.htm (2015).

[21] 10 USC 4342(USMA)(Nominations to USMA).

[22] Aric Jackson, "Navy and President Donald Trump, commissioning USS Gerald Ford Aircraft Carrier, Naval Station Norfolk, (Fortune Tech) July 22, 2017

Chapter 4. Breaking In the Lieutenant

[1] *Parachute Jump Towers, Fort Benning, Columbus, GA*. (Google: International Chimney, 2014).

[2] http://www.goarmy.com/soldierlife/Rangerschool.html;www.military.com/military-fitness/Army-ranger school-pup (2014).

Chapter 5: My Pacific Cruise

[1] *May 3, 1965: 173rd Airborne Brigade deploys to South Vietnam*, http://www.history.com/.../173rd-airborne-brigade-deploys-to-south-vietnam... (2014)

[1] NavSource Online: Service Ship Photo Archive USS General J. C. Breckinridge (AP-176) (1945–1946) USS. (2014)

[2] http://www-03.ibm.com/systems/services/briefingcenter/poughkeepsie/topics.htm(2014).

[3] http://www.taiwandc.org/history.htm (2014).

4   https://history.state.gov/milestones/1945-1952/chinese (2014).

5   Eui Young Yu, *Components of Population Growth in Seoul:1960-1966*(California State College, Los Angeles, 2014),1

6   *Seoul Sees Rapid Growth as Global Metropolis* (Korean Times, 08.15.2005)

7   *The Official Homepage of the 2nd BN, 503rd Infantry Regiment,* http://www. EUR.Army/173ABCT/2-503 (2014)

8   http://www.2id.korea.army.mil/ (2014).

9   http://www.panorama.org/panoramas/corregidor (2014).

Chapter 6: Romance—From Cornhuskers, Boilermakers to the Black Knights

1   Henry Morgenthau, Sr., US Ambassador, *The Murder of a Nation,* (ch. XXIV, 1919)52–53, (written 1916, before Greece entered war on the side of Allies in 1917, before further massacres of Greeks between 1916 and 1923)

2   *Decisions at Smyrna: A Speech at the American Hellenic Institute,* www.ahiworld. org/ahi-forum-commemorates-91st…of…/1799.html (2015).

3   www.usma57.org/MemorialArticles/Poulos.htm (2014).

4   www. USMA.edu/dca/sitepages/CullumHallissitory.aspx (2014).

5   *Christ John Poulos,1957 Howitzer Yearbook,* (New York: Comet Press, 1957) 430.

6   http://www.ladycliff.org/history_of_ladycliff.htm(2014).

7   http://www.history.com/this-day-in-history/johnson-approves-operation-rolling-thunder (2014).

8   http://www.usma.edu/chaplain/SitePages/Jewish/20Chapel.aspx (2014).

9   http://www.biography.com/#!/people/norman-schwarzkopf-9476401# synopsis (2014).

10   Alex Johnson, Daniel Arkin, Jason Cummings, Bill Karins, *Hurricane Irma Leaves 1Million without Power* (NBC News), (2017).

11   Matt Zapotosky, David Nakamura, Abigail Hauslohner, *Revised (Presidential) Executive Order bans travelers from six Muslim majority countries from getting new visas.* (the *Washington Post*, 2017).

Chapter 7. Rubber Plantation

[1] Helene Copper, Charles Shander, *Combat, Fighting for Promotions* (*New York Times* 04.20.2014).

[2] http://www.u-s-history.com/pages/h1871.html (2014).

[3] http://www.history.army.mil/Chapter VII: Across the Border: Sanctuaries in Cambodia and Laos (2014).

[4] http://www.archives.gov/research/military/vietnam-war/casualty-statistics.html (2014).

[5] Robert Timberg, *Blue-Eyed Boy, A Memoir* (Penguin Press, 2014).

[6] http://www.militaryfactory.com/aircraft/detail.asp/ (2014).

[7] http://history1900s.about.com/od/vietnamwar/a/vietnamtimeline.htm (2014).

[8] http://www.nytimes.com/interactive/2010/08/31/world/middleeast/20100831-Iraq-Timeline.html?r=0#/#time111_3262 (2014).

[9] http://thevietnamwar.info/vietnam-war-draft/ (2014).

[10] http://www.wartimecontracting.gov; *Final Report to Congress, Commission on Wartime Contracting in Iraq and Afghanistan"* (August 31, 2011) (2014).

[10] http://www.nbcnews.com/id/33210358/ns/world_news-south_and_central_asia/t/us-war-afghanistan/ (2014).

[12] http://www.historylearningsite.co.uk/agent_orange.htm (2014).

[13] http://www.history.comn/topics/vietnam-war/agent-orange (2014).

[14] http://www.nytimes.com/2004/05/01/politics/campaign/01CHEN.html (2015).

[15] http://www.nytimes.com/1992/02/14/us/the-1992-campaign-the-60-s-clinton-and-draft-issue-vietnam-era-revisited.html (2015).

[16] "Pentagon Papers." History (US TV Channel). Retrieved 26 October 2013.

[17] Apple, R.W. (1996-06-23) "Pentagon Papers," the *New York Times*, New. 2013-10-23.

[18] "In Speech Trump Sets US Strategy for Afghan War," Mark Landler and Maggie Haberman, NYT, p A10, 08.22.2017; "Expanding Role in Conflict He Once Called Futile" Julie Hischfield Davas, and Mark Landler, NYT, pA10, 08.22.2017

Chapter 8: Traversing the Pentagon Rings

[1] http://www.raytheon.com/capabilities/products/hawkxxi/ (2014).

[2] http://olive-drab.com/od_firepower_hawk.php (2014).

[3] http://www.history.com/topics/vietnam-war/pentagon-papers (2014).

[4] http://www.army-technology.com/projects/grafenwohrarmybase/ (2014).

[5] http://globalnews.ca/news/1203882/israels-mobile-missile-defence-system-what-is-the-iron-dome(2014).

[6] http://online.wsj.com/articles/ukraine-says-missile-shrapnel-destroyed-mh17-1406544088 (2014).

[7] http://www.infoplease.com/spot/pentagon1.html#ixzz3GiKzlW8c (2014).

[8] http://www.globalsecurity.org/military/library/policy/army/accp/ad0699/lesson5.htmS(2014).

[9] http://www.global security.org/military/facility/adelphi.htm (2014).

[10] Norman Freidman, *Implausible Deniability* (World Naval Developments, USNI Proceedings, 09.2014) 90,91.

Chapter 9. Cold War Command

[1] http://history.redstone.army.mil/miss-honest john.html (2014). Researched and written by: Capt (N) (Ret'd) M. Braham, Edited by: Trevor Clayton. The MGR-1 Honest John rocket was the first nuclear-capable surface-to-surface rocket in the US arsenal.

[2] http://olive-drab.com/od_firepower_honest_john.php(2014).

[3] http://history.redstone.army.mil/miss-lance.html(2014).

Chapter 10. The Horse Holder

[1] *Warnings from the Post-Vietnam Era* (*Armed Forces Journal*, March 1, 2013).

[2] http://armed forces journal.com/rebuilding-the-army-again/(2014).

Chapter 11. The Frequency-Hopping Radio

1   http://www.army.mil/article/49970/Retired_Army_Lt__Gen__Thomas_M __Rienzi_laid_to_rest_at_Punchbowl/(2014)

2   Interim DoD Instruction 5000.02, *Operation of the Defense Acquisition System* (November 25, 2013)

3   DoD Directive 5000.1, *Defense Acquisition System* (May 12, 2003).

4   news.bbc.co.uk/2/hi/europe/6314559.stm, Feb. 12, 2007(2014).

5   http://grad-schools.usnews.rankingsandreviews.com/best-graduate-schools/ top-law-schools/law-rankings/page+4(2014).

6   David P. Smole and Shannon S. Loane, *A Brief History of Veteran's Benefits and Their Value* (CRS Report for Congress, June 25, 2008).

Chapter 12. The Rookie Barrister

1   The International Traffic in Arms Regulations, ITAR (22CFR 120-130); https://www.pmddtc.state.gov/.../itar.ht... (2014).

2   Michael Mineiro, *Space Technology Export Controls and International Cooperation in Outer Space,"* (google.com/books?isbn=9400725671(Comparative Analysis of ITAR and *EAR* Regulations, 2014)

3   The Great American Eclipse, USA Today, p.8A, August 18, 2017.

Chapter 13. Seasoned Counsel

1   Bill C. Giallourakis, *Cost Analysis Software For Contract Administration (CASCA)* (1983).Small Business Innovative Research (SBIR) Phase I, program winner for Air Force (ASD/YZD).

2   http://www.nifa.usda.gov/fo/sbir, United States Department of Agriculture Jun 20, 2014—*Small Business Innovation Research Program:* Phase I. See the *2015* USDA *SBIR Program* Solicitation (2014).

3   Funding Opportunity Announcements (FOAs) | US DO...science.energy. gov/sbir/funding-opp...United States Department of Energy Grant Start Date, Late February *2015*.4. (2014).

4   *mall Business Innovation Research Program* Phase I Solicitation (*SBIR*) December

Submission … 2014 *SBIR*, HHS, Jan 17, 2014, Mar 5, 2014, Jan 7, *2015.*

[5] Program Contract Solicitation grants.nih.gov/grants/National Institutes of Health, Aug 15, 2014—NIH Funding Opportunities and Notices in the NIH Guide for *Grants* and Contracts: *Small Business Innovation Research (SBIR) Program …(2014.*

[6] Program Schedule and Selection Announcements
| NAS.sbir.nasa.gov/prg_sched_anncmnt *Program* Solicitation, Open Date, Close Date,
Selection Announcement Date … Apr 23,*2015.* NASA *SBIR* Select *2015* Phase I Solicitation, Nov 14, 2014, Jan (2014).

[7] http://www2.ed.gov/programs/sbir/appli…United States Department of Education Apr 21, 2014—The Institute of Education Sciences.(2014).

[8] Bill C. Giallourakis, *Contracting with Uncle Sam, The Essential Guide for Federal Buyers and Sellers* (USNI, 2008).

[9] Federal Acquisition Regulation(FAR) Part 25-1, *Buy American Act.*

[10] http:/www.uscfc.uscourts.gov/Vaccine-program/(2014).

[11] The Vaccine Act became effective October 1, 1988 comprises Part 2 of the National Childhood Vaccine Injury Act of 1986 ("Vaccine Act"). See Pub. L. No. 99–660, 100 Stat. 3755 (1986)

[12] http://www.cdc.gov/mmwr/preview/mmwrhtml/mm64e0213a1.htm(2015).

[13] http://www.cdc.gov/measles/cases-outbreaks.html(2015).

[14] http://www.webmd.com/children/vaccines/measles-mumps-and-rubella-mmr-vaccine (2015).

[15] Michael T. Kaufman, *Peter W. Rodino Dies at 96; Led House Inquiry (*New York Times, May 8, 2005).

[16] http://www.dhs.gov/xlibrary/assets/st-safety-act.pdf (2014); codified as amended at 42 USC §§ 300aa-1 to -34) 2014.

[17] http://www.uscis.gov/working-united-states/students-and-exchange-visitors/students-and-employment (2014).

[18] http://www.uscis.gov/working-united-states/temporary-workers/l-1a-intracompany-transferee-executive-or-manager (2014).

[19] http://www.uscis.gov/about-us/our-history(2014).

[20] Streiff Diary, *New York Court Allows Uncle and Niece to Marry* (New York Post October 31, 2014).

[21] http://www.wipo.int/pct/en/pct_contracting_states.html(2015).

[22] http://wipo.int/patentscope/en/ (2015).

23   *The Homeland Security Act of 2002*, Pub L. No.107-296, 116 US Statute 2135.

24   https://j1visa.state.gov/

25   *Here's what America's biggest companies plan to do with all the cash coming back to the US,* Business Insider, Jonathan Garber, December, 2017)

26   *ISIS has been militarily defeated in Iraq and Syria,* Business Insider, Alex Lockie, November 21, 2017

Chapter 14. When Love Calls—The Sneak Cancer

1   http://www.destinationpaloalto.com/pages/ (2014)

2   http://www.nationalcenter.org/MacArthurFarewell.html(2014)

3   *CDC—What Can I Do to Reduce My Risk for Ovarian Cancer?* (March 10, 2014); www.cdc.gov/cancer/ovarian/basic_infor/prevention.htm(2014).

4   *Ovarian Cancer Prevention—Web MD*, October 22, 2002, www.webmd.com/ovarian-cancer/guide/ovarian-cancer-prevention.(2014)

5   *American Cancer Society Ovarian Cancer,* http:www.cancer.org/cancer/ovarian cancer/detailed guide/ovarian-cancer-prevention (2014).

6   http://www.medicinenet.com/ca_125/article.htm (2014).

7   *Transvagina Sonogram,* www.nlm.nih.gov/medlineplus/ency/article/003779.htm (2014)

8   *Patient Information Chemotherapy Fact Card, Carboplatin, Paclitaxel, Cisplatin,* (MSKCC 1995).

9   Introduction: What is DNA? Learn Science at Scitable-Nature, http://www.nature.com/scitable/topicpage/introduction-what-is-dna-6579978(2014).

10 "*PET Scan: Medline Plus Medical Encyclopedia,* http://www.nlm.nih.gov/medlineplus/ency/article/003827.htm(2014.

11 http://www.nlm.nih.gov/medlineplus/ency/article/003574.htm(2014).

12 *BRCA1 and BRCA2: Cancer Risk and Genetic Testing Fact Sheet,* www.cancer.org/cancertopics/factsheetbrca-gene–test.(2014).

13 http://www.cancer.gov/cancertopics/factsheet/Risk/BRCA(2014).

14 http://www.hindwi/journals/ju/2013/481806(2014).

15 http://www.imdb.com/name/nm0001659/(2014).

16 http://www.cancer.org/cancer/ovariancancer/detailedguide/ovarian-cancer-staging (2014).

17 http://www.biography.com/people/christopher-reeve-9454130(2014).

[18] http://www.imdb.com/name/nm0001659/ (2014).

[19] *Hospice Care-What is Hospice?* www.hospice.org(2014).

[20] "Claire Burke Gallagher and Antonia P. Giallourakis, *Eyes on Insects, An Interdisciplinary Teacher's Guide*" (Eyes on Architecture Series, G&G Educational Consultants, 1993).

Chapter 15. The Centenarian Calls

[1] http://www.stanthonythe great.org/saint-anthony.html(2014).

[2] http://www.britannica.com/EB checked/topic/167547/Dodecanese(2014).

[3] Certificate of Naturalization No. 5473346, Petition Number 5826, Department of Justice, USA, Stamatia Gerakis Giallourakis, 01. 18. 1944, Edwin Williams Clerk, US District Court.

[4] orthoinfo.aaos.org/topic.cfm…American Academy of Orthopedic Surgeons (2014).

[5] http://www.hopkinsmediciine.org/gec/seruies/fixing_hip_fractures (2014).

[6] Jonathan Cluett, MD, *Intertrochanteric Hip Fractures. What is an intertrochanteric hip fracture?*", http://orthopedics.about.com/cs/hipsurgery/a/brokenhip_3.htm(2014)

[7] http://www.asyouage.com/difference between _Nursing _Homes_ and Skilled_nursing_ facilities.html(2014)

[9] http://www.webmd.com/alzheimers/guide/alzheimers-dementia(2014)

[10] http://www.webmd.com/alzheimers/guide/alzheimers-basics(2014)

[11] "Decubitus Ulcers or Bed Sores; Causes and Treatments, July 25, 2012, http://www.healthline.com/health/pressure-ulcer(2014)

[12] http://www.mayoclinic.org/tests-procedures/mohs-surgery/basics/definition/prc-20014261(2014)

[13] *Durable Power of Attorney Containing Health Care Surrogate Provisions and Provisions Relating to Real Property Including Homestead Property, Stamatia C. Giallourakis* (January 31, 2006).

[14] George N. Klimis P.A.*Declaration, Stamatia C. Giallourakis*, (July 6, 2000).

[15] http://www.medicinenet.com/percutaneous_endoscopic_gastrostomy/article.htm. (2014).

[16] Fee Schedule August 1, 2014 (St. Mark Village), www.stmarkvillage.org (2015).

[17] *How to Avoid Costly Mistakes in Search Senior Living,* http://www.aplaceformom. com,(2015).

Epilogue

[1] *Life Lessons from Dad* (*Wall Street Journal,* Weekend Edition.,06.28-29, 2014) C1

[2] Maureen Dowd, *A Cup of G.I. Joe* (Sunday Review, *New York Times,* 11.2.2014)

[3] Ahmed Tolba and Yara Bayoumy, *Egypt bombs Islamic State targets in Libya after 21 Egyptians beheaded,* (Cairo, Reuters, 02.15.2015)

[4] Jim Garamone, *Secretary of Defense Hagel Announces Nuclear Force Reforms* (DoD News, Defense Media Activity, 11.14.2014) NR-567. 145.http:// www.defense.gov/pubs/(2014)

[6] Jim Garamone, *Hagel Says Vietnam War Teaches Sacrifice, Need for Questioning Policies"* (DoD News, Defense Media Activity, 11.11.2014).

[7] Mark Perry, *The Most Dangerous Man in America: The Making of Douglas MacArthur,* Mark Perry, (NY Basic Books, 2014); review by Cdr. John T. Kuehn, Book Reviews, Proceedings, USNI Press 2014) 73

[8] Michael Perlman, *Truman and MacArthur* (Indiana U. Press, 2008).

[9] Paul Sonne, "US Is Overhauling Its Nuclear Arsenal," *Wall Street Journal,* August 10, 2017, p. A6.

[10] Linda Qiu, "Trump Claims undue Credit on Nuclear Arsenal," *New York Times,* August 10, 2017, p. A7

[11] Christopher Woody, "The US-Led bombing campaign against ISIS set a record in August," Business Insider, September 13, 2017.

Photo Gallery (See included photographs)

PHOTOGRAPHS

Antonia, the Art teacher at Shreswbury Borough School (K-8),
just graduated from Monmouth University in West Long Branch,
New Jersey and after the ceremony is standing with Bill, holding
her diploma, a Master of Science in Education (1977).

A carriage ride through Central Park in New York City—a break from Memorial Sloan Kettering Cancer Center treatments (1998).

Bill and his beloved Aunt Ypapanti. Aunt Ypapanti's birthday celebration.

Bill, as a student cadet, at Georgia Military
Academy(GMA) during high his school graduation.

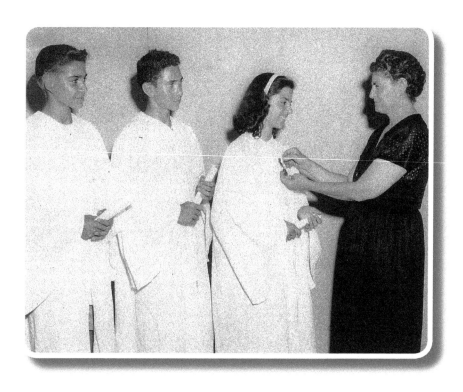

My Mom, the Principal, congratulating graduating
seniors of the Saint Nicholas Greek School.

The brothers, Mike and Bill, standing in front of their Mom
Stamatia and Dad Cosmas dressed for marching in the
Epiphany Day celebration wearing Greek Evzon Uniforms.

Bill being promoted to the rank of Lieutenant Colonel on October 07, 1969 in the Pentagon by Lieutenant General A.W. Betts, the Chief of Research and Development (OCRD). Antonia is assisting General Betts pinning one of the silver leafs on the left shoulder while little Stamie stands amazed at the photographer.

Bill in the field after a Parachute Jump onto the Han
River on the outskirts of Seoul, Korea satisfying his thirst
before heading with his artillery battery to the DMZ for
artillery firing in 1962 from his base in Okinawa.

The Engaged Couple—Antonia, a sophomore at Nebraska
and Bill, a captain in the Army at Purdue U. (1962)

Antonia and Bill, married on June 13, 1965 in the Holy
Trinity Greek Orthodox Churh in Grand Island, Nebraska
shown flanked by my brother Mike on the left and my two
cousins, Kathryn and Manoli from Nassau on the right.

Bill and Antonia at their wedding crossing hands,
showing their wedding bands/rings.

Christ Poulos, USMA Class of 1957, who introduced
Bill to his sister, Antonia who became Bill's wife.

West Point U.S.M.A. Bill's Class of 1958 Photograph

Memorial of John K. Cheyney at the entrance of the
Tarpon Springs Sponge Exchange; who was instrumental
in promoting the sponge industry in Tarpon Springs.

The current concrete Sponge Docks with a
preserved sponge boat on exhibit.

Statue of Sponge Diver at the Docks in Tarpon Springs Florida

Tile plaque in front of the Tarpon Springs Sponge Exchange

Family Photo at Stanford Graduation

Stanford Graduation Bill, Orry, and Alex.

INDEX

BILL C. GIALLOURAKIS is an attorney and lecturer. He served in the Army for twenty-three years, retiring as a colonel. He initially served as an artillery officer in the Eighty-Second Airborne Division at Fort Bragg, 503rd Infantry Combat Team in Okinawa and in South Vietnam.

Assignments followed in Vietnam from July 1967 to July 1968, as the executive officer of the Second Battalion, Thirty-Third Field Artillery Battalion, First Infantry Division. His awards for service in Vietnam include Legion of Merit; Bronze Star with oak leaf cluster for Valor, February 8, 1968; the Army Commendation Medal for Valor, January 31, 1968; and the Air Medal.

Later, he served with the Army general staff working on R&D Air Defense Missile Projects IHAWK and Air Traffic Control Systems in the Pentagon. While in the Pentagon, he served as military assistant to the chief scientist of the Army and later held command positions first in Europe, commanding a rocket (nuclear) battalion, and later in the US where he served first as the project manager for the test and evaluation of the SINCGARS Combat Net Radio System. While in Europe, he also served on the Seventh Army Staff in Heidelberg, as an assistant for two deputy chiefs of staff for operations.

He served as an associate professor, Department of Electrical Engineering, USMA, West Point, New York and was an instructor for the Professional Development Center, Armed Forces Communications-Electronics Association (AFCEA) on government contracting.

Bill remains a Florida-licensed attorney with specialization in federal contracting, construction, and intellectual property law. He is the author of *Contracting with Uncle Sam: The Essential Guide for Federal Buyers and Sellers*. He resides on the Whitcomb Bayou near the sponge docks in Tarpon Springs, Florida.

Education: BS, USMA, West Point, NY, 1958; Purdue University, MSE, 1964; MBA, Fairleigh Dickinson University, 1978; JD, Seton Hall University School of Law, 1980.

CPSIA information can be obtained
at www.ICGtesting.com
Printed in the USA
LVHW072016120721
692484LV00022B/2587